D1710570

For additional information on Profit Streams™, please visit **www.appliedframeworks.com** or email **profit-streams@appliedframeworks.com**

Software Profit Streams

Written by

Jason Tanner & Luke Hohmann

Release 1.0.0

We'd like to thank the following people who have helped and inspired us in writing this book.

Dan Murphy
Tammie Hollis
Jesse Fewell
Em Campbell-Pretty
Daniel Dorion
Monica Foley
Ken France
Lisa Hammond
Gregor Hohpe
Peter Jessen
Niko Kaintantzis
Haresh Keswani
Carol McEwan
Isaac Montgomery
Odile Moreau
Nicholas Muldoon
Saahil Panikar
Kevin Rosengren
Harpreet Singh
Siraj Sirajuddin
Will Stockwell
Nader Talai
Eric Willeke
Gianpaolo Baglione
Ron DiFrango

Tariq Juneja
Mark Lichman
Mike Miracle
Joe Montalbano
Toby Owen
Craig Palli
Scott Paradis
Aaron Proeitti
Michael Schrage
Jeff Smith
Jane Tudor
Jackie Vanover
Mark Saymen
David McFarlane
Igor Altman
Nathan Anderson
Mackenzie Baines
Brian Barr
Tim Bertheau
Steffen Bilde
Alex Bould
Alicia Castillo Holley
Daniel Chapellin
Rune Christensen
Calvin Chu

Mark Crager
Vijay Dafal
Kyle Dukes
Ben Emrick
Jennifer Fawcett
Mark Flnnern
Benjamin Fornarino
Marc Fortin
Chen Gongyuan
Greg Head
Jerome Levadoux
Christophe Louvion
Shawn Lowe
Kamal Manglani
Mikko Mannila
Sam McAfee
Grigori Melnik
Kay Overand
Konstantin Popov
Simon Porro
Cassandra Salud
Bria Schecker
Jeff Shupack
Mahesh Singh
Michael Smith

Jemmie Wang
Brad Waugh
Marcus Willson
Ken Yagen
Guy Duncan
Cliff Pollan
Steven Savage
Deb Ludewig
Pete Behrens
Tracey Wilson
Florian Reuter
Kanaiya Vasani
Don McGreal
Heidi Araya
Rich Arnold
William Avila
Janna Bastow
Peter Beck
Alex Brazie
Brendan Burns
Simon Chesney
Alvin Crawford
Marc Danzinger
Charles Fleet
Paul Germeraad

Todd Girvin
Praveen Goel
Adam Grill
Nicholas Hauff
Barry Hawkins
John Heimstra
John Hoye
Zafar Iqbal
Marc Kohler
Carrie Kritzer
Laurent Laffite
Matt Lievertz
David Luzquinos
Daniel Marcos
John Matthesen
Joel Meyer
Megan Miller
Anand Murthy Raj
Mark Musselman
Kiran Naik
Ramesh Nori
Padma Satyamurthy
Andreas Schliep
Scott Shagory
Peter Shanley

Bryan Smith
Kurt Stangl
Dwayne Stroman
Andy Taylor
Wayne Trattles
Pieter Van Osch
Benjamin Watkins
Derrick Wesley
Valerio Zanini
Max Zelaitis
Gil Aires
Martha Amram
Walter Ariel Risi
David Baer
Carlos Baradello
Brent Barton
Timothy Bates
Aloke Bhandia
Steven Birdsall
Kim Brainard
Heather Bronson
Evan Campbell
Catherine Cartwright
Alistair Cockburn
Alex Constantin

Büşra Coşkuner
Ty Crocket
Krishna Dunthoori
Thomas Ecker
Shawn Flynn
Nick Foster
Andreas Frei
Danielle Gerber
Markus Giesen
Clint Gossett
Raphael Goumot
Dan Greening
Dan Griffith
Marshall Guillory
Bijan Hafezi
Brent Harrison
Neil Hays
Darren Heaphy
Stacia Heimgartner
Brandon Hickie
Jim Hilbert
Tim Hockin
Chris Hohman
Vaughn Jackson
Sandy Johnson

Steve Johnson
Suzette Johnson
Saeed Kahn
Terrin Kalian
Hande Kazgan
Keith Klundt
Jason Knight
David Koontz
Dimitri Kusnezov
Kyler Laird
Derek Lane
Edrick Larkin
Matt Lasee
Brad Lehman
Morgan Livermore
Anders Lund
Nuria Macia
Lys Maitland
Olli Mannerkoski
Wiselin Mathuram
Harry Max
Kevin McCabe
Russ McClelland
Micheal McCullough
James McElroy

Phil Montgomery
Rich Moran
Nitin Motgi
Dave Neuman
Toby Owen
Steve Pfiffner
Andrew Phelps
Bala Pitchaikani
Hrishi Raman
Mark Rennie
Marc Rix
Diane Robinette
Bill Rochell
Felix Ruessel
George Schlitz
Moustapha Seck
Bill Seitz
Marcio Sete
KJ Sethna
Bharat Shah
Al Shalloway
Bradley Shaw
Jordan Sheffield
Raphael Sigg
Andy Simon

Deborah Simon
Dharmesh Singh
Anu Smalley
Randy Smith
Parthib Srivathsan
Bryan Stalllings
S. Sundukovskiy
Robert Szustakowski
Peter Tapley
David Tarver
Wayne Trattles
James Tremlett
Samuel Vaden
Marc Visent
Kim Werner
Anissa Williams
Brian Witten
Jan Ydens
Marc Emmons
Tyler Simons
Phil Hornby
David Pollak
John Miller
Sam Diener
Saim Abbasi

Rodney Adkins
Rohan Bhokardankar
Lee Counselman
Anna Hamilton
Lori Harmon
Gail Hoffman
Brian Kardon
Dave Krupinski
Pietro Maffi
Daniel Stevenson
Perry Tancredi
Spiros Theodossiou
David Vap
Ralph Verrilli
Harry Koehnemann
Karin Wiberg
Chon Chua

Bryan Vaughn
Stephen St. John
John Mulligan
Mike Robertson
Bob Ternes
Laura Caldie
Carlton Nettleton
Michael Whitaker
Travis Moorer
Joel Bancroft-Connors
Rachele Maurer
Charlene Newton
Kim Poremski
Phil Gardiner
Andrea Starr
Brooke Dever
Ted Dikmen
Scott Heffield
Kristen Harrison
Julie Teeter

AND OF COURSE, OUR MOMS!

FOREWORD

Page 49

As someone who learned about building software the hard way —by making mistakes and picking myself up along the way— I can attest to the importance of having the right tools and tactics in your toolkit. That's why I was delighted to see ***Prune the Product Tree*** in Jason and Luke's latest book, Software Profit Streams™. I first discovered this exercise early in my career, from Luke's previous book "Innovation Games", and it opened my eyes to new ways of drawing insights and learning before making costly product decisions. It's been a staple in my approach ever since.

Page 182

As the CEO and Co-Founder of a successful and fast-growing SaaS company, it was in the crowded hallways of a SaaS conference, searching for ways to improve my business, where I stumbled upon the **Van Westendorp Price Sensitivity Meter** from another SaaS builder.

I quickly realized that these kinds of gems—tools and tactics that can make a real difference in your approach—aren't always widely shared. There's an element of serendipity in voicing the right pain to the right person, unlocking some new insight along the way. That's why this book is so important. It brings all of these tactics, and so much more, **together in one place.**

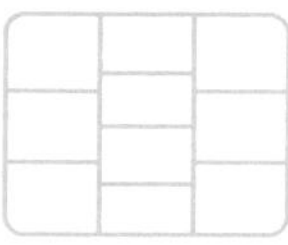
Page 125

Software Profit Streams is essential reading for anyone involved in creating, pricing, selling, and marketing software-enabled solutions. The authors explore everything from roadmapping to pricing sensitivity, solution maps, value exchange models, pricing the first release of a solution, and pricing the 5th release as the solution evolves. They provide essential tips and tactics that are key to any team looking to build a sustainable, profitable software business.

Page 341

And I do mean everyone: CEOs, venture capitalists, private equity investors, aspiring founders, CROs, CFOs, and product managers can all benefit from this book's ability to help you increase profit, improve customer satisfaction, and create an ongoing stream of value. It's the kind of resource I wish I had ten years ago, and I know it will add real value to those who read it today.

Page 184

JANNA BASTOW
CEO and Co-Founder, ProdPad
Inventor of the Now-Next-Later Roadmap and Mind the Product

IS THIS BOOK FOR ME?

We are adding software to an existing solution.

* LIKE A SMART APPLIANCE

Our customers are not renewing their subscriptions.

We need to fund innovation.

* CHANGING PEOPLE'S LIVES!

We are facing price competition.

We need to quantify the 'value' of our 'value streams'.

* DATA ALL THE WAY!

We are a startup and we are unsure of how to price our solution.

* SMART CHOICES. GOOD OUTCOME!

We want to improve profitability of our company.

* YES! WE ALL WANT THIS!

We want to create a **sustainable business!**

If you answered  **"YES"** to any of these questions,

THIS BOOK IS FOR YOU

You will use this book to create **sustainably profitable software-enabled solutions.**

Let's get to it!

This book introduces **Software Profit Streams**, the essential tool you will use to create sustainably profitable software-enabled solutions. It will explain where they come from and how to maximize the benefits of Profit Stream design.

You're going to love Profit Streams because you can...

Use Profit Streams to **increase profit** through more effective pricing and licensing.

Use Profit Streams to **increase customer satisfaction** because your profits can be used to create more features and improve product quality: an ongoing **stream of value**.

Use Profit Streams to create a **sustainable business,** one that promotes long term, beneficial relationships with employees, suppliers, investors, and of course customers.

Profit Streams are a team sport

This book will help all business leaders involved in **creating, pricing, selling, distributing, and licensing** software-enabled solutions.

HOW THIS BOOK IS ORGANIZED

01

Software Profit Streams

We start with an overview of the conceptual foundations that guide the design of Profit Streams.

02

Profit Stream Canvas

We provide an overview of the Profit Stream Canvas, detailing each block of the canvas and how it relates to sustainability.

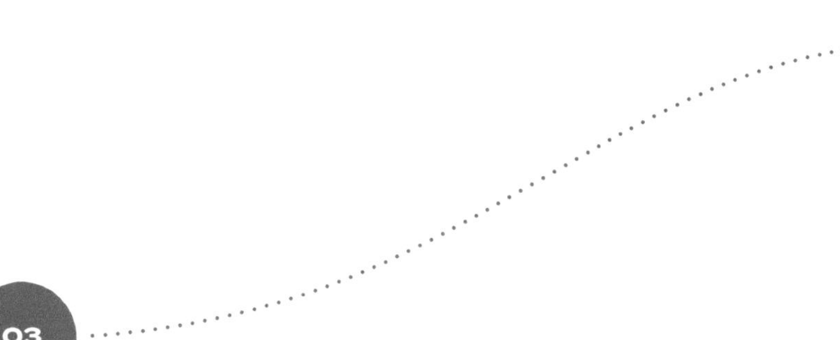

Applications

We show how to use the canvas to design and evolve Profit Streams over time.

Continuing your journey...

This book is just the start! Continue your journey at **www.profit-streams.com** where you can join the Profitable Software Community, access additional content, download tools, and much more!

SECTION 01

Software Profit Streams

ofit Streams

Profit fuels sustainability

Just as mother nature relies on the energy from the sun to sustain life on earth...

Every business relies on profit for sustainability.

Creates a **virtuous cycle** between a business and the customer it serves.

A profitable business can invest in the ongoing development of its solutions.

This book will help you design sustainably profitable

Software-Enabled Solutions.

WHAT IS PROFIT? WHY DOES IT MATTER?

One way to define profit is the net income resulting from revenue minus expenses (salaries, sales and marketing, development, production, overhead, etc.). What may be even more important than the definition of profit is to explore what profit means and why it matters, as profit often means different things for different businesses and is used to accomplish different goals.

"In our P&L, I don't have the word profit. On my P&L, it says freedom." — SIMON SINEK

Profit fuels sustainable businesses. Without profit, we cannot maintain or grow our business, we cannot serve our customers or provide benefits to our employees and other stakeholders. Without profit, the goals of the business are unattainable.

Even well-funded startups eventually need to make a profit!

MORE PROFIT? MORE FREEDOM!

Profit is the result of a system that provides value to customers in ways that are sufficiently differentiated from your competitors and that generates more revenue than costs.

The system must include defining this value and charging a fair price for it—*not just once*, but also over time.

This book is specifically about creating sustainably profitable software-enabled solutions because the knowledge, techniques, and best practices you find in traditional books on pricing regular goods and services cannot fully address the complexities business leaders face designing a Profit Stream.

 ***This is critical because Software is eating the world.***[(1)]

Software is now in everything

Smart Shoes

TESLA FARTS!

Safer/Faster Cars

CARS THAT
MAKE US
GIGGLE!

Door Locks

Which means every business must become proficient at creating profit from software.

An understanding of **software-enabled solutions** provides the foundation needed for this proficiency.

A **software-enabled solution (SES)** has four attributes:

Before software we had...

Hardware, Services, and Data.

Wrench, steam engine, ticker tape machine

Generating and managing stock quotes

Stock prices printed on ticker tape, stock orders printed on paper

Software

The instructions, data, and/or programs used to operate computers to perform a specific task.

Hardware

The chips, computers, and related infrastructure required to run the software.

Services

In some SES, people use and/or complement the software (like a Registered Investment Advisor who uses special software to provide investment advice).

In other software-enabled solutions, engineers and developers enhance the software, a topic discussed extensively later in the book.

Data

Most SES generate some data. The nature of this data can determine the value provided to the customer.

Profit Streams

Designing a Profit Stream starts with an understanding of value streams.

A value stream is the sequence of activities that an organization undertakes to design, produce, deliver, and as needed, maintain and/or extend a product or service to a customer.

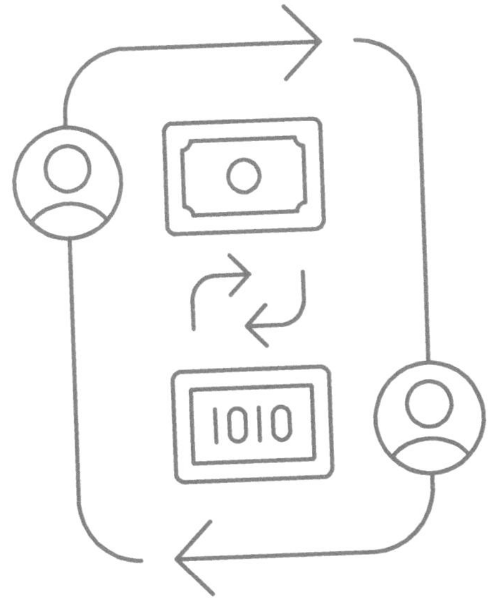

Value streams are everywhere!

They define everything from how a complex agricultural supply chain enables us to purchase milk in a supermarket, how a car company upgrades the software in a car, and even the recycling and disposing of an obsolete smart phone.

A solution is the product and/or service delivered to the customer.

Customers value a solution in proportion to its ability to meet their present and future needs.

Economic value is based on tangible and intangible attributes

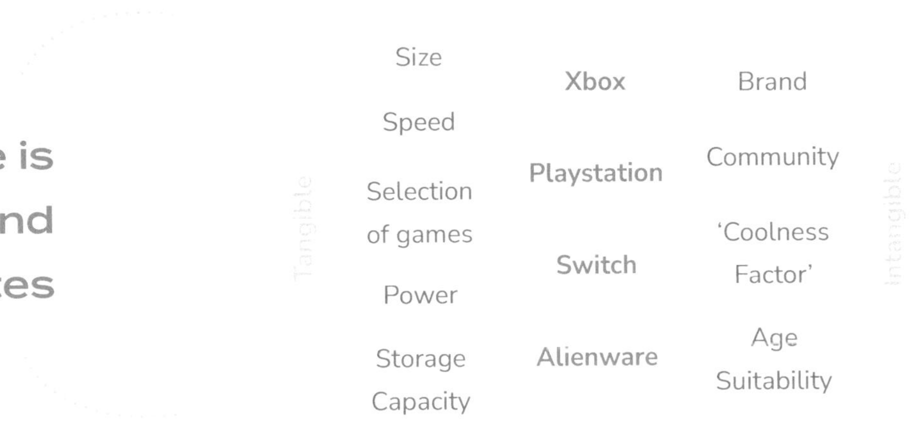

As we will explore later, customers vary significantly in their perceptions of value and what they are willing to pay. These differences can significantly change your ability to generate a profit.

A **Profit Stream** is a value stream designed to create a sustainable business.

Profit Streams:

- Quantify the **economic value** of the solutions they create...
- Are sold through **pricing** and **licensing** choices that...
- Ensure the **revenue** generated from these solutions exceed the **costs** required to serve across the solution lifecycle.

THE TYPICAL SOLUTION IS NOT PROFITABLE ON A SINGLE CUSTOMER, BUT INSTEAD FACTORS THE ECONOMICS OF MULTIPLE CUSTOMERS OVER TIME.

What is value?

Value is the benefits a customer receives less the total cost of ownership.

Profit Streams are the necessary evolution of value streams.

These four techniques will help you evolve your value streams.

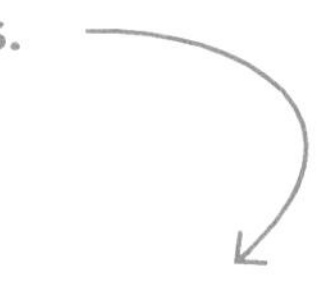

Customer Benefit Analysis is how you will identify and quantify the economic value of your solution.

Pricing Strategy, Structure, Specifics, and Policy design is how you will generate revenue.

PAGE 149

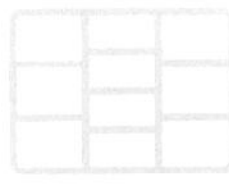

Total Solution Cost analysis is how you will identify and model your costs and pricing.

PAGE 175

Customer and Solution ROI modeling is how you will ensure all parties benefit.

PAGE 199

While a business can - and should - make a profit on one sale, **sustainable profits** come from an ongoing stream of sales between a business, the market it is serving, and its customers.

Sustainability starts with market share

You have developed a software-enabled solution to help paint companies match color samples. You estimate that there are 100,000 paint stores. Your path to sustainability starts by selling your solution to your first customer. It continues as you acquire market share.

Sustainability through Customer Lifetime Value

The right choices in pricing ensures that each customer is profitable. And while this may take some time, and even a few generations of releases, the inescapable fact is that a sustainable solution must make a profit.

Sustainability requires profitable unit economics so that you're not losing money as you scale. While this can take time and substantial capital investments, eventually the unit economics must be such that each additional sale is profitable.

In a healthy solution, both customers A and B contribute to profit. It is likely that A has a greater TLV. However, depending on the business, B might have greater unit profits.

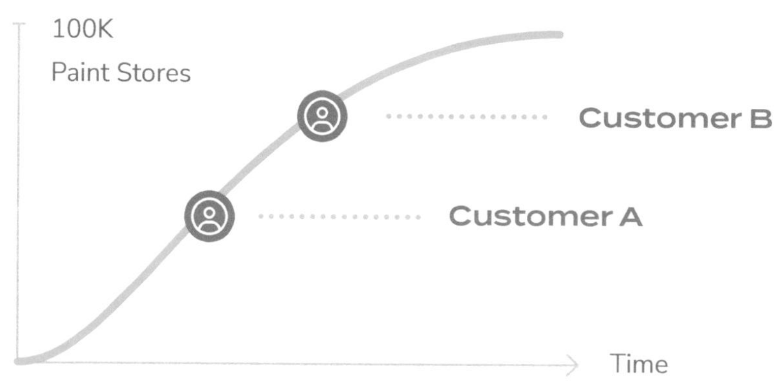

Profit Stream design integrates three aspects of sustainability, all of which are interdependent and evolve over time.

Solution Sustainability means...

Customers are receiving a continuous flow of value. The timing of this flow of value is determined by customer and market needs and the nature of the solution.

The frequency of value delivery is enabled—or constrained—by technical choices in the design and delivery of the solution, compliance requirements, and other contextual factors.

Economic Sustainability means...

Your customer's assessment of value is greater than the price they've paid, and your revenues exceed your costs to create, maintain, and operate your solution—which often vary by customer segment.

Selecting your solution also means that it provides more value than alternative solutions, including the status quo.

Relationship Sustainability means...

The legal agreements (such as contracts, terms and conditions, and licensing agreements) that govern the interactions between the solution, customers, suppliers, and regulatory agencies promote mutually beneficial outcomes.

Software Profit Streams should deliver an ongoing sequence of different 'sizes' of value, from a small bug fix to a major release.

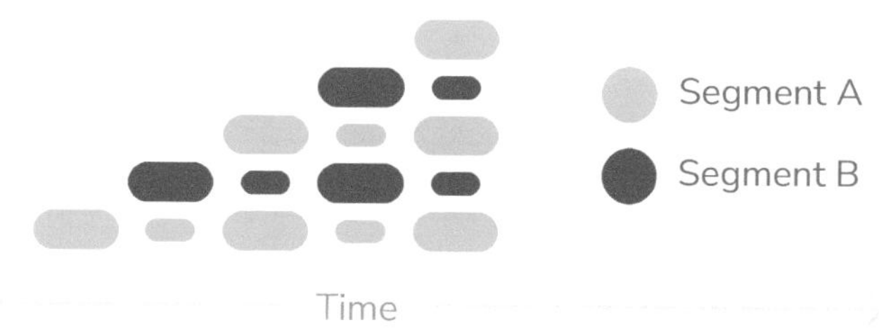

In this picture, each block represents the value created by a specific Feature. These accumulate over time.

Discrete features can be combined to create even more value: in a software-enabled solution, 1+1 really can be equal to 3!

For instance, a mobile game can be updated with a new level, new items, new roles, and other improvements.

As long as the value continues to attract new customers and/or retain existing customers, the solution is sustainable.

If you want to learn more about under what condition the addition of a new 'block of value' warrants a price increase, turn to page 341 on Solution Lifecycle Management.

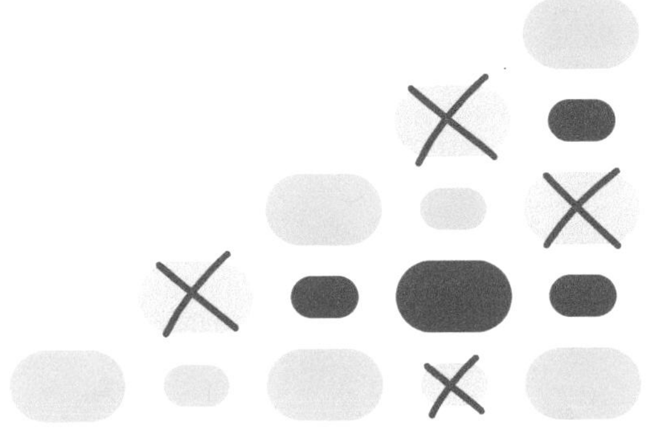

Blocks of value can deteriorate over time.

Because the perception of value changes over time, Profit Stream design encompasses the inevitable evolution of customer needs.

Accordingly, Profit Stream design is based on an understanding of customer needs over time, a topic explored starting on page 40 in our discussion of the solution lifecycle.

A game company that must decide which versions of smart phone to support will find the greatest value in supporting the most recent versions of the phone, eventually declining to support the oldest models who do not have enough customers to justify the costs of supporting the older hardware.

There are two kinds of value streams:

Operational Value Streams and Development Value Streams.

Operational Value Streams

Operational Value Streams (OVS) define how a customer interacts with the enterprise. The sequence of activities involved in the value stream are commonly drawn as boxes or chevrons that capture the flow of work.

OVS ARE USED TO MODEL VALUE

Development Value Streams

Development Value Streams (DVS) capture the 'behind the scenes' activities that support and/or create some or all of the solutions offered to a customer.

DVS ARE INPUTS INTO COST MODELS

PROFIT STREAMS ARE USED TO MODEL PROFIT!

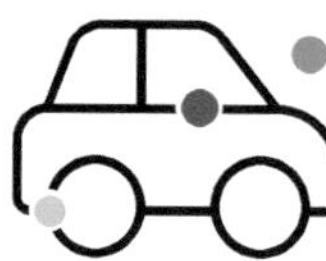

- The fulfillment of a car order from a website through a dealership is an **OVS**
- The team building the power train is a DVS
- The team building the entertainment system is a **DVS**

Some software-enabled solutions provide value over many years, such as the financial applications that help consumers and businesses manage taxes.

Other solutions can be considered disposable, used only for a specific problem for a short period time, such as mobile games that are played for a few days or weeks or a conference app that allows attendees of an event manage their schedule.

All software-enabled solutions have to make a profit. How they make a profit varies based on their underlying business model. Solutions used for a limited period of time must have a low-cost basis and a strategy designed to support future sales. Hosted or Software-as-a-Service solutions based on recurring revenues must charge enough to support the ongoing investments which create sustainable value. Enterprise solutions targeted to B2B customers and associated with large license fees must be designed to support a longterm relationship with customers who rely on these solutions.

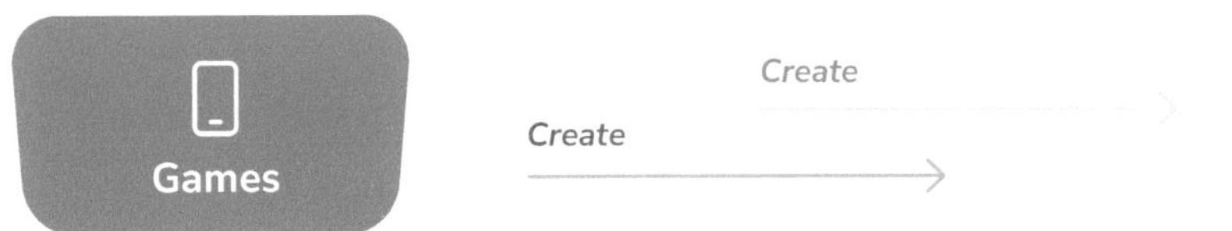

A game studio's business model is often based on selling new games to the same customers by using the profit from one successful game to create a new game. These profits can be further enhanced through the sale of digital goods to all customers.

An enterprise software provider's business model is typically based on extending a core platform by using the profits of previous releases to fund the development of subsequent releases.

Every sustainable software-enabled solution has a set of ongoing expenses. One objective of the Profit Stream is to ensure the sustainability of the business.

Systems Thinking

Designing a sustainable **Software-Enabled Solution** involves making—and remaking—a system of **interdependent choices.**

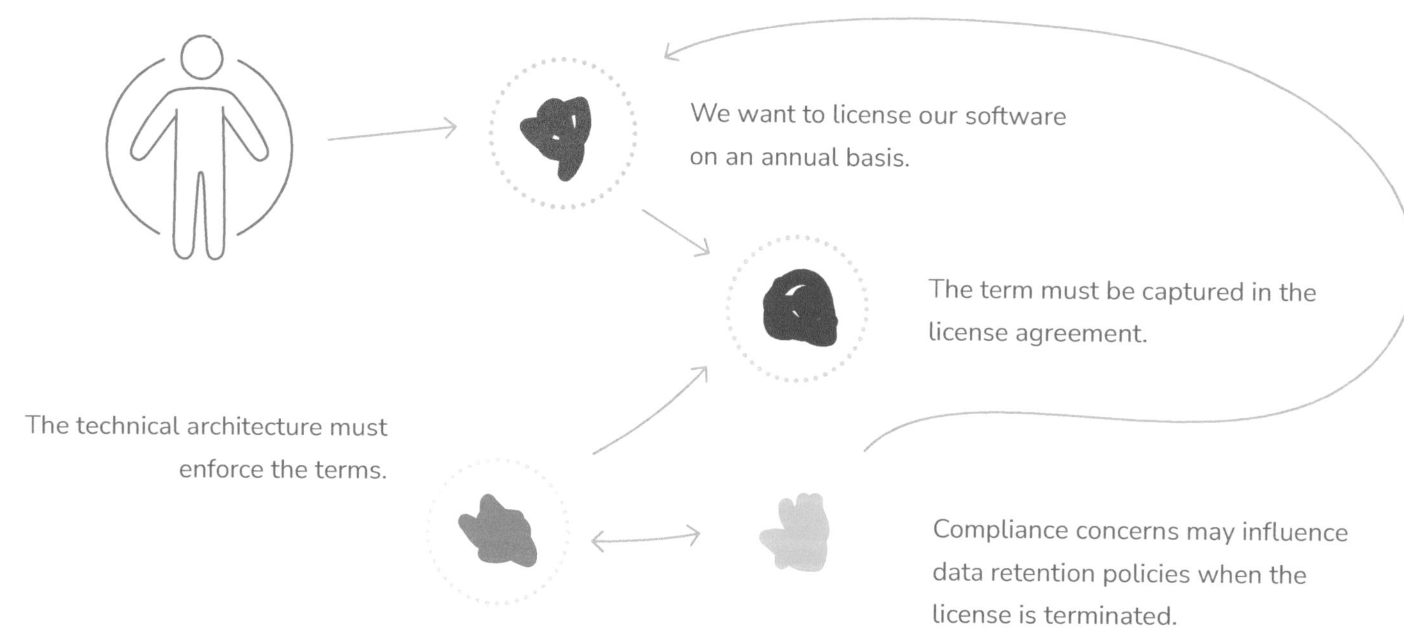

We want to license our software on an annual basis.
The term must be captured in the license agreement.
The technical architecture must enforce the terms.
Compliance concerns may influence data retention policies when the license is terminated.

The choices we make can be captured as a set of nodes and relationships. Your sequence exploring this system will vary.

Starting with one node may lead us through the system in an entirely new way — even if we end up at the same place.

By organizing the elements of our system as a canvas, we create a highly compact representation that promotes **holistic innovation, collective wisdom, and collaboration.**

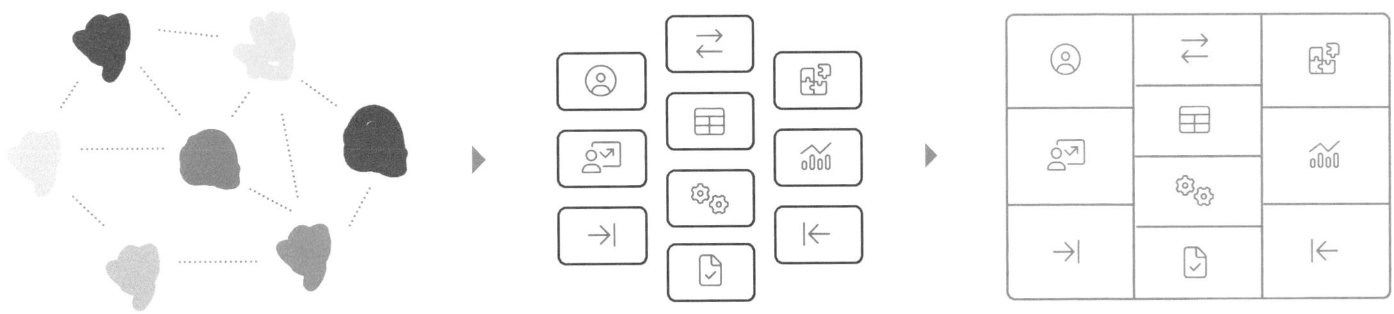

Systems Thinking and Sustainability

Here are some of the ways in which the systems thinking promoted by the **Profit Stream Canvas** creates more sustainable solutions.

Let's explore a data-centric solution that ingests raw data, reprocesses it, and generates new value-added results.

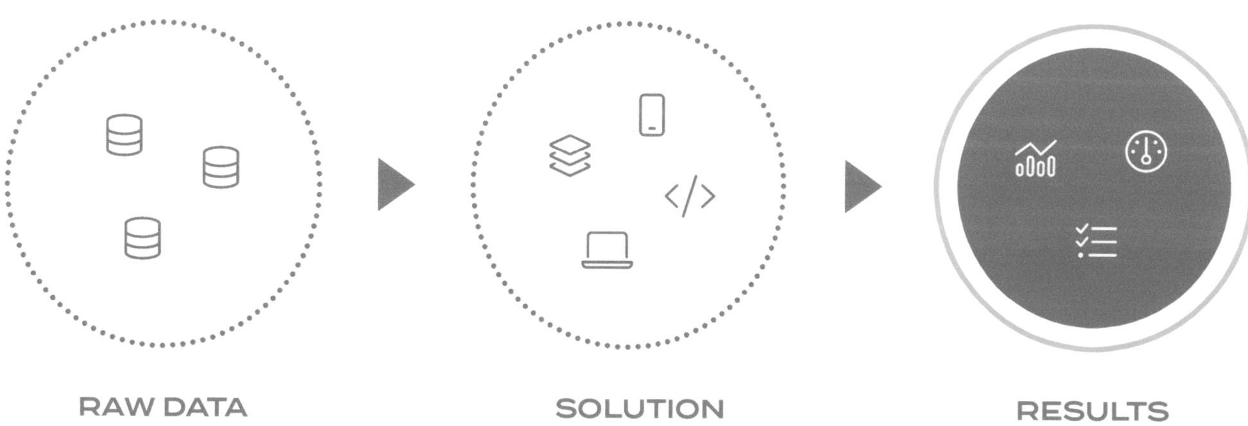

Here are some of the ways the **Profit Stream Canvas** uses **systems thinking** to create more sustainable solutions.

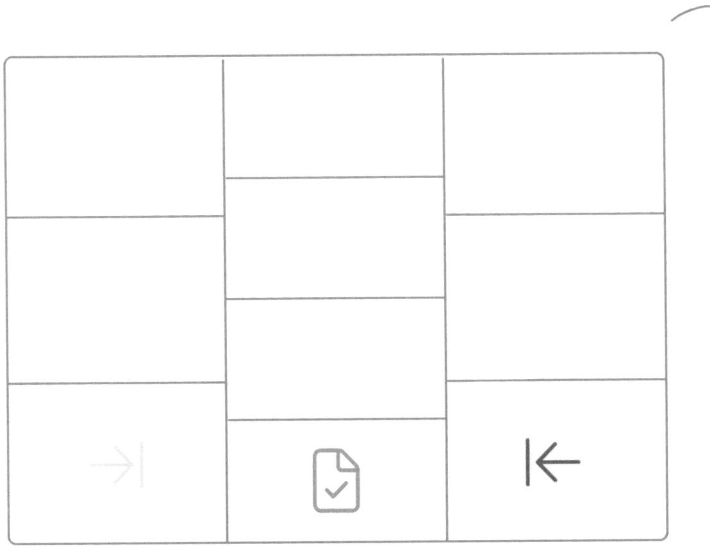

The Profit Stream Canvas will help ensure you're managing your in-licenses.

The Profit Stream Canvas will help you comply with in-license and regulatory concerns.

The Profit Stream Canvas will help you develop your license agreements with your customers.

Let's consider a different example. Consider a solution that has been consistently evolving over several years.

In this case, the canvas will help you plan and execute price changes.

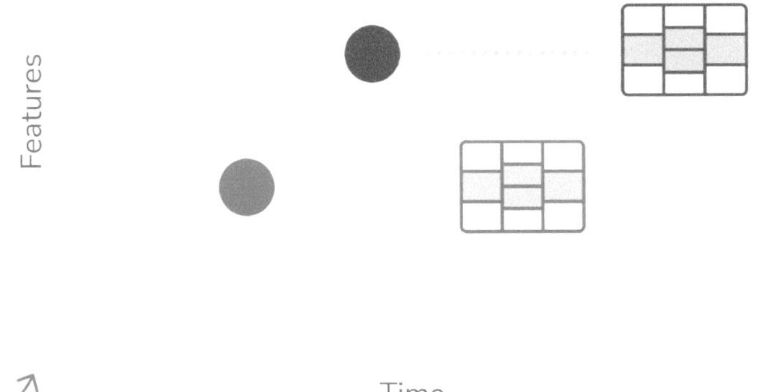

Systems Thinking Mindsets

The Profit Stream Canvas supports different systems thinking mindsets.

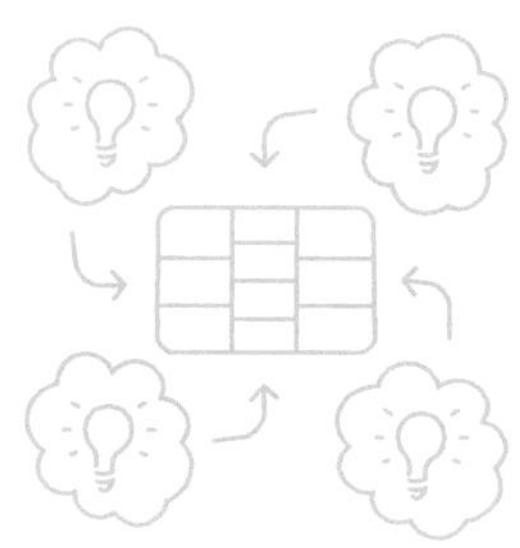

The Explorer

I use the canvas to explore ideas without missing something important.

The Designer

I use the canvas to realize my vision for a new or improved Profit Stream.

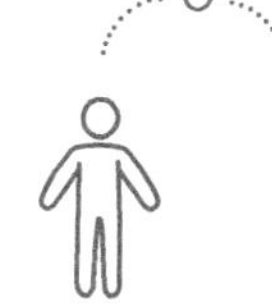

The Strategist

I use the canvas to plan ahead for a better future.

The Technician

I use the canvas to focus on key aspects of the solution.

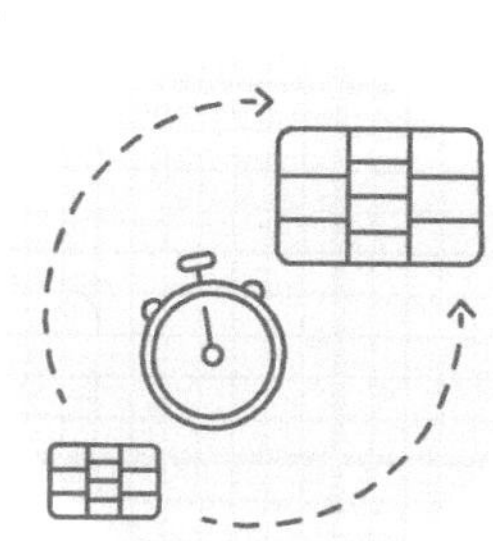

We are all of these (sometimes).

The New System Innovator

A special application of the Profit Stream Canvas occurs when you are designing entirely new systems. Instead of a single canvas you may have multiple canvases that enable you -and your team- to design the broader solution - including a new system.

You might create two canvases:

OVEN WITH AI

IN-STORE RECIPES

For example, let's consider the design of a new portable oven with an AI cooking engine and a cloud-based catalog of recipes.

The recipes may be stored in a proprietary format. The oven will have standard connections for power and a custom battery pack.

Looking for the biggest impact?

Start by developing your Profit Stream in the context of an existing system. Identify how this context influences your current design.

Change the external forces of the system and you'll get a new Profit Stream.

Navigating the future

Navigating the Future

Creating a software-enabled solution is a commitment to a future shrouded in a fog of uncertainty.

- **How should we design our business model?**
- **What is our pricing and licensing model?**
- **What features should be removed? Or added?**
- **How might we take advantage of emerging technologies?**
- **What macro-economic, cultural, societal, and environmental forces will most impact our solution?**

Sustainable businesses use a variety of models, frameworks, and maps to navigate through the fog of uncertainty.

It is hard to navigate through the fog of uncertainty without **models, maps** and **frameworks.**

Effective business leaders use these tools to promote business agility through the design and evolution of software-enabled solutions.

Ineffective business leaders use these tools to ignore market feedback, maintain outdated policies, and inhibit the natural innovation within their organization.

There are a few general approaches to **navigating through a fog.**

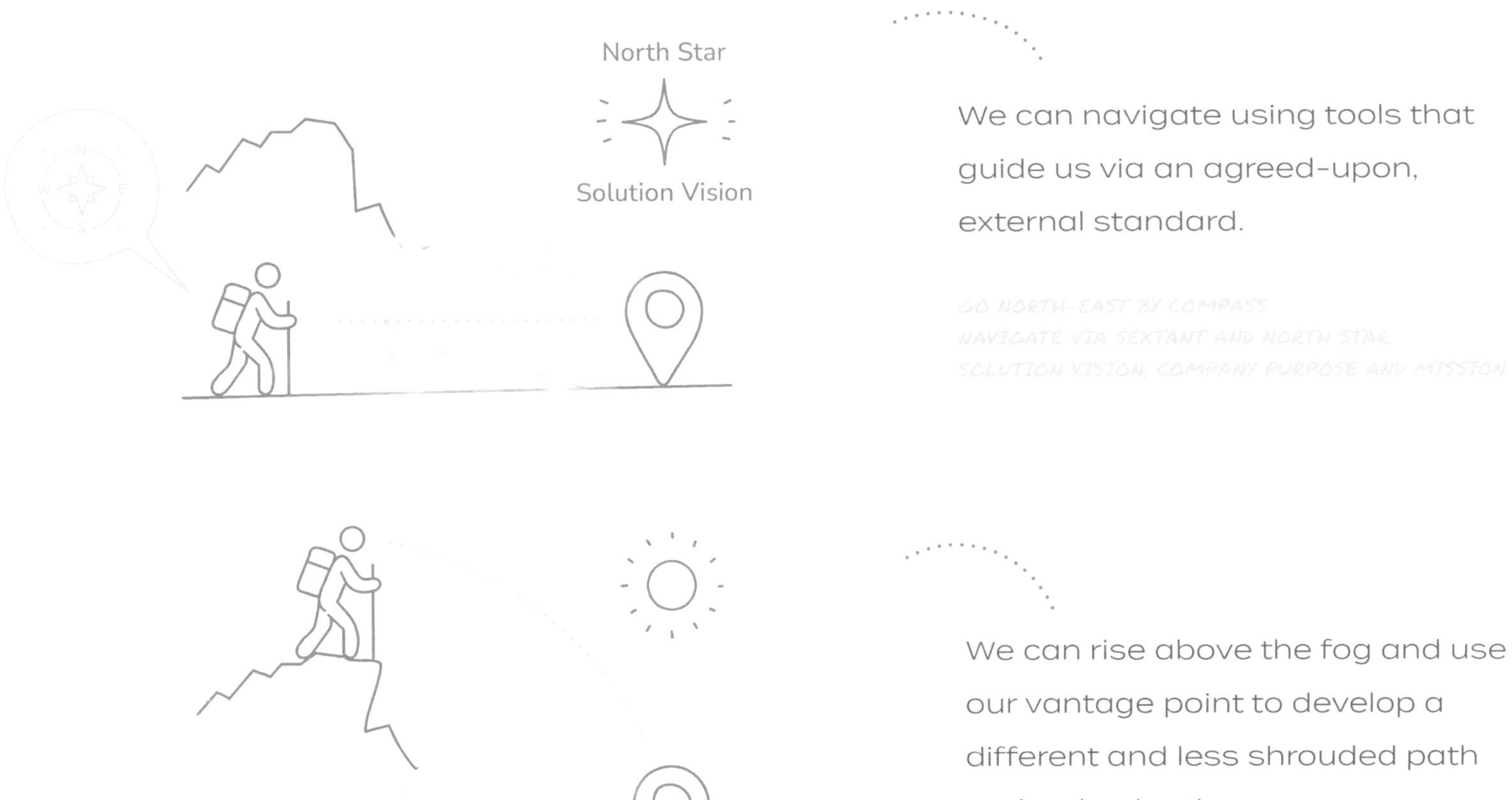

We can navigate using tools that guide us via an agreed-upon, external standard.

We can rise above the fog and use our vantage point to develop a different and less shrouded path to the destination.

Together, these approaches provide guidance to brave navigators of the future.

While **models, maps, and frameworks** guide us through the fog, sustainable business leaders are adept at navigating the realities of the market.

Sustainable business leaders know that your **final destination** may vary based on what happens during your journey. Whether you call this a pivot or just a new choice, the result is created from using these models and adjusting based on the customer and market terrain.

There are many tools business leaders use to navigate the fog of uncertainty. Because this fog becomes more dense the further we project into the future and the farther we stray from our own solution, we organize tools in two dimensions:

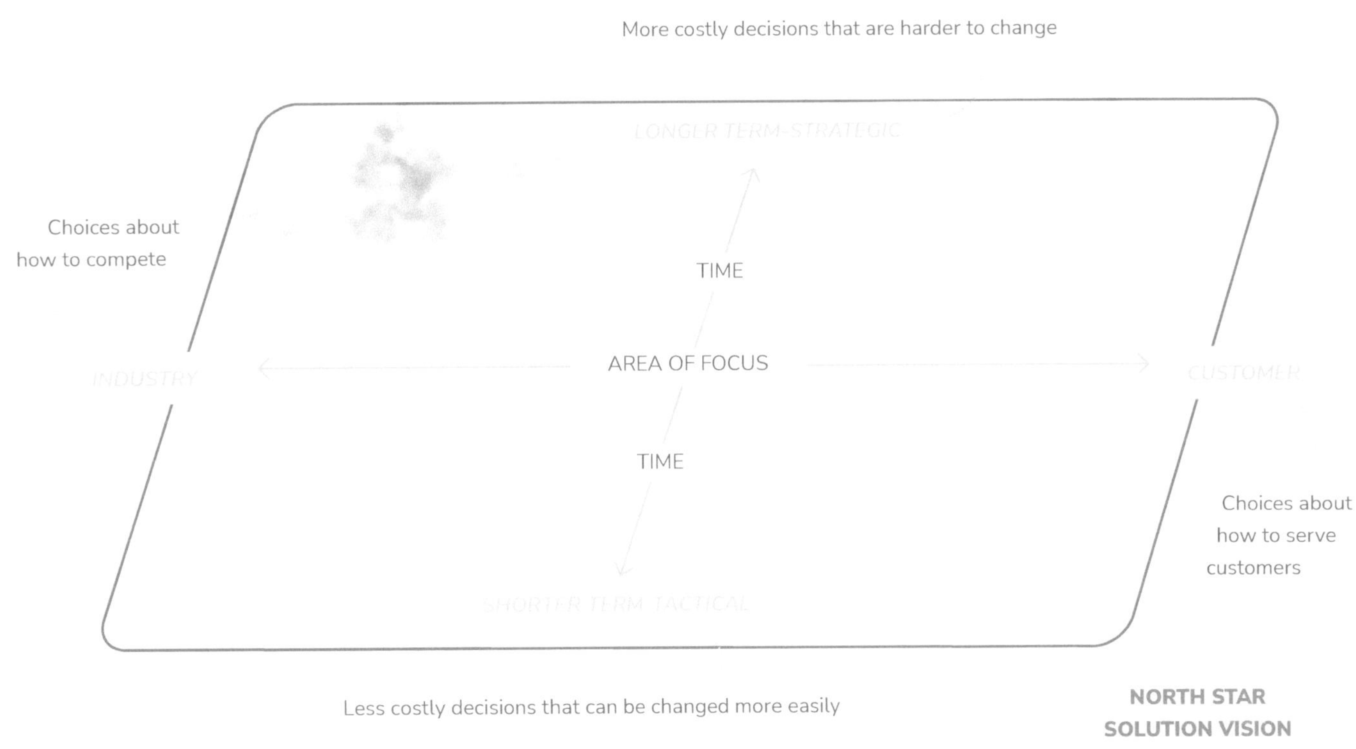

SEVEN TOOLS TO NAVIGATE THE FOG OF UNCERTAINTY

The Industry Lifecycle captures the broad structure of all solutions serving a given market.

The Solution Lifecycle captures the development, launch, and ongoing success of your solution.

Prune the Product Tree captures the evolution of solution features over time, emphasizing organic growth.

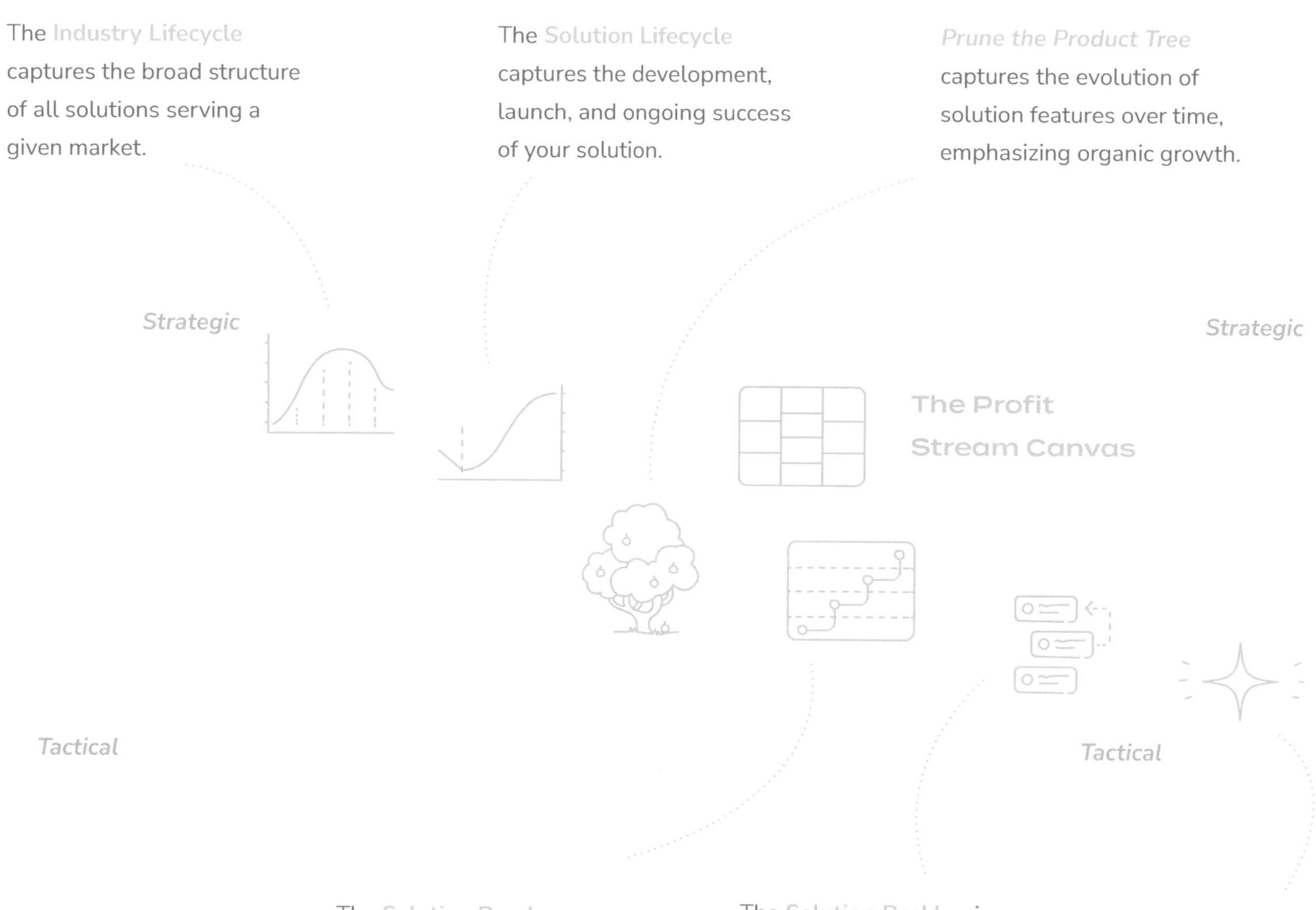

Visit www.profit-streams.com/navigating-uncertainty for additional tools.

The Solution Roadmap captures planned commitments, milestones, and releases, typically for 1-3 years.

The Solution Backlog is a prioritized list of near-term work items, where near-term ranges from 1 week to 3 months.

The North Star Solution Vision informs cohesive usage of the other tools.

The Industry Lifecycle

It provides a model for the creation, growth, maturation, and eventual decline of a collection of companies that serve common market needs.

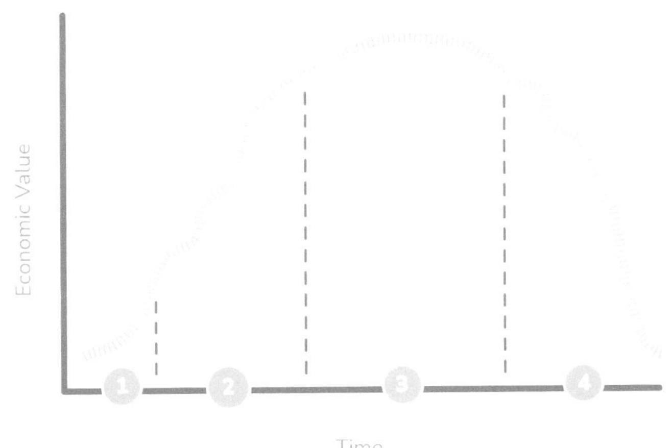

1 INTRODUCTION

Introduction is the domain of startups that are creating a new industry. Highly volatile, many companies fail because they are 'too early' for the market.

2 GROWTH

The growth phase is where new companies become sustainable, existing companies decide to join, and overall success emerges.

As the industry matures, weaker companies fail, competitors merge or are acquired, and the industry coalesces around leaders.

3 MATURITY

In the maturity phase, companies are well-established, and profits tend to be highest.

4 DECLINE

The decline phase captures the end of the need for a given set of solutions in a market. Companies evolve to new industries or fail.

Three things you need to know about the **INDUSTRY LIFECYCLE**

Know your location.

Your position in the Industry Lifecycle helps determine your pricing power, how you will compete, and other strategic choices.

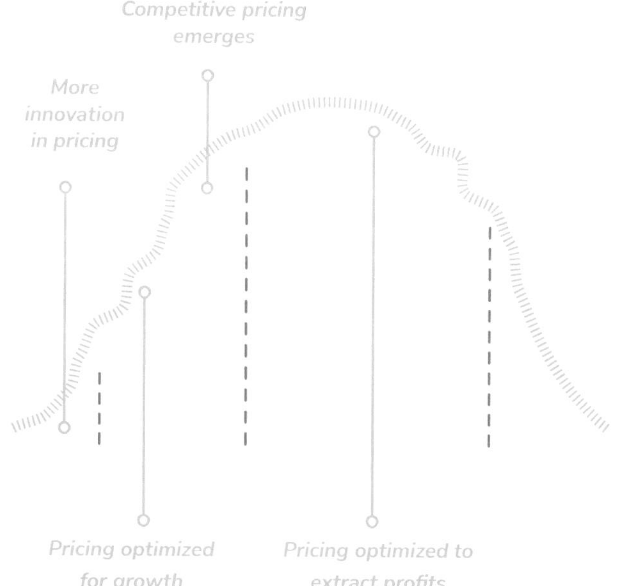

The maturity phase is often longer than you think.

Technology advances and innovation can extend the Maturity phase by decades, providing plenty of room for continued competition.

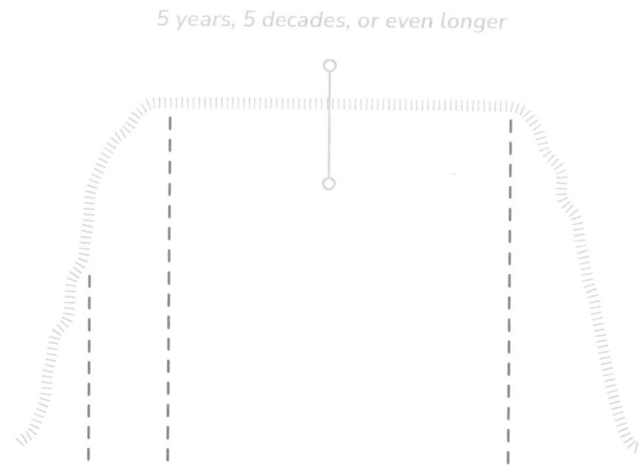

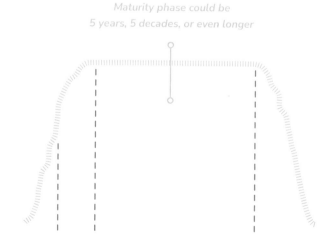

WE LISTENED TO MUSIC ON COMPACT DISCS FOR ABOUT A DECADE... AND WE'VE BEEN DRIVING CARS FOR MORE THAN A CENTURY!

3

There are opportunities in every stage!

ZOOM, SLACK, AND WORKDAY ARE SOME COMPANIES THAT STARTED BY TARGETING A MATURE MARKET.

You can acquire, merge, or otherwise join (or fight!).

The maturation phase is often the perfect place to introduce a superior offering — you know a market exists, so serve it better than competitors.

The decline phase can create lucrative opportunities to profitably serve niche segments.

While most of the world has moved to streaming music services, there remains a market for records and record players.

You can join fellow innovators and create the industry.

For hundreds of years, patent analysis was a slow and costly process, often limited to patent attorneys. It was a mature industry, with a known problem, ripe for disruption.

Aurigin Systems saw an opportunity to use advanced data warehouse and search technology to distrupt this industry.

Traditional Patent Analysis

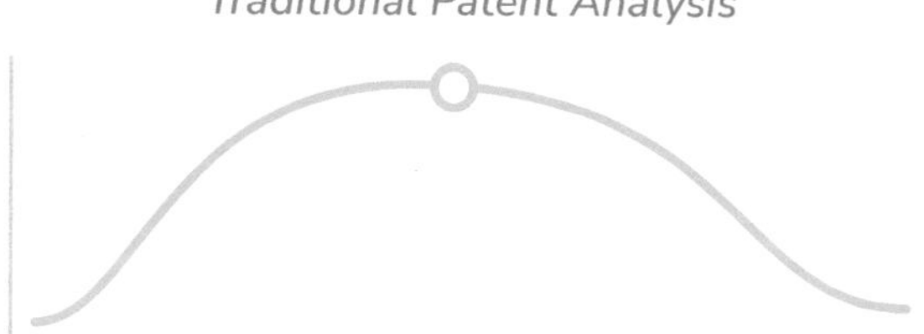

Patent Analysis

NEW industry called "Intellectual Property Asset Management"

Aurigin created an entirely new industry—Intellectual Property Asset Management—that far exceeded traditional patent analysis.

In creating an industry that unlocked billions of dollars of value buried in patent portfolios, Aurigin secured millions of dollars in VC funding, and was acquired by an incumbent who wanted to gain the benefit of acquiring a company who had defined a new industry.

The Solution Lifecycle

The Solution Lifecycle captures the **development, launch, growth, maturation, and decline** of a specific solution within a market.

As described in the book *Diffusion of Innovations*, every successful solution follows an S-Shaped **curve of adoption,** in which categories of adopters acquire the solution according to durable traits and the relationship between the entity adopting the solution and the solution itself.[5]

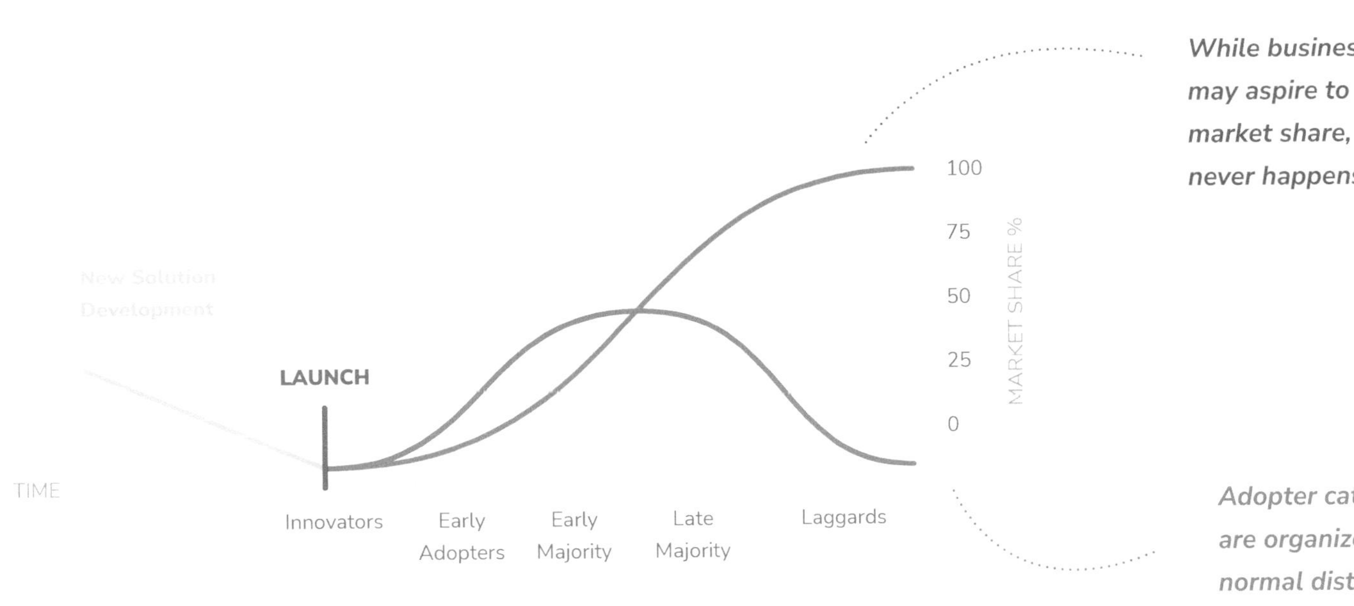

While business leaders may aspire to reach 100% market share, it virtually never happens.

Adopter categories are organized in a normal distribution.

These adopter categories can be found in all consumer, professional, and business markets.

Adopters are categorized on innovativeness, measured by the time at which an individual or organization adopts the solution.

INNOVATORS: VENTURESOME

Adventurous customers who actively pursue new technology and are willing to take the highest risks.

EARLY ADOPTERS: RESPECT

Customers who seek new solutions, albeit with less emphasis on the technology, and more emphasis on gaining early access to the benefits of the solution.

B2C - B2P

Typically more affluent and more driven by psychometric factors, including the intrinsic motivation of 'trying new things for fun'.

B2B

Typically seeking the earliest possible competitive advantage; may be quiet about their adoption.

EARLY MAJORITY: DELIBERATE

Pragmatic in nature, early majority customers adopt the new solution after risks are mitigated and the solution has a more proven track record of providing value.

B2C - B2P - B2B

Individuals and businesses in this category tend to be more skeptical, often waiting until a new solution matches a convenient and known market rhythm.. They typically require more support and more financial proof.

LATE MAJORITY: SKEPTICAL

These customers are the most skeptical. They tend to purchase when solutions are known to be stable, support options are plentiful, and the company is stable and mature.

B2C - B2P - B2B

Individuals and businesses in this category are likely to wait as long as possible to adopt a solution, often skipping market rhythms and avoiding potential risky changes. Changing your focus to improving intangible attributes ('fewer features, better support') helps attract the late majority.

LAGGARDS: TRADITIONAL

These customers adopt the solution when prior alternatives are no longer available or when the solution has been fully integrated into another solution in such a way that it is not material.

B2C - B2P - B2B

Because individuals and businesses in this category do not seek to change from their existing solutions, they are not typically a financially attractive portion of the market. Indeed, they may only seek a change when required because of regulatory compliance or product obsolescence.

The category of an adopter is based on the nature of the innovation—A given customer may be an early adopter of one solution and a laggard of another.

"I'm a gamer, and I always buy the newest game console!"

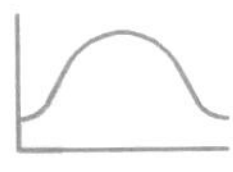

"When buying a car, my goal is to keep it for as long as possible."

"We always look for software to reduce cost and increase profit."

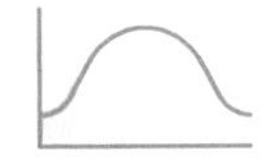

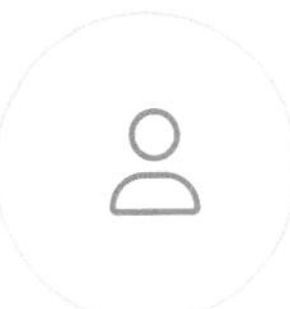

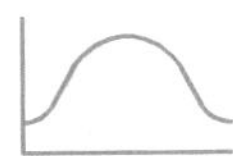

"I love movies, and I usually upgrade my TV faster than my friends."

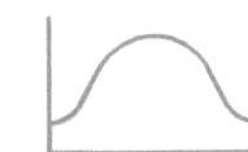

"As a salesperson, I look for software that helps me close deals faster."

"We only buy new equipment when it wears out, even if it's depreciated."

Business leaders who can identify the adoption category of their customers are in a better position to **design pricing strategies that close sales faster.**

Geoffrey Moore identified that in many technology markets the gap between the early adopters and the **early majority** was so great it created a **'chasm'.**

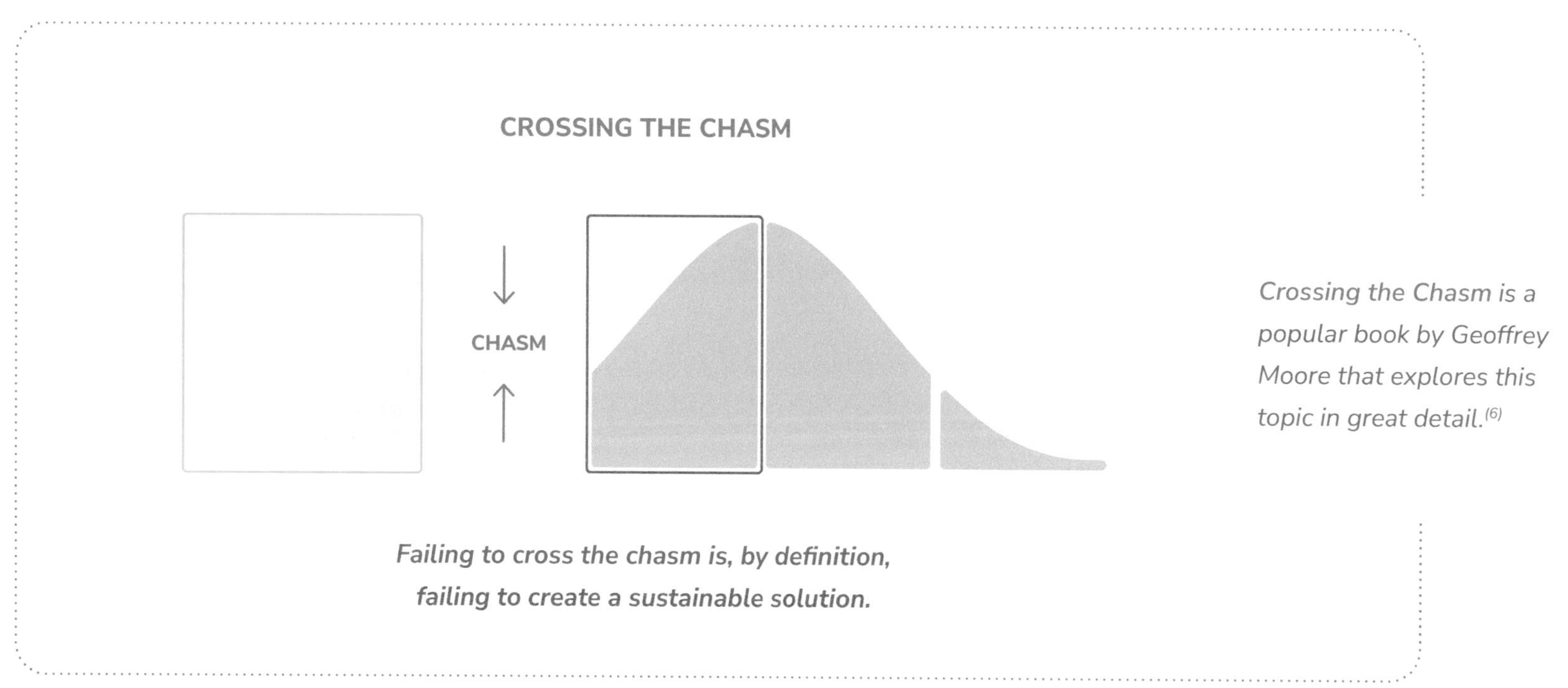

Crossing the Chasm is a popular book by Geoffrey Moore that explores this topic in great detail.[6]

Failing to cross the chasm is, by definition, failing to create a sustainable solution.

To help customers cross the chasm, solution providers must pay special attention to intangible benefits.

For example, minimizing the fear of losing data may be more important than adding more features.

Five things to know about the **Solution Lifecycle.**

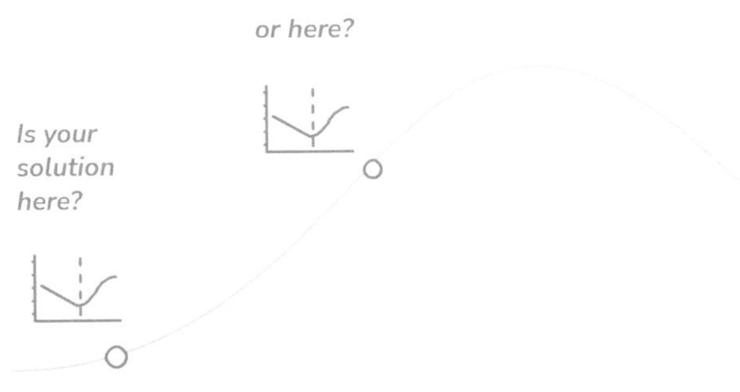

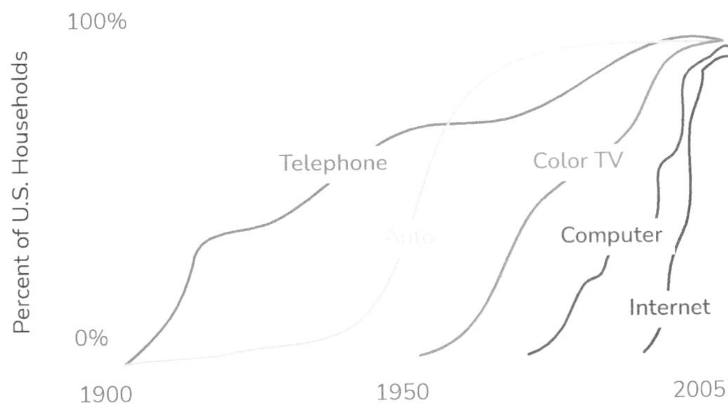

1 Know where you are

There are many Solution Lifecycles within the Industry Lifecycle. Knowing where your solution is situated creates a competitive advantage in navigating the fog.

2 Avoid too much precision

Do not be overly precise about your analysis because estimates of the precise number of customers within an adopter category are imprecise and fail to capture growth and decay. Focus more on the reasons behind your adopters' behaviors.

3 Use Agile to move faster

The increased density and sophistication of communication networks and the consistent reduction of global poverty means that new solutions are adopted and discarded at a faster pace. If you're not using Agile frameworks, chances are good you won't be able to match the pace of your competitors.[7]

Each release provides a unique set of opportunities.

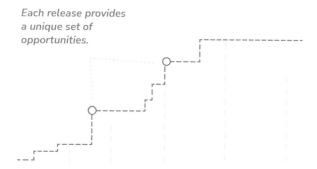

4 Time releases with market rhythms

The smooth curve hides the stair-step nature of discrete releases of a solution. By timing these releases with your customer's buying patterns, business leaders can increase profits.

Prepare for the next curve

There are multiple solution curves, one for every solution. The collection of these curves vary based on the Industry Structure, the size and growth rate of the market, and the rate of innovation of the provider.

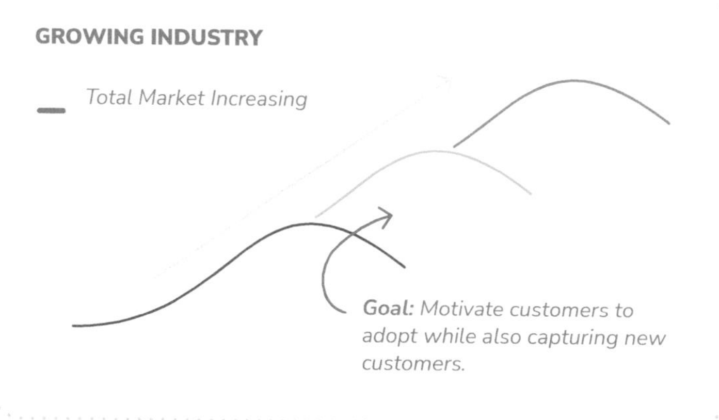

GROWING INDUSTRY
Total Market Increasing
Goal: Motivate customers to adopt while also capturing new customers.

STABLE INDUSTRY
Goal: Steal customers from competitors and/or motivate them to migrate from older to newer versions of your solution.
Market size is stable

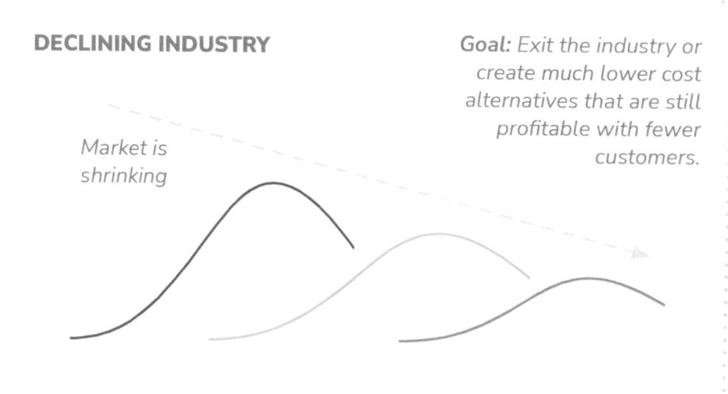

DECLINING INDUSTRY
Goal: Exit the industry or create much lower cost alternatives that are still profitable with fewer customers.
Market is shrinking

YOUR SOLUTION PORTFOLIO SHOULD CLEARLY SHOW THE STATE OF ALL SOLUTIONS

EACH NEW SOLUTION CREATES AN OPPORTUNITY TO DEVELOP NEW PRICING & LICENSING OPTIONS

Using the Solution Lifecycle to raise prices

The first principle of the Agile manifesto states: "Our highest priority is to satisfy the customer through early and continuous delivery of valuable software".

While inspiring, this principle fails to provide guidance on when a company should raise prices to account for the increase in value.

Knowify is a fast-growing SaaS platform that helps electricians, plumbers, and other trades, and construction companies, manage finances, subcontractors, and projects.

Knowify used the Solution Lifecycle to help identify that their solution had started to move from visionaries to early adopters. This change in buyer created an opportunity to raise prices to better reflect the increased value of the Knowify platform.

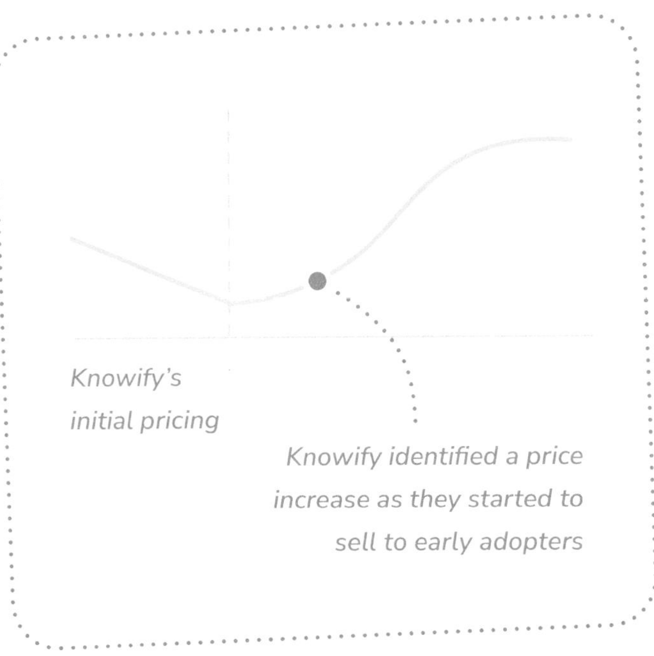

Because **Profit Streams** are designed to serve the needs of external and internal stakeholders over time, we augment the conceptual models of the Industry and Solution Lifecycles with a Vision, a Prune the Product Tree, and a Customer-Centric Solution Roadmap.

These tools guide the organization with a perspective of the future that integrates customer and market feedback.

Vision

A vision is a model or depiction of a future state that guides the development of one or more solutions. It can be delivered in many forms:

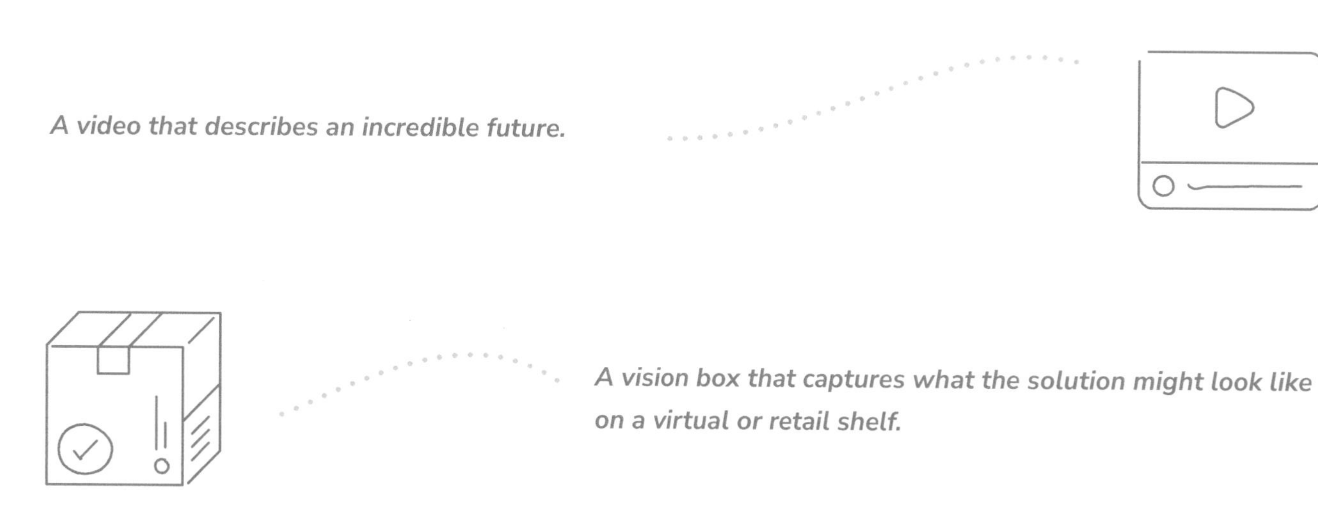

A video that describes an incredible future.
A vision box that captures what the solution might look like on a virtual or retail shelf.

A vision box is based on the Product Box Innovation Game. [4]

A graphic novel that shows how your customer succeeds with your solution.

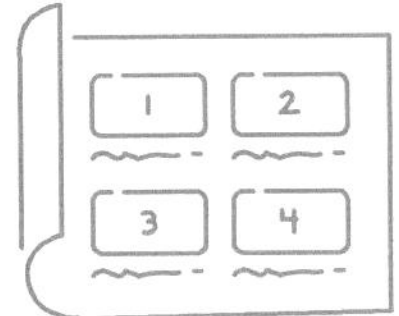

A press release that describes the solution.

Visions that strike the right balance of time, technology, and a better future for our customers inspire us.

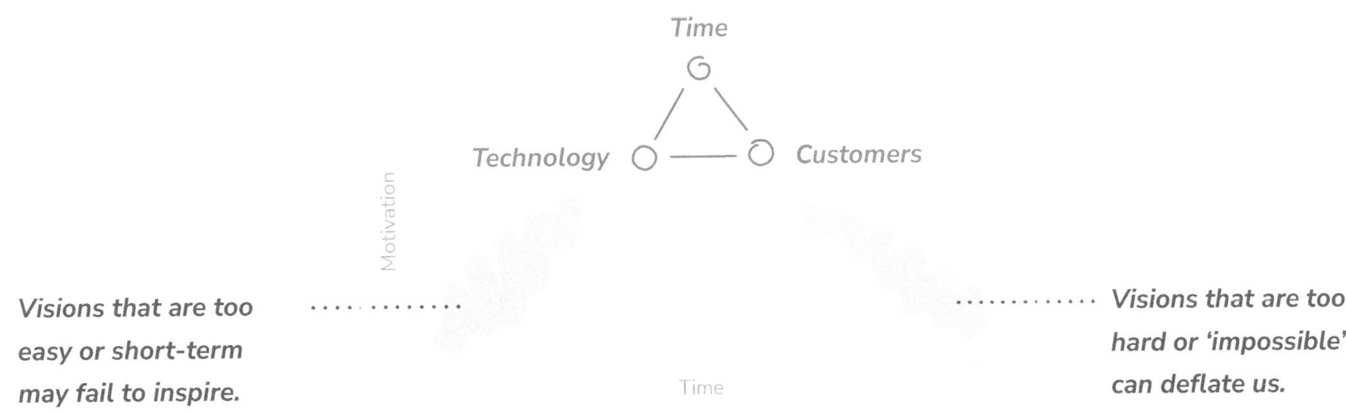

Time
Technology
Customers
Motivation
Time
Visions that are too easy or short-term may fail to inspire.
Visions that are too hard or 'impossible' can deflate us.

Prune the Product Tree*

This technique uses the organic metaphor of a growing tree to capture the evolution of a solution.

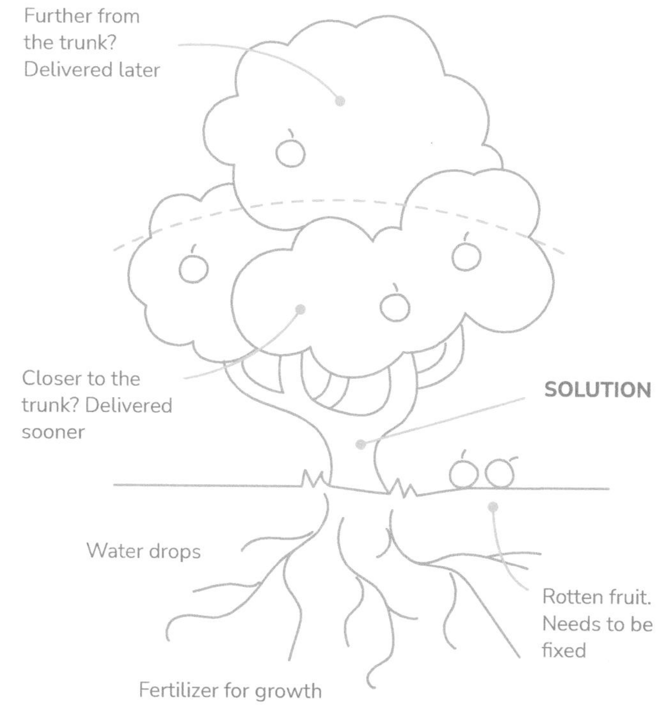

Tailor these to meet your needs.
Use a fruit that aligns to your market, such as Apples and Peaches in North America, Pears in Europe, Dates in Africa, Figs in the Middle East, Mangoes in India, and Avocados in Latin America.

FRUIT	Tangible benefits
LEAVES	Intangible benefits
ROOTS **WATER** **FERTILIZER**	Infrastructure or technical requirements that sustain the tree or support a specific set of fruits.
BRANCHES	Related sets of features or broad capabilities.

Originally described in the book Innovation Games: Creating Breakthrough Products Through Collaborative Play, Prune the Product Tree is also known as Prune the Future, The Product Tree game. [4]

Like the gardener who prunes trees to promote the growth of high-quality fruit, business leaders need to prune the features of their solution so they too can thrive.

There are **lots** of ways to use *Prune the Product Tree*...

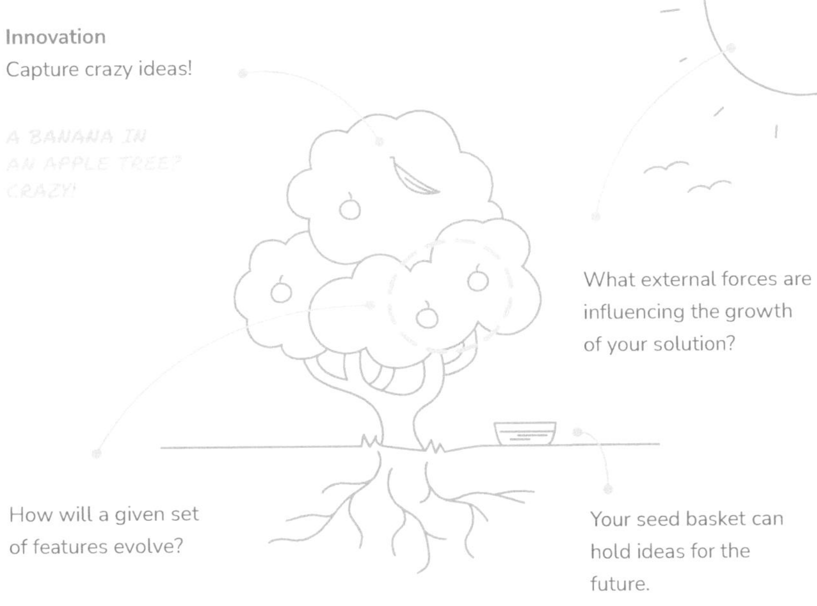
Innovation
Capture crazy ideas!
A BANANA IN
AN APPLE TREE?
CRAZY!
What external forces are influencing the growth of your solution?
How will a given set of features evolve?
Your seed basket can hold ideas for the future.

Create one tree for every solution:
The Portfolio Orchard
Mature solutions
Young/Emerging Solutions

Prune the Product Tree creates a warm and inviting forum for customers to share how they think your solution should evolve.

Create a starting tree capturing your perspective of growth 1

   2

Invite groups of customers to shape these trees to their needs.

   3

Use the results to shape your roadmap

What was pruned? What was added? What was moved?

Roadmaps

A roadmap clarifies and communicates how business leaders intend to execute on key strategies needed to achieve their goals over a period of time.

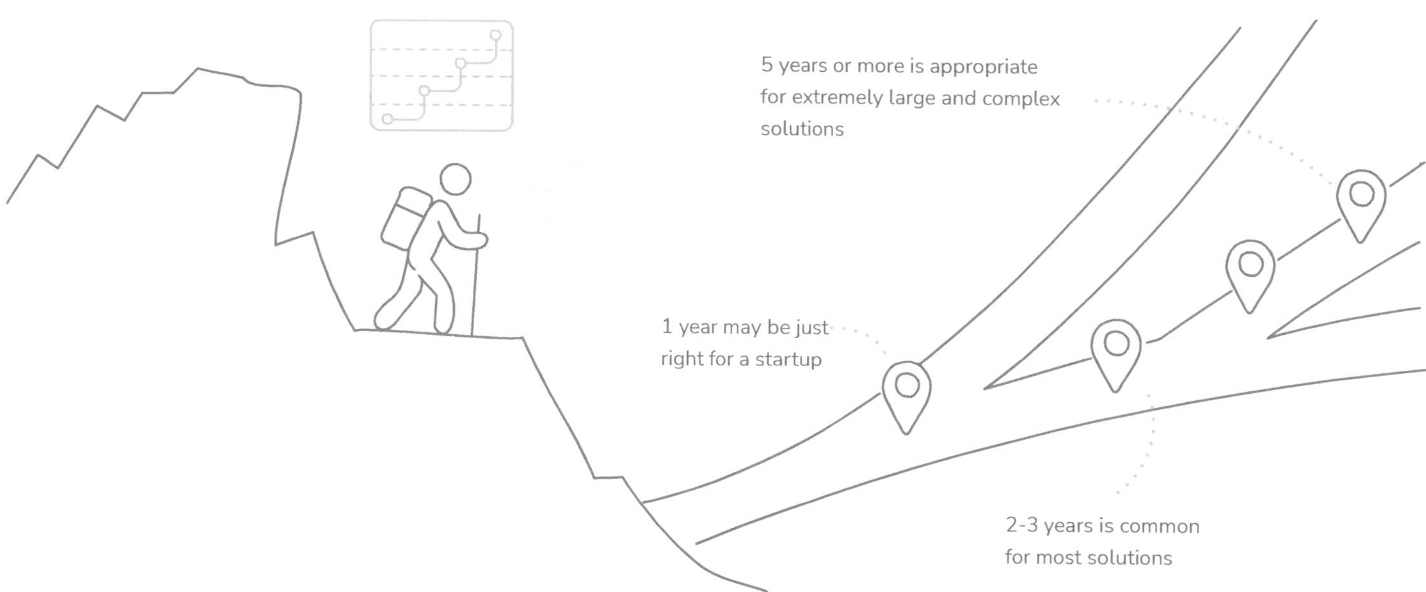
5 years or more is appropriate for extremely large and complex solutions
1 year may be just right for a startup
2-3 years is common for most solutions

Roadmaps evolve over time based on the dynamic interplay between the solution and the larger context in which the solution exists. This evolution perfectly captures the balance between creating a plan for the future while responding to reality.

Beyond Software Architecture

The roadmapping format used here was first introduced in Beyond Software Architecture by Luke Hohmann.

4 QUARTERS
2 HALVES
1 YEAR

Structured as a grid with time on the horizontal axis, roadmaps capture information in rows, or swimlanes.

Q Q Q Q H H Y

WHO	Who are we serving?	*Market Map*
WHAT & WHY	What features are we delivering and why do they matter? What problems are we solving? What benefits are we creating?	*Features & Benefits*
WHEN	What are the predictable, repeating events of your market?	*Market Rhythms*
	What are one-time events that are likely to influence your solution?	*Market Events*
PROFIT	How will you create sustainable profits?	*Profit Stream*
HOW	How should your technical architecture evolve?	*Technical Architecture*

FIDELITY DECREASES AS WE FORECAST FURTHER INTO THE FUTURE....

Additional swimlanes can *-and should-* be added as needed.

Common additions include swimlanes for *Partners, Suppliers, or Competitors.*

WHO? / WHAT? / WHY?

The first two swimlanes focus on who we're serving, what we're delivering, and why they care.

Market Map

The market map captures the market segments you're targeting over the planning horizon.

PRO TIP - There should be a small number of market segments on your map. Startups should have one. Mature companies may have a few.

Examples:

- High school students
- Technicians who manage HVAC control systems for apartments
- Non-profits that need to manage their finances

Features & Benefits

The features & benefits swimlane captures what you're delivering and why your customers care. Short statements are all that is needed!

PRO TIP - If your feature doesn't provide a benefit related to your Customer Benefit Analysis, why are you creating it? *(See page 75)*

Examples:

- Automated flight rebooking saves time for busy travelers

WHEN? / HOW FREQUENTLY?

The value of your solution varies considerably based on when and how frequently it is released. Market windows are defined by those periods of time when your release has optimal value. Use **Market Rhythms** & **Market Events** to identify market windows.

Market Rhythms

These rhythms often correlate to predictable customer buying patterns.

We capture these insights in our roadmap and use them to guide releases:

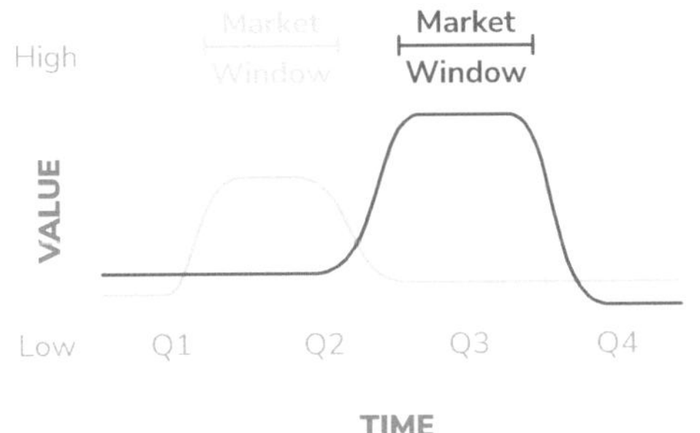

Retailers don't like to install new systems during Q4 holiday shopping season.

Software for farmers has to be delivered before the growing season.

Examples:

- New car buying season
- Summer vacations in Europe or North America
- Religious or cultural holidays
- Professional trade shows and conferences

The value of a release is relatively constant, and you can release at any time.

- Software that produces credit reports
- Software that manages small business finances
- Core banking services
- Antivirus software

Once you have defined your **market window** you can further determine how frequently you can **release your solution.**

Making your software easy to install/update, ensuring that it is reliable and stable, and creating license agreements that promote currency with the latest version all contribute to enabling your customers to fully realize the benefits of your solution as it evolves.

MARKET EVENTS

Market events capture significant forthcoming events that will influence your solution.

Examples:

- A change in regulations
- A release of a competitor's offering
- A new technology released by a supplier
- A planned release of your solution ······ YES! INCLUDE SIGNIFICANT RELEASES

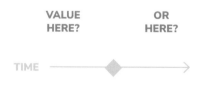

You will have to choose if releasing before or after the event has the most value.

NEW REGULATION
Releasing in advance of a new regulation gives your customers time to prepare.

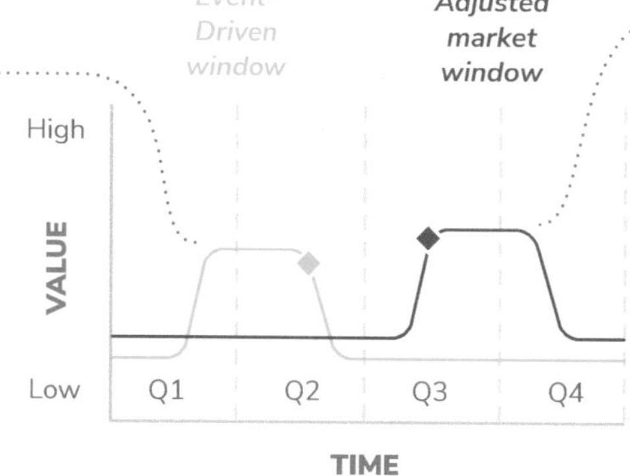

SUPPLIER CHANGE
Because supplier changes induce risk, it is often desirable to release your solution after a technology change to reduce risk. This choice can also make it easier for customers to prepare for the change.

PROFIT

The profit swimlane captures events that affect the financial model of your solution. These include, but are not limited to:

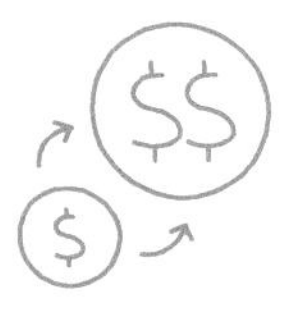

Planned price increases

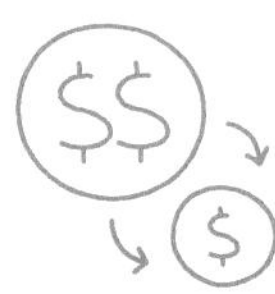

Planned price decreases

Discounts or promotions tied to market events or rhythms

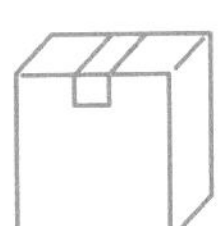

Introduction of new solutions or new packaging

Increases or decreases to your cost model, such as replacing a high cost Supplier with a lower cost alternative.

Use your Roadmap
to capture significant
events.

Use your Solution and Customer ROI financial models to capture the forecasted impact of these events.

We discuss how to evolve your solution based on these events in the Applications section of the book.

TECHNICAL ARCHITECTURE EVOLUTION

No matter how skillfully your technical architecture was created, it will need to evolve over time. These changes are captured in the technical architecture swimlane, which serves to power many of the other swimlanes.

Add these to your technical architecture swimlane:

Technical innovations ranging from new programming languages, new manufacturing techniques, to new technologies.

Opportunities to deliver benefits to customers using not-yet-invented technologies.

The entries in this swimlane should be connected to content contained in other swimlanes to reinforce how the evolution of the technical architecture provides value to customers.

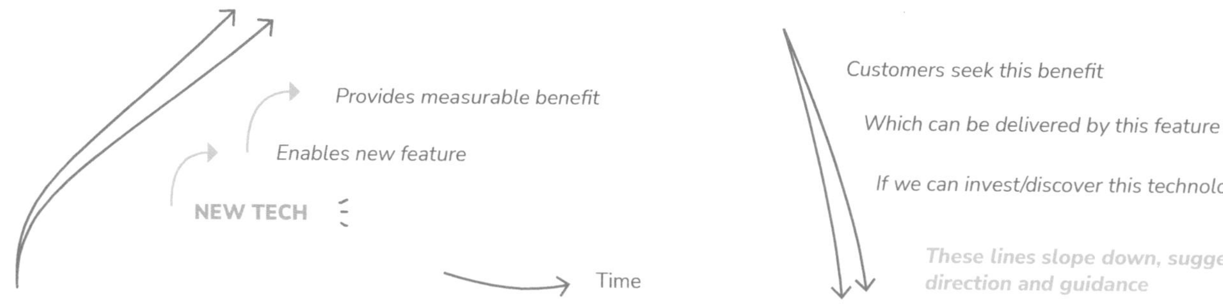

Roadmaps or Roadblocks?

Used properly, roadmaps are high-impact, Agile planning tools that provide numerous benefits. Roadmaps...

Promote collaboration between all of the groups that **contribute to a sustainable solution.**

Enable customers to **plan for new solutions along with other significant changes.** Especially important in B2B!

Enable organizations to **plan for significant, multi-term development initiatives that support corporate strategy.**

Promote **compliance with emerging government regulations,** which are often published years in advance.

Support teams in making high integrity commitments to release windows—and even specific dates—as they explore potential futures.

10 tips to help ensure your roadmaps do not become roadblocks

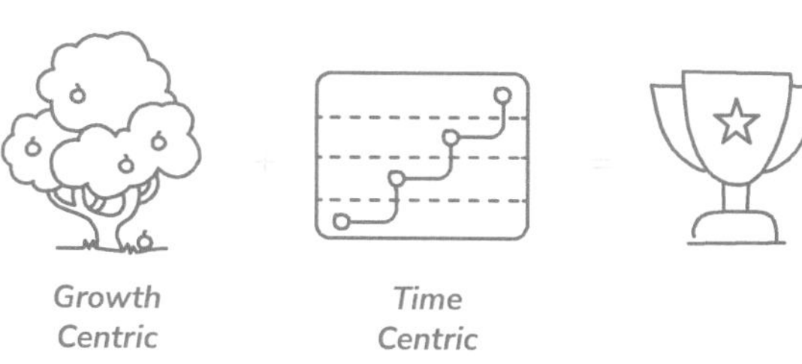

Create two Roadmaps for growth and time. These two representations of the future complement each other, enabling business leaders to explore complex topics from multiple perspectives.

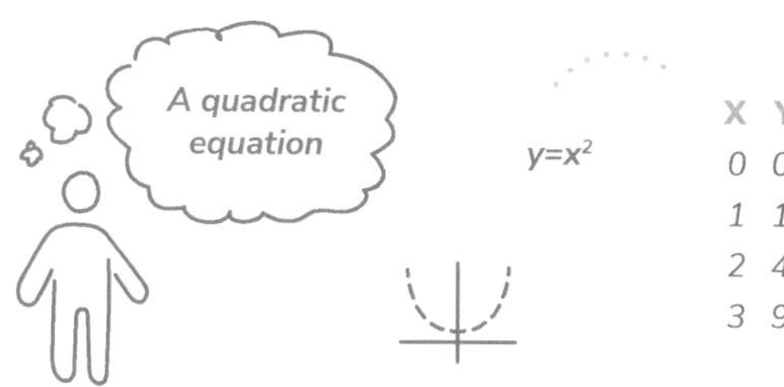

We use multiple representations to capture different facets of complex concepts.

Explore multiple formats. Different solutions need to emphasize different information. Tailor Profit Stream roadmapping techniques to meet your needs.

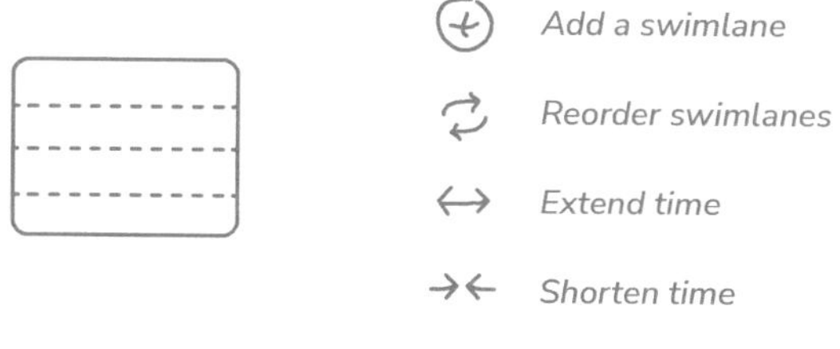

Use the Press Release Test. Roadmap-worthy features should be important enough to put into a press release, highlight in a sales presentation, or call out on your website.

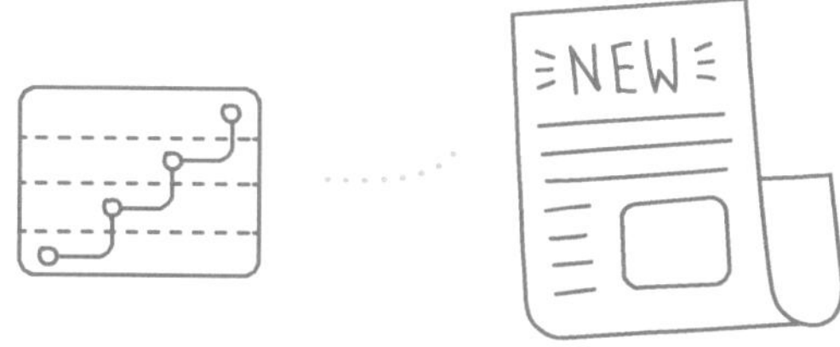

What's
coming?...

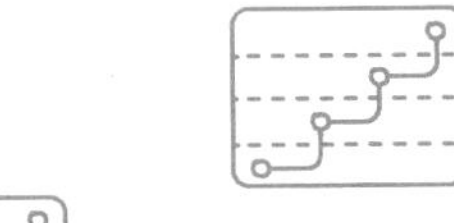

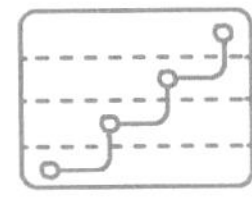
Don't wait to
update!

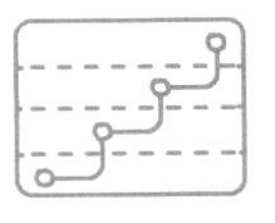
Next update on...

Competitive events & market events are compelling reasons to update your roadmap.

4

Next update on. Stale roadmaps lead to stale solutions. Keep your solution - and your roadmap - fresh by putting a 'next update on YYYY-MM-DD' on your roadmap.

5

Skip the past. Don't version your roadmap and don't save older versions. A roadmap is a future-oriented planning tool.

Let old roadmaps fade
into the fog
PAST
NOW
FUTURE

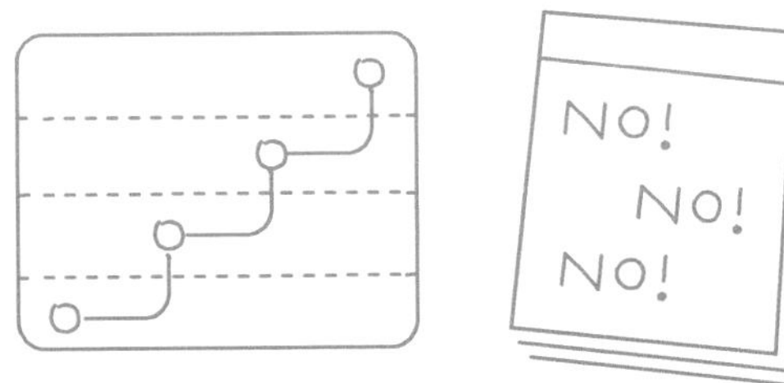
NO!
NO!
NO!

6

Say YES to NO! By providing a thoughtful forecast of a desired future, a roadmap by its nature suggests what you will not be doing. In other words, if it isn't in the roadmap, you're not planning on doing it.

Some organizations keep a short list of what they are NOT doing as part of their roadmap.

10 tips to help ensure your roadmaps do not become roadblocks

The Intihuatana stone at Machu Picchu casts no shadow at noon on either equinox.
Image source: Wikipedia

7

Look for Rhythms. We form all manner of groups, communities, schools, cities, and associations in our personal and professional lives to help us perpetuate our societies. We then create rhythms around these entities: regular meetings, predictable school schedules, holidays, and conferences. Find the rhythms of your market(s).

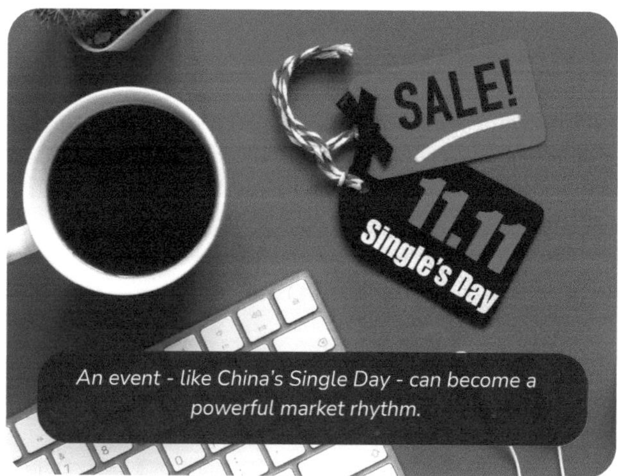

An event - like China's Single Day - can become a powerful market rhythm.

8

Create Rhythms. High impact business leaders create rhythms around their solutions.

+ Start with an event
+ Repeat it
+ After 3 years it is a Rhythm

Explore Profit Stream Rhythms at **www.profit-streams.com/rhythms**

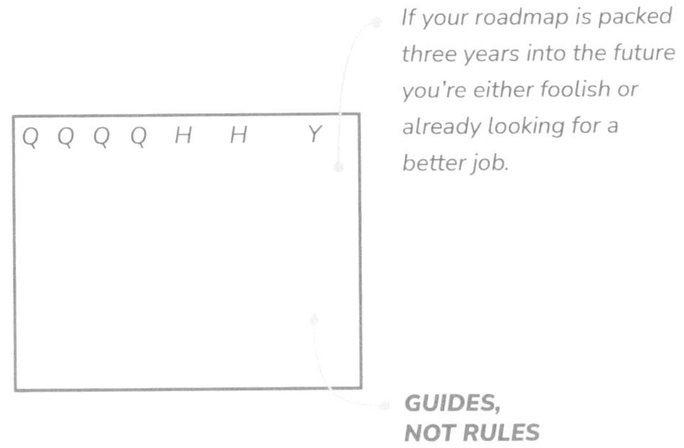

Q Q Q Q H H Y
If your roadmap is packed three years into the future you're either foolish or already looking for a better job.
GUIDES, NOT RULES

Leave space. Every forecast of the future carries with it the risk that business leaders will resist changing it. Mitigate this risk by leaving space in your roadmap for the future to unfold.

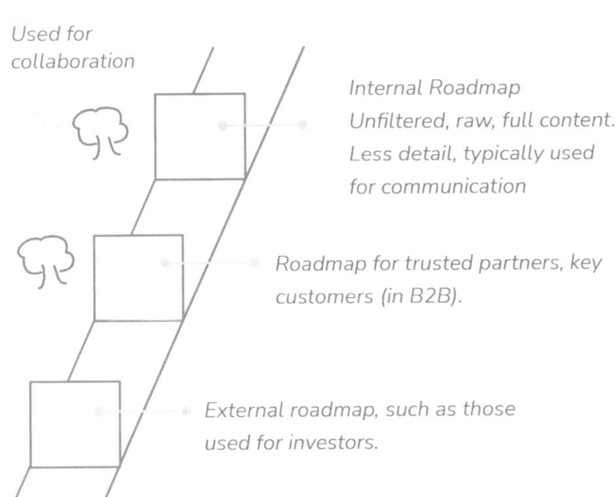

Used for collaboration
Internal Roadmap Unfiltered, raw, full content. Less detail, typically used for communication
Roadmap for trusted partners, key customers (in B2B).
External roadmap, such as those used for investors.

Choose what to share. There are times when sharing some or all of your roadmap externally advances your solution. And there are times when you need to carefully manage who has access to your roadmap. There is no universally correct answer… just a choice you'll need to make.

Our preference is to use the growth-centric representation of a roadmap of ***Prune the Product Tree*** to solicit feedback from stakeholders and the **time-centric** roadmap of columns and swimlines to communicate events, rhythms, and Profit Stream changes.

Market and solution events

Markets and the solutions that serve them interact in a complex dynamic system. Business leaders can gain significant, sustainable advantage by planning for and responding to these events.

Strategic market events are often hard to identify, as they tend to be associated with markets moving through the market lifecycle. Once identified, sustainable businesses find the means to capitalize on them faster than competitors.

Strategic solution events are events that have a significant long term impact on your solution, such as replacing the supplier of a core component with a new supplier or introducing a new pricing model.

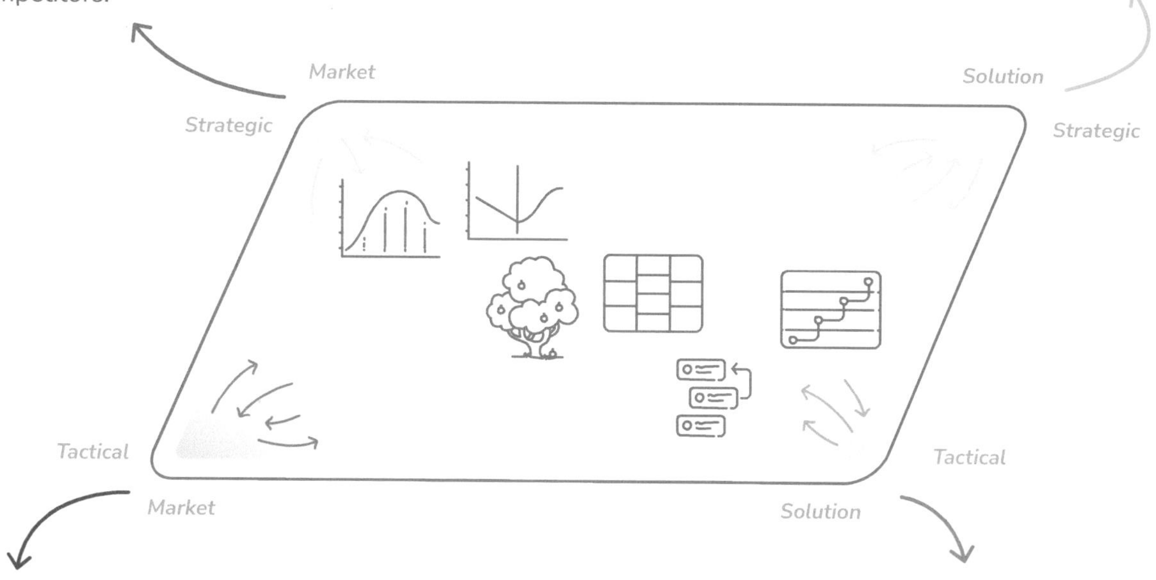

Tactical market events impact all stakeholders. Actions of competitors are one class of market events, as are regulatory changes.

Tactical solution events range from customer feedback to supplier feedback. The most impactful events can often appear tactical in nature and become strategic as their ramifications are known.

Clearing the fog with customer feedback

The GE Predix solution team wanted to obtain customer feedback on the evolution of the GE Predix platform. Working together, we organized a strategic marketing event in which groups of customers played Prune the Product Tree to help.

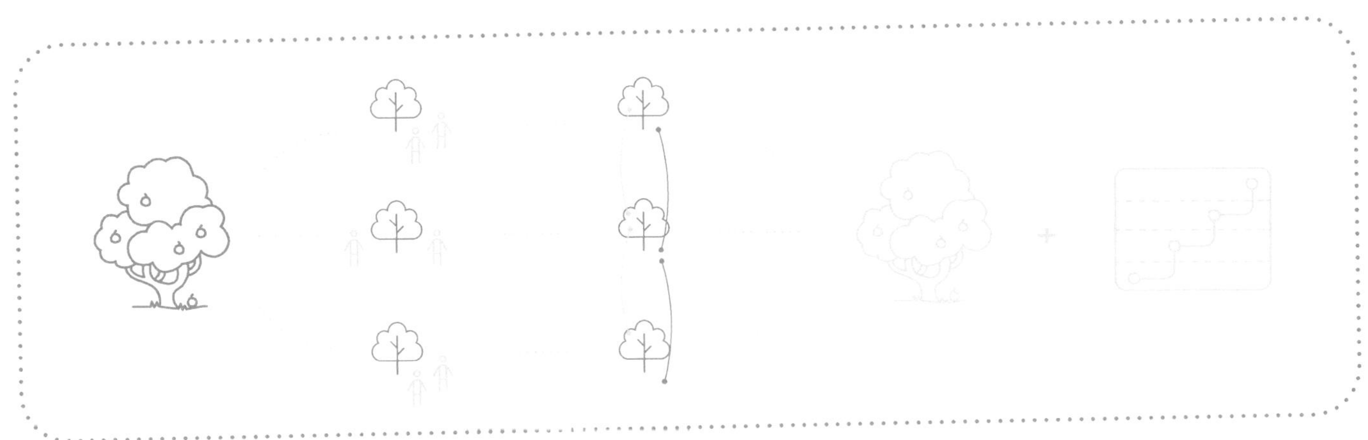

01

The GE Predix solution team created an initial tree. A copy was given to each customer team.

02

Teams of 5 to 8 customers pruned their tree. Customers were segmented by different kinds of manufacturing operations to identify segment-specific details.

03

Patterns of feedback in the results were analyzed to determine which adjustments GE should make to their roadmap.

04

The final results were captured in a new tree and a new roadmap.

Backlog

A backlog is an ordered list of work items. Roadmaps feed the backlog... with some work! Specifically, the "larger" and "more strategic items" contained within the roadmap are decomposed into many smaller items in a backlog.

The specific approach to decomposing larger items into smaller items varies by Agile methods. Most Agile organizations will use one backlog to guide the development of the solution and create additional backlogs from this solution backlog to guide the work of the Agile teams building the solution. These backlogs are coordinated to maintain a cohesive work plan that delivers a continuous flow of value to customers (the 'value stream') that when priced properly creates a Profit Stream.

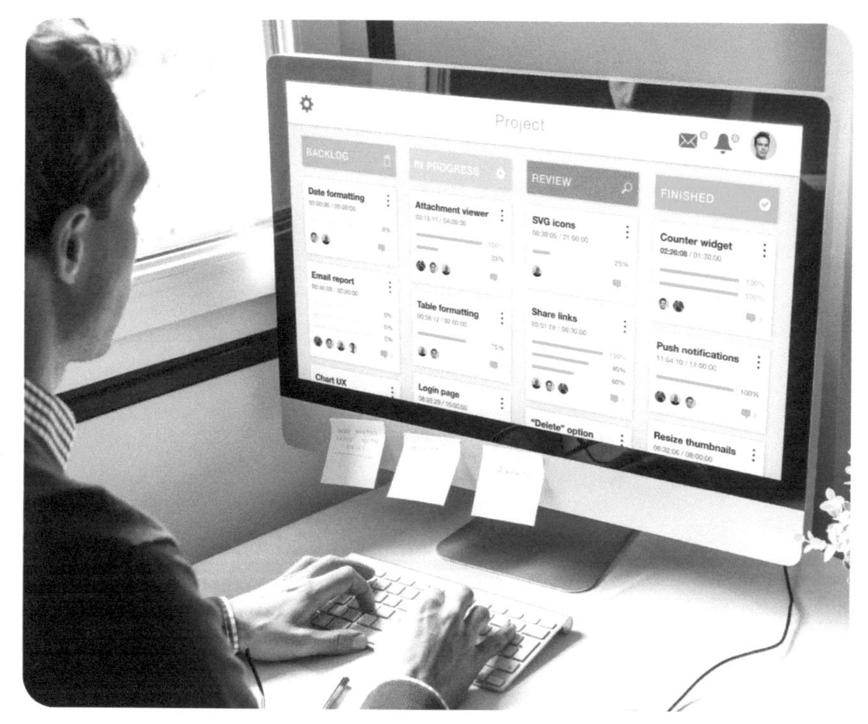

The dominant organizational structures used for backlogs are the ordering of the items and the time horizon of backlog items.

BONUS.

Every Agile development method has at least one backlog!

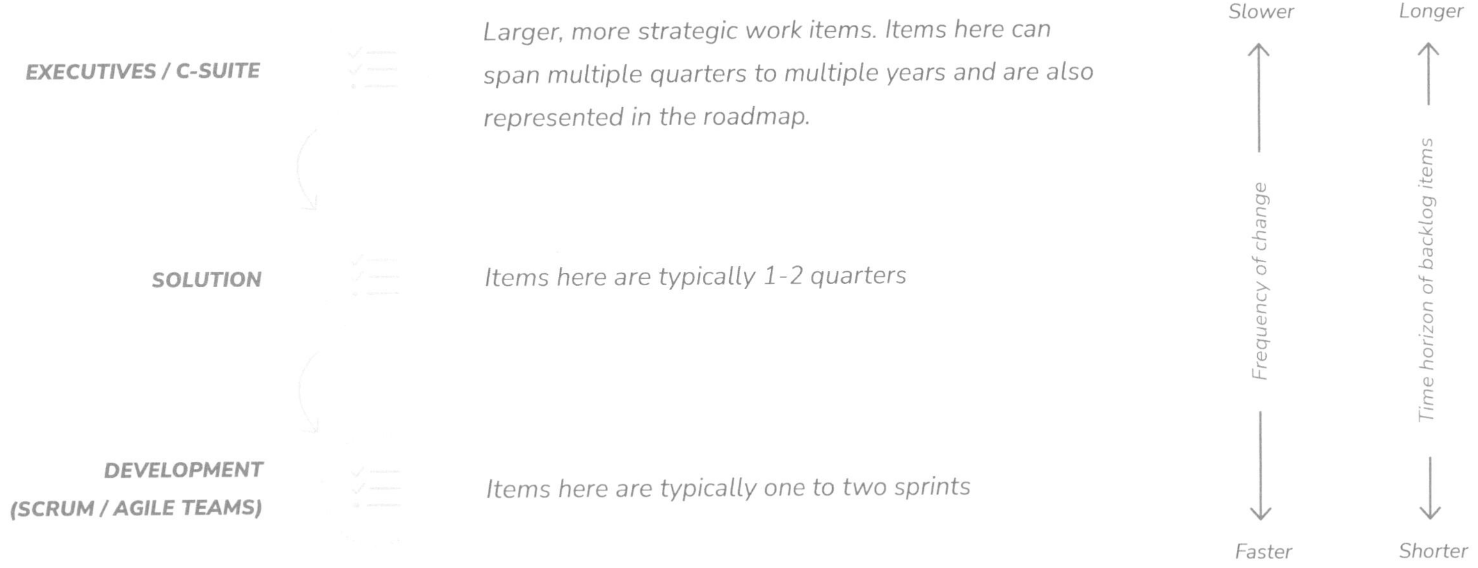
EXECUTIVES / C-SUITE
Larger, more strategic work items. Items here can span multiple quarters to multiple years and are also represented in the roadmap.
SOLUTION
Items here are typically 1-2 quarters
DEVELOPMENT (SCRUM / AGILE TEAMS)
Items here are typically one to two sprints
Slower
Frequency of change
Faster
Longer
Time horizon of backlog items
Shorter

The roadmaps and backlogs used by executives to guide the organization are similar in structure to the roadmaps and backlogs used to guide the solution and the agile teams, tailored to the such things as key investment decisions and strategic outcomes.

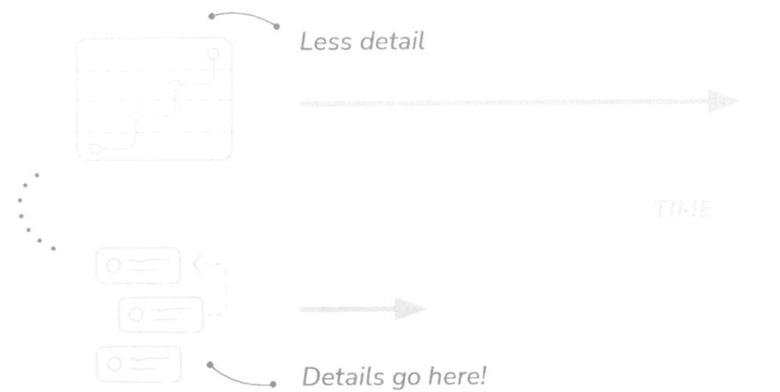
Less detail
Details go here!

Roadmaps & Backlogs can exist at different levels, where a level captures a consistent time horizon.

Profit Streams embrace Agile methods — and their backlogs.

SCRUM?
YES!

SAFe®?
YES!

SCRUM @ SCALE?
YES!

Kanban?
YES!

LeSS?
YeSS!*

Your own method?
YES!

Every Agile method is designed to create value for all stakeholders.

This means that every Agile method can help you create Profit Streams.

Want to make your Agile methods even better?
You're doing it by reading this book!

Aligning distributed Agile teams through **market rhythms and roadmaps**

United Technologies Aerospace Systems (UTAS) faced a challenge common to large scale Agile development: How should they organize the releases across hundreds of teams working on a complex solution based on sophisticated hardware and software?

The answer was found by analyzing the market rhythms of their customers' customers.

UTAS makes the landing gear sub-assemblies for airplanes. Boeing and Airbus are two main customers. In turn, Boeing and Airbus sell airplanes to major airlines, such as United Lufthansa, or Turkish Airlines.

Through a very simple process, UTAS identified the market rhythms of the airlines, which included an understanding of the long development process of a new airline and the buying cycles of the biennial Farnborough Airshow. These rhythms, a key part of the UTAS Agile roadmap, helped align hundreds of Agile teams on a common objective.

Steve Mann - stock.adobe.com

Farnborough Airshow, Paris Airshow

SECTION 02

Profit Stream Canvas

am Canvas

The Profit Stream Canvas is the key to designing and evolving Profit Streams.

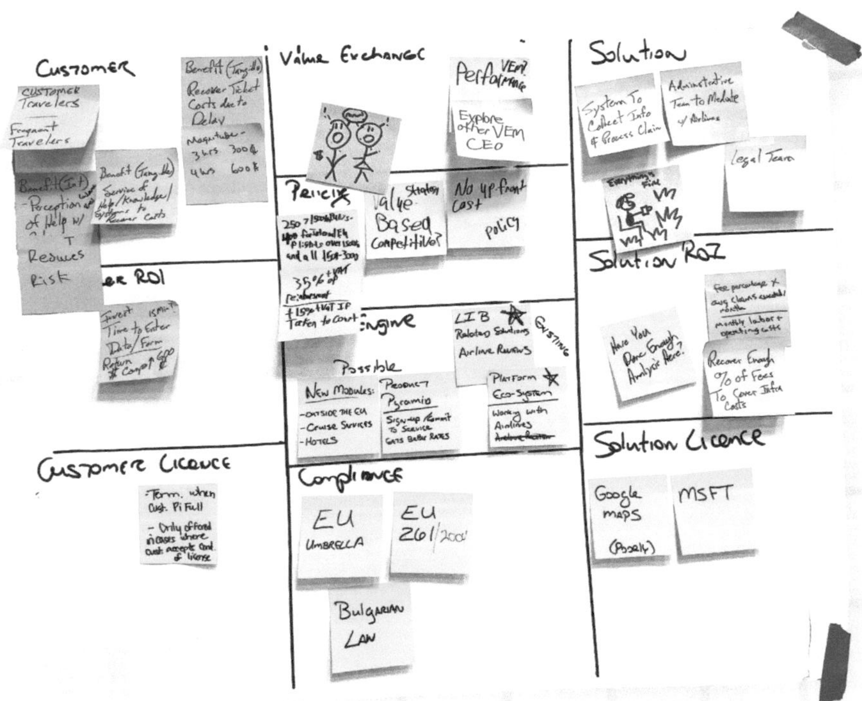

THE PROFIT STREAM CANVAS

Solution

Version

Customer

What does my customer value?
+ Hard / Tangible
+ Soft / Intangible

What might my customer pay for this?

Customer ROI

Is this sustainable for my customer?
+ TCO vs. Benefits

Is it better than competing or alternative offers?

Customer Licenses

What are the Terms and conditions of the use of the solution?
+ Rights / Restrictions

Are they fixed? Negotiated?

Value Exchange

How do I 'trade value for money'?
Annual license? transaction?

Pricing

How much money will this cost?
What is the Price?
+ Strategy
+ Structure
+ Specifics
+ Policies

Profit Engine

How do I design/engineer a sustainable business?

Compliance

How do I maintain / honor my relationship with external stakeholders? (societal stakeholders)
+ GDPR, FERPA, HIPAA, COPEA

Solution

What are the ways I can provide value to my customers?

What are the features / (other) I can provide / create?

Solution ROI

Is this sustainable?
+ Costs
+ Revenue

Improvements over time?

Solution Licenses

What are my in-licenses?
How do I manage them?
How do they impact my model?

The Profit Stream Canvas is organized to help you manage the choices you will make as you design your Profit Streams.

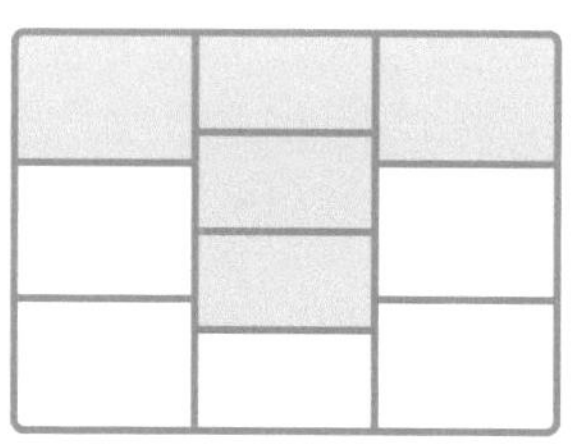

Solution Sustainability

Delivering value to your customer over time.

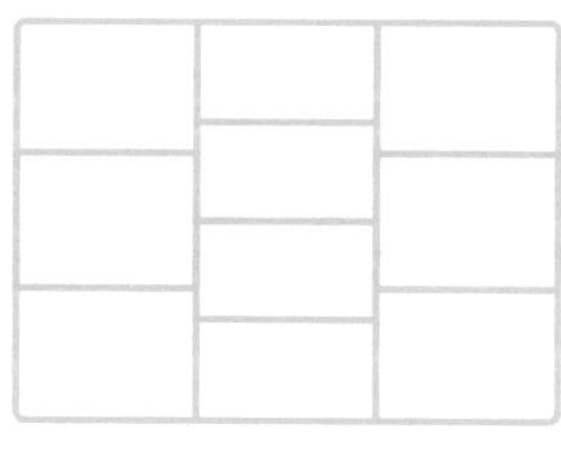

Economic Sustainability

You are making a profit. Your customers' assessment of value is greater than their total cost of ownership.

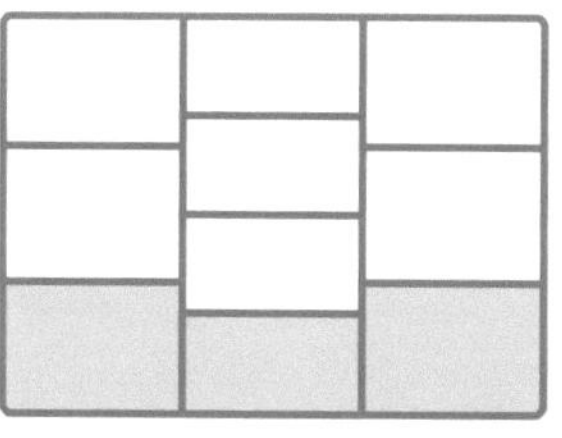

Relationship Sustainability

Designing longterm relationships that benefit all stakeholders.

The **Profit Stream Canvas** helps you focus on...

Monetization

How are all elements of profit working in harmony?

GET THESE RIGHT AND YOU HAVE A HAPPY CUSTOMER

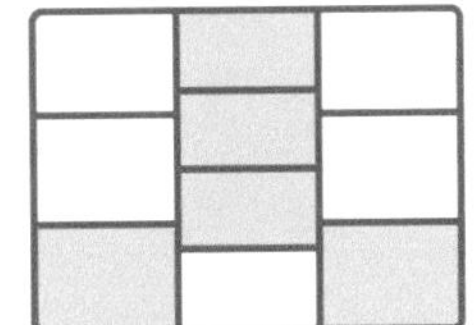

GET THESE RIGHT AND YOU HAVE A PROFITABLE SOLUTION

Customer

What are their goals and aspirations?
What problems are they trying to solve?
How do they perceive value?
What are their economic choices?
What licenses do they require?

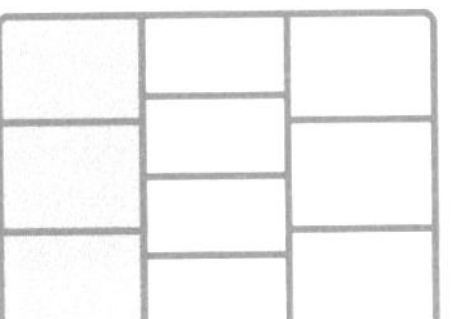

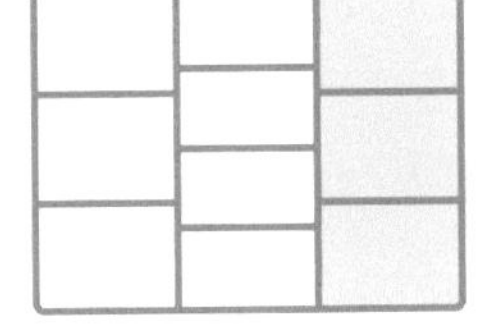

Solution

What solutions might you create?
How will they promote sustainability?
How will they generate a profit?
How will you manage supplier relationships?

GET THIS RIGHT AND YOU'LL HAVE STABLE, HEALTHY BUSINESS RELATIONSHIPS

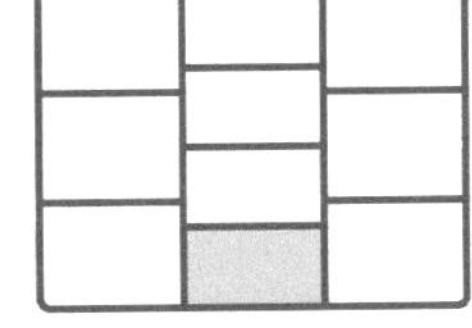

GET THESE RIGHT AND YOU HAVE A GREAT SOLUTION

Compliance

How does our solution ethically and responsibly comply with applicable regulations and laws?

CUSTOMER BLOCK

SOLUTION SUSTAINABILITY

CUSTOMER FOCUS

Customer

We serve one or more customer segments through solutions that provide a system of tangible and intangible economic benefits.

The customer block defines the economic benefits of our solutions:

→ *the customer segments we're serving*

→ *the tangible and intangible economic benefits of our solutions*

→ *how technical choices provide current and future value*

→ *the manner in which different customers may assess the system of value*

Customers are the individuals or organizations that benefit from our solution.

The heart and soul of every business is its ability to understand and serve its customers, as customers are the only source of economic wealth.

This entails understanding four essential questions:

1. Who is your customer?
2. What are the benefits provided by your solution?
3. How might your customer value these benefits?
4. How does your strategy enable you to serve your customer over time?

What is value?

Value is the benefits a customer receives less their total cost of ownership.

Solutions are sustainably profitable when their total revenue exceeds their total costs.

Total Revenue > Total Costs

There are three broad categories of customers...

These categories share common sets of motivations...

CONSUMER B2C	HOME COOK PARENT	• Help me live a better life (make and save money) • Entertainment and pleasure • Experience
PROFESSIONAL B2P	DOCTOR DESIGNER	• Help me do my job • Help me work with others • Help me feel competent
BUSINESS B2B	BANK HOSPITAL SUPERMARKET	• Lower costs • Increase revenue and profitability • Perform critical tasks like sales, manufacturing, marketing, development, HR, etc. • Deliver a better customer experience

The most direct measure of success is economic

Segments emerge as we identify groups of customers that share similar attributes.

Common attributes used to create segments include:

- Customers with different needs
- Customers who value different outcomes
- Customers who value different aspects of our solution
- Customers who are willing to pay more based on brand
- Customers who require unique sales or distribution

Defining a segment can be easy: scheduling software for dentists. Defining a segment can also be hard, especially when customers use solutions in novel ways. If you're having trouble defining your segments, you're going to have trouble defining how your solution provide value. Invest the time to clearly define your customer.

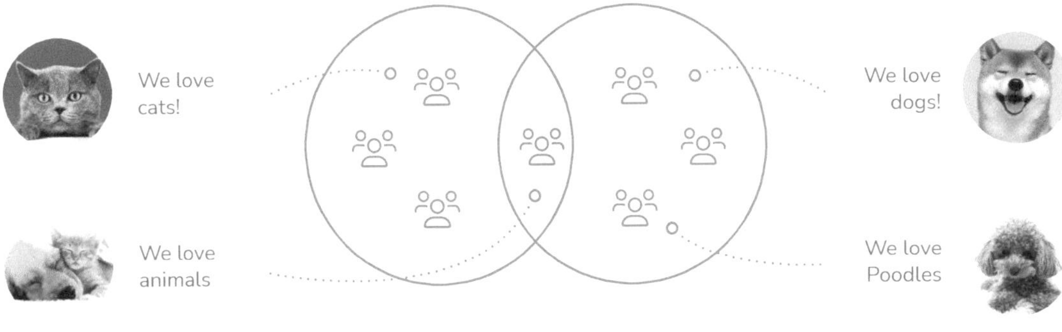
We love cats!
We love animals
We love dogs!
We love Poodles

We can segment by business type. We're a bank — We're a manufacturer

We can segment by geography. We're a regional company — We're a European company

These are very coarsely defined, large segments and could be usefully refined by company size, the types of customers they serve, degree of digital transformation, etc.

A Profit Stream is designed to serve customer segments with the highest profit potential. This requires business leaders to quantify the value they can create for their customers.

Customer Benefit Analysis is a structured process designed to answer two key questions:

What dimensions of our solution provide benefit to our customer?

What is the magnitude of these benefits to your customer?

Customer Benefit Analysis captures the answers to these questions in a unified economic model based on **tangible** and **intangible** economic benefits.

Tangible

Tangible benefits are established through objective analysis. The two main dimensions of tangible benefits are:

- Cutting costs
- Increasing revenue

②

Intangible

Intangible benefits are established through subjective analysis and must be converted into an economic benefit. Intangible dimensions include such things as:

- Brand
- Customers who align with the company's social mission
- Making decisions more confidently by using the Profit Stream Canvas

Tangible benefits can be captured through a verb that modifies a dimension of value relevant to your customer.

The two main verbs are **REDUCE** and **INCREASE**

Common pairings of verbs and dimensions can help you create your **Customer Benefit Analysis**

Other verbs you can explore for **REDUCE:**

Conserve
Eliminate
Decrease
Cut
Lower
Share
Shorten
Lessen
Shrink
Minimize
Weaken

Other verbs you can explore for **INCREASE:**

Expand
Upgrade
Grow
Maximize
Accelerate
Strengthen
Enhance
Spur
Enlarge
Boost
Promote

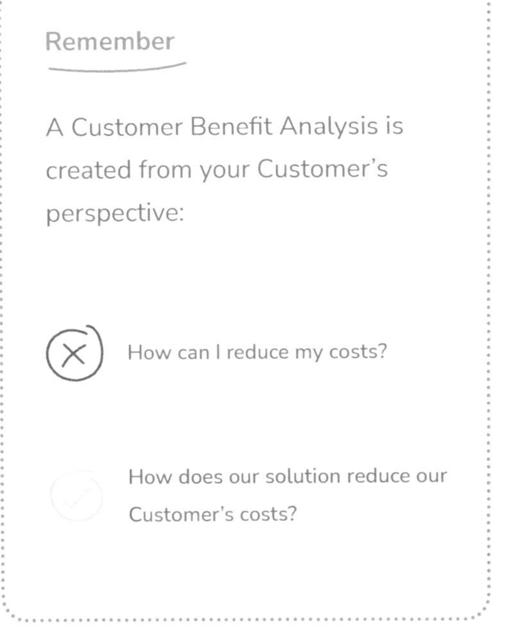

Remember
A Customer Benefit Analysis is created from your Customer's perspective:
How can I reduce my costs?
How does our solution reduce our Customer's costs?

6 dimensions customers seek to reduce

01. Reduce cost

Your solution reduces direct or indirect costs.

- Your solution costs less than alternatives.

- Your solution provides recommendations on how to spend less.

  Personal finance software helps consumers save money and pay lower taxes.

  ERP software helps corporations find the lowest cost suppliers.

- Your solution eliminates the need for another solution.

Reduce Compliance Costs

A special case in cost reduction is reducing your customer's compliance costs.

Comply Advantage uses AI to help financial institutions implement Anti-Money Laundering (AML) policies.

DFIN automates the filing of financial statements to the U.S. Securities and Exchange Commission (SEC)

Intuit helps ensure U.S. taxpayers are compliant with U.S. tax laws.

PRO TIP: *If there is a government regulation... you can find software to help you comply with it!*

02.
Reduce Capital Investment

Your solution helps your customer reduce capital investment costs.

***Fleet.io** provides a truck maintenance solution to help trucking companies lower maintenance costs and reduce capital expenditures.*

***Upkeepr** is a consumer app that plans, manages, and records upkeep (maintenance) to help homeowners avoid expensive repairs and make their most valuable assets last longer.*

Capital investment reductions are a special case of cost reductions, distinguished by the different ways your customers account for capital and operating expenses.

03.
Reduce time

Your solution reduces the time to complete a task.

- Your solution eliminates steps or automates a workflow.

  Automated workforce scheduling solutions can create schedules faster than individual managers scheduling workers.

- Your solution computes a result faster than alternatives.

  Parallel computing solutions built on specialized hardware can solve a wide range of computational problems faster than traditional, serialized solutions.

- Your solution converts manual, slow steps to faster, software-augmented steps.

  An app for recipes or photos enables chefs and families to find the food and photos they desire far more quickly than thumbing through a photo album.

PRO TIP: Time savings can often be converted into an increase in another dimension. Saving a truck driver's time can enable them to deliver more packages. Pick the economic framing most relevant to your customer.

6 dimensions customers seek to reduce

04.
Reduce Risk

Your solution reduces risk for your customer.

Many software solutions help customers manage information security risks

Anti-Virus solutions help consumers protect their machines from malware, phishers, and identity theft.

05.
Reduce Effort

Your solution reduces the effort required to accomplish a task.

Warehouse Management Systems can optimize worker schedules and activities, reducing overall effort.

Appointment management solutions help busy office professionals manage scheduling complexities.

06.
Your solution reduces a dimension of value not yet discussed.

These hidden gems of value enable your solution to sparkle and can create tremendous benefit for your customer...
...AND YOU!

The primary dimension associated with the tangible economics verb 'increase' is **REVENUE.**

CONSUMERS

Consumers want investments and assets that make money.

Automated investment solutions ('Robo Advisors') automate stock market investing in an attempt to make consumers more money.

Lyft, Didi, Grab, Curb, and other 'side hustle' platforms enable consumers to increase personal income, often by leveraging underutilized assets.

AIRBNB TOO

PROFESSIONALS

Professionals want solutions that advance their careers and help them land better, higher paying jobs.

Credential verification apps help professionals increase income by managing certifications.

BUSINESSES

Businesses seek to increase revenue / profits by...

- Raising prices
- Selling to new customers
- Selling new items to existing customers
- Retaining existing customers / preventing churn

Customer Relationship Management (CRM) solutions help businesses manage new and existing customers.

Price optimization solutions recommend specific prices that optimize retail revenue.

Here are 4 additional dimensions customers seek to increase.

(AND YES, MANY OF THESE CAN BE CONVERTED INTO AN INCREASE IN REVENUE)

01.
Increase Productivity

Your solution helps your customer increase productivity.

Semi-automated to self-serve checkouts enable retailers to increase the productivity of sales clerks:
X number of customers served by Y number of clerks.

Digital torque wrenches enable technicians to increase manufacturing productivity

Vacation planning apps help consumers maximize vacation activities.

Increasing productivity can be framed as...

Increase X by Y

Where X and Y are defined in ways that excite your customer.

MORE TIME ON THE BEACH
MORE TIME TO GO HIKING
MORE ADVENTURES PER DAY!

Increasing productivity or quality requires a deep understanding of how your customer measures these dimensions.

A tired truck driver is more likely to cause an accident. In order to minimize accidents, truck drivers are highly regulated, with separate limits on how many hours they can drive before taking a mandatory rest and how many hours they can drive in a single day. Truck drivers are required to maintain records of their driving to demonstrate compliance with these and other regulations. Trucking companies face severe fines if their drivers are not in compliance with these regulations.

Your solution automates the record keeping process by determining when a driver is driving through a combination of a smartphone app and special hardware that integrates with a truck's On-Board self-diagnostic and reporting system.

Your research indicates that your solution can save a truck driver between 20 and 40 minutes per day, with much higher accuracy.

While that time savings may be real, it may also be irrelevant to a trucking company.

Consider a trucking company with unionized drivers. These drivers are paid for an 8-hour workday. Saving them 30 minutes per day will not actually lower the cost of the trucking company. In this case, you must translate the time savings into an increase in productivity. Let's assume that the trucking company measures productivity by 'on-time deliveries per driver, per day'. One option for showing an increase in productivity is to show that the time saved by your solution can increase the number of deliveries.

Alternatively, you can show that the time savings improves the percentage of on-time deliveries because it enables routes to be designed with greater flexibility.

The most successful analysis of customer value is always framed in terms that matter to your Customer.

02.
Increase Optionality

Your solution helps increase the number, type, or scope of options consumers may pursue.

Financial planning software enables businesses and consumers to explore and even increase the options available.

Optionality can also be increased by your pricing choices, including payment terms, a topic explored in greater detail in the pricing block.

03.
Increase Ease of Use

Your solution is easier to use than an alternative - which includes making your own solution easier to use over time.

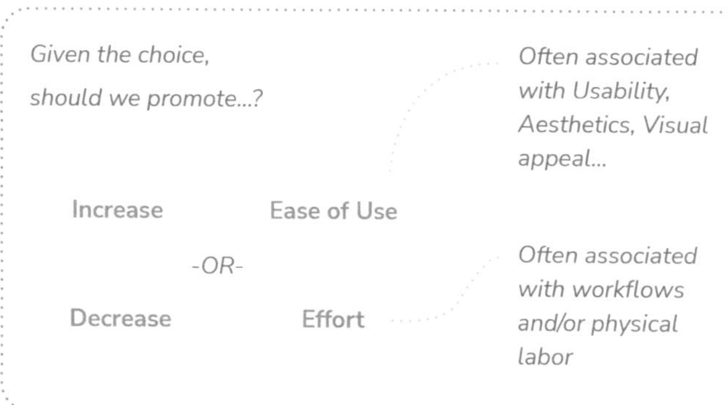

Given the choice,
should we promote...?
Increase
Ease of Use
-OR-
Decrease
Effort
Often associated with Usability, Aesthetics, Visual appeal...
Often associated with workflows and/or physical labor

04.
Data-Centric Attributes

Software-Enabled Solutions that focus on data have unique, data-centric attributes.

Timeliness:
Data that is delivered faster is generally more valuable

|·· *Slow* ·························· *Fast* ··|

Breadth:
Data that includes related data may be more valuable

|·· *Narrow* ·························· *Broad* ··|

Accuracy:
More accurate data is generally more valuable

|·· *Low* ·························· *High* ··|

Precision:
Data that is more precise is generally more valuable

|·· *Low* ·························· *High* ··|

Scarcity:
Unique and/or scarce data may be more valuable

|·· *Common* ·························· *Scarce* ··|

Examples:
Credit scores, stock quotes, patent data, digital goods in video games. An NFT is, by design, an example of a perfectly scarce item - there is only one.

Here are some ways you can objectively measure **tangible economic benefits.**

01.

Laboratory Testing

Demonstrate the performance of your solution through testing by yourself or a third party.

Dimensions you can verify include: Performance claims, such as battery life, visibility, transaction processing speed, storage required, and so forth.

02.

Field Testing / Observation

Demonstrate solution performance through monitoring solution data, field testing, or direct observation of changes.

Dimensions you can verify include: Workflow improvements, operational changes, increases in quality, reductions in errors.

Like tangible economic benefits, many **intangible economic benefits** can be captured as a verb that modifies a dimension.

INCREASE SAFETY

Anti-virus solutions help us feel safe at home;
Collaboration solutions can help us feel safe at work;
Building access control solutions help us feel safe at work by ensuring the right people are in the building at the right time.

INCREASE SECURITY

Intrusion detection solutions help businesses feel secure, while password managers help individuals feel secure.

INCREASE STATUS

Many software-enabled hardware solutions, from smartphones to advanced appliances, are new forms of status symbols.

BETTER/PRETTIER AESTHETICS

Some software solutions are simply prettier.

ENHANCE CREATIVITY

Software solutions become magical when they support new forms of creative expression, such as software controlled LED lighting or new kinds of collaborative play.

IMPROVE CONFIDENCE

Lifestyle and self-help apps increase our confidence—how we look, how we feel.

REDUCE FRUSTRATION

We seek to minimize frustration. Example:

Grr... This software is so buggy!

Macro trend: Agile Software Development methods have improved software quality to the point where 'low-quality' providers are losing ground.

INCREASE FUN/PLEASURE

Most commonly associated with the B2C market for games, music, and media, a feeling of fun or pleasure is not an intrinsic attribute of an object, but instead a relationship that exists between a customer and the object.

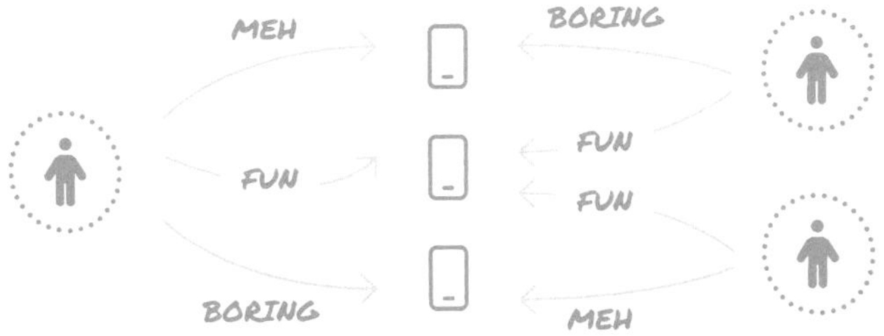

When enough users feel the same positive association, you have a hit!

REDUCE/INCREASE FEAR/ANXIETY

Software can help reduce the fear of the unknown or uncertainty.

When will my car arrive? I don't want to miss my doctor appointment! Oh—I can see it on a map!

Fear for the safety of a loved one...

Where are my children?

Fear of not having enough money for personal or professional reasons...

Will our business be able to run payroll this month? Can we afford that new manufacturing plant?

While most of the times we want to reduce fear/anxiety, sometimes we *choose* to increase it, such as when we're facing a horrific monster or trying to solve a complex logic puzzle in a video game.

REDUCE LONELINESS

Social software can help us organize activities with other people who have similar interests; online counseling services combat feelings of loneliness or isolation; social media platforms can help us feel connected with friends and families.

REDUCE STRESS

Software enabled solutions can help us reduce a significant number of stresses in our lives - a family can reduce scheduling stress through shared calendars; workplace monitoring software can reduce stress felt by workers; personal meditation apps help individuals reduce stress.

Creators of software-enabled solutions must recognize that there is also a dark side to the understanding of negative emotions, especially in the B2C market.

Many social media companies have economic models that generate profit by creating, nurturing, growing, and/or otherwise exploiting negative emotions and addictive behaviors.

Examples of some of the worst outcomes include targeting young people who may feel inadequate about their physical appearance with ads for products and services that make their feelings worse, or promoting violence towards others. Solutions that exploit negative emotions and addictive behaviors for financial gain are not aligned with our objectives of promoting sustainability.

Other **intangible economic benefits** are more effectively captured by the relationship that may exist between the customer and the Solution or Solution Provider.

Values

Your solution or company promotes one or more personal values important to your customer.

A **personal value** is any concept deemed worthy or important that motivates action.

Some values include:

- Freedom
- Fairness + Equity
- Collaboration + Connectedness + Interdependence.
- Independence
- Care + Concern for others
- Environmental + Social Causes

A special intangible dimension is **brand,** which can have a disproportionate impact on value.

To illustrate the influence of brand, imagine that you were involved in a purchase decision.

Which of the brands listed below do you perceive as favorable? How might this assessment impact your decision and the attribution of value?

YOU CAN BE HONEST! WE'RE NOT GOING TO ASK YOU ABOUT THIS

CONSUMER

Apple ... Google

Netflix ... Disney

Xbox ... PlayStation ... Switch

Facebook ... TikTok

PROFESSIONAL

Adobe ... Canva

Microsoft Office ... Google G Suite

Autodesk ... SketchUp

BUSINESS

Oracle ... SAP ... Workday

AWS ... Azure

Google Cloud ... IBM

Facebook ... TikTok

Don't like any of these brands? No problem! Add your own!

Customer Value and Technical Architectures

The technical architecture of a Software-Enabled Solution is a designed set of relationships between the software modules, the hardware they require, and the data they consume or generate.[(2)]

Architecture defines how the relationships can be and are expected to be modified and/or extended, and on which technologies they depend, from which one can deduce current and likely future capabilities, and from which one can form a plan for the implementation or modification of the system.

Practically speaking, these choices enable the delivery of value. The economic worth of the architecture depends on how effectively it enables the solution to meet customer needs.

To help determine the relevance of architectural choices, we define a set of *"ilities"*.

> An *"ility"* is a characteristic or quality of the architecture that applies across a set of customer needs.

Because *"ilities"* are relevant across all kinds of consumers, we selectively illustrate their relevance.

"ilities" can be organized in two categories:

Watch designed by DANIEL WILL-HARRIS

PRESENT

Attributes or characteristics of how the solution performs NOW.

FUTURE

Attributes or characteristics of how the solution may be modified to perform differently in the FUTURE.

11 Present-Focused "ilities:

01

Availability/Reliability

Is your solution available when your customer wants to use it?

- Remember the Twitter 'fail whale'? Availability is often part of your brand!
- Are there legal requirements for availability, such as MTTF/MTBF? *(We'll explore further when we discuss Customer License)*

02

Usability

Can your customers easily learn, use, and otherwise control the solutions?

Because usability may also be assessed as a tangible benefit (saves time, reduces errors) and an intangible benefit (more enjoyable, more beautiful), you should take time to understand the specific aspects of usability that are most important to your customer.

03

Performance / Performability

How effectively your solution performs under defined loads? Does your solution respond quickly enough to customer use? While the answer to this question varies tremendously based on the nature of the customer and the type of work, the reality is that there is always a minimum performance requirement that typically gets harder over time.

04

Survivability

Can your customer recover what is important to them if your solution experiences a catastrophic event?

Most closely associated with cloud or hosted services.

Will my photos of my kids be safe?

Will our employee payroll data be available if we're audited?

Will my art portfolio be available if my hosting provider fails?

05

Interoperability

Can your customer use some or all of your solution on other devices, hardware, or environments?

Grr! Why can't I play Apple Music on my Samsung phone?

Can our CRM system exchange data with our conference management system?

06

Supportability

How effectively does your solution enable your customer to get the help they need when they need it?

Grr! Why can't they help me figure out why my game is so glitchy?

07

Internationalization

Does your solution support the language, data presentation, and even societal norms of your customers?

For businesses and professionals, does your solution support your customer's customers?

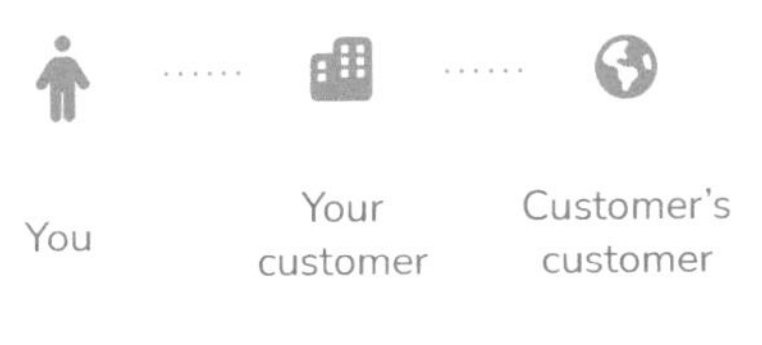

08

Security

Does your solution ensure the right people can perform the right operations? Does it ensure only the right people can access data?

"You must be over the age of 16 to create an account"

09

Backward Compatibility

How does your current solution support customers using older versions?

While you may live in the present and the future...

Most of the time, your customers will use solutions from the past.

Supporting them may be a wise economic choice... until it isn't.

10

Tailorability

How can you control which customers can access specific functionality?

I need to upgrade my plan to access this new feature.

This feature is not allowed in this region.

11

Compliance

How thoroughly does your solution comply with relevant legal, technical, or accessibility standards?

What standards are relevant to your customer?

Compliance is covered in greater detail starting on page 297.

These five **"ilities"** are associated with how well you can meet future customer needs.

Telemetry

How does your solution collect, store, and analyze usage, operational, and operational data so you can monitor and improve your systems over time?

Maintainability

How easily / effectively can you fix defects and resolve issues without causing new issues, i.e. low fragility.

Extensibility

How easily can you add new features or enhance existing functionality without changing the source code? or replacing original hardware?

Scalability

How effectively can your solution meet the demands of increased usage?

Portability

To what degree can the solution run on multiple hardware environments? Portability can increase the number of customers. Example: iOS *OR* Android?... iOS *AND* Android!

Customer Benefit Analysis focuses on one and only one segment.

Different segments value different dimensions, with different magnitudes.

Change the segment and you change the analysis.

Example: Grammarly is an AI-based writing assistant that targets all three categories: Students (Consumers), Professionals, and Businesses.

Here are some of Grammarly's tangible and intangible benefits from the perspective of a business professional.

Tangible Benefits	Money saved from not hiring a copywriter Reduced time and effort to create production-ready manuscripts
Intangible Benefits	Greater confidence and satisfaction in my writing Pleasure in using a well-designed solution

Use **Dimension and Magnitude of Benefit** cards to capture the results of your Customer Benefit Analysis for each segment.

A short title makes managing collections of cards easier.

Who is receiving the benefit? Clarifying the "who" helps maintain focus while also helping identify potential new segments.

What is the value of the solution? Can you describe it as a narrative?

What is the economic impact of the benefit? How can it be measured?

Expressing the magnitude of a tangible benefit in a financial formula makes pricing and financial modeling easier. Capturing the strength or importance of intangible benefits informs pricing strategies.

Every Solution demands something from your customer. Even the app you download on your phone requires a phone.

Understanding the demands your solution places on your customer improves total cost of ownsership analysis and helps you design more elegant solutions.

Organizing your cards by tangible and intangible benefits enables you to capture the total economic benefit of your solution.

Title

Who

Dimension

Magnitude

Solution Demands / Costs

Tangible

Intangible

Who *What segment is receiving the value?*	VP of RevOps		
Summary *What value does the solution provide the customer?*	Time Savings		
Magnitude *What is the economic impact of the value? How can this potential value be measured?* *How can the economic impact be expressed as a formula?*	Salary Cost Time saved x Salary		
Implementation *What changes does the customer need to make in order to realize the value?*	Adopt Best Practices ☐ Easy ☒ Medium ☐ Hard		
Revenue, Cost or Risk	☐ Increase Revenue	☒ Decrease Cost	☐ Avoid Risk

Example of **Dimension and Magnitude of Benefit** cards.

Who *What segment is receiving the value?*	CRO		
Summary *What value does the solution provide the customer?*	Increased Revenue from Sales Territoies		
Magnitude *What is the economic impact of the value? How can this potential value be measured?* *How can the economic impact be expressed as a formula?*	ARR 7% increase in ARR		
Implementation *What changes does the customer need to make in order to realize the value?*	☐ Easy ☐ Medium ☒ Hard		
Revenue, Cost or Risk	☒ Increase Revenue	☐ Decrease Cost	☐ Avoid Risk

Fullcast is a fast-growing SaaS startup that provides a Revenue Operations (RevOps) Management Solution that integrates strategy, marketing , and sales into a cohesive platform. The Fullcast team grounds their growth and pricing changes in their Customer Benefit Analysis.

Who *What segment is receiving the value?*	CRO		
Summary *What value does the solution provide the customer?*	Increased revenue through more ramped sales reps		
Magnitude *What is the economic impact of the value? How can this potential value be measured?* *How can the economic impact be expressed as a formula?*	Cost of replacing fully ramped AE Headhunter fees + lost productivity		
Implementation *What changes does the customer need to make in order to realize the value?*	☐ Easy ☒ Medium ☐ Hard		
Revenue, Cost or Risk	☒ Increase Revenue	☐ Decrease Cost	☐ Avoid Risk

Like Fullcast, you can modify the structure of the cards to meet your needs.

Identify as many **Dimension and Magnitude of Benefit** cards as possible:

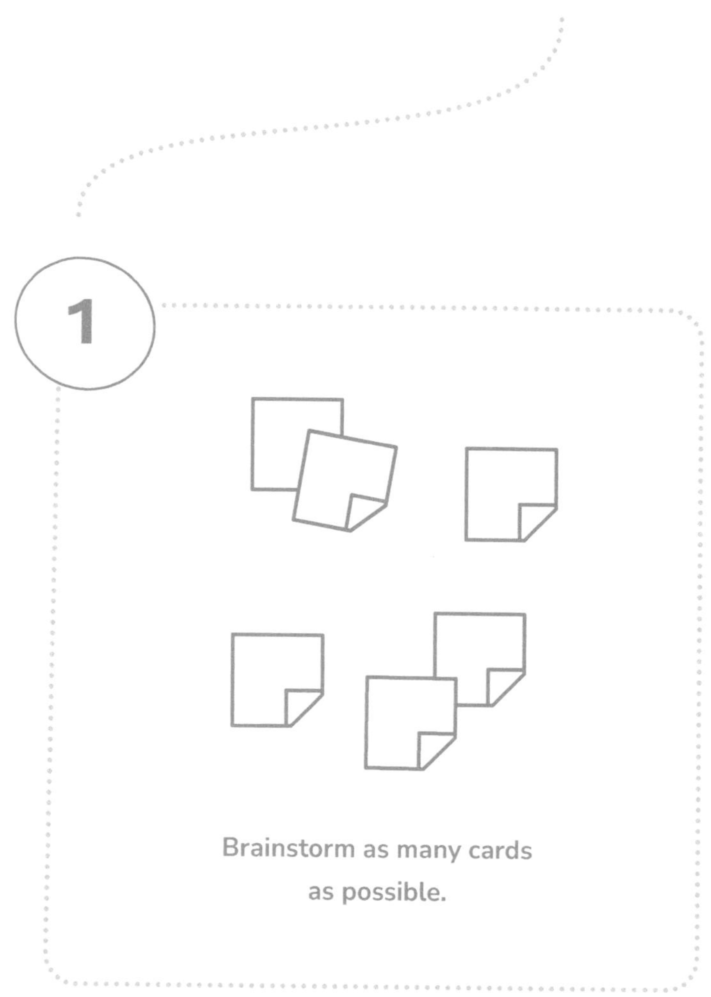

Brainstorm as many cards as possible.

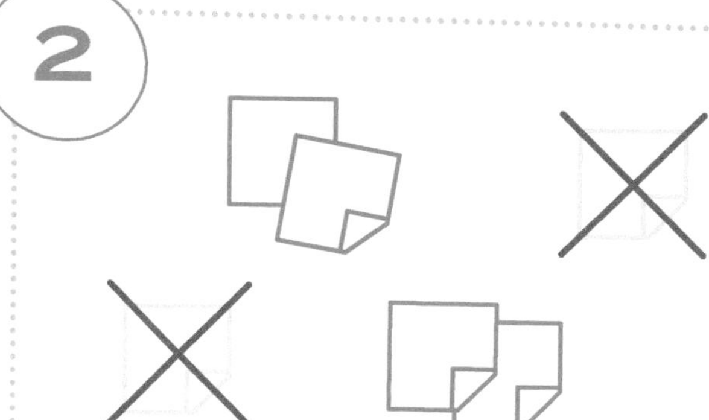

Organize the cards into those that have been validated vs. those that remain to be validated. Validated benefits have a greater impact in pricing, while assumed benefits can guide the design of experiments and development activities in building future solutions.

Prioritize experiments based on prevalence and severity of problem before proposing solution hypotheses and experiments for them.

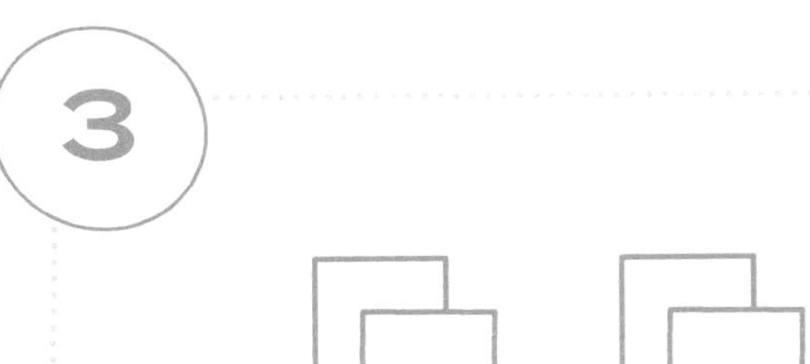

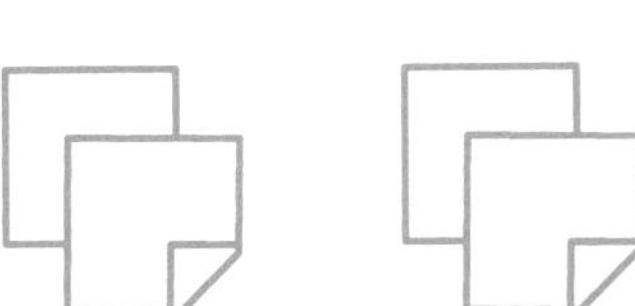

Consolidate similar cards and prioritize the remaining cards according to those benefits that provide the greatest economic value.

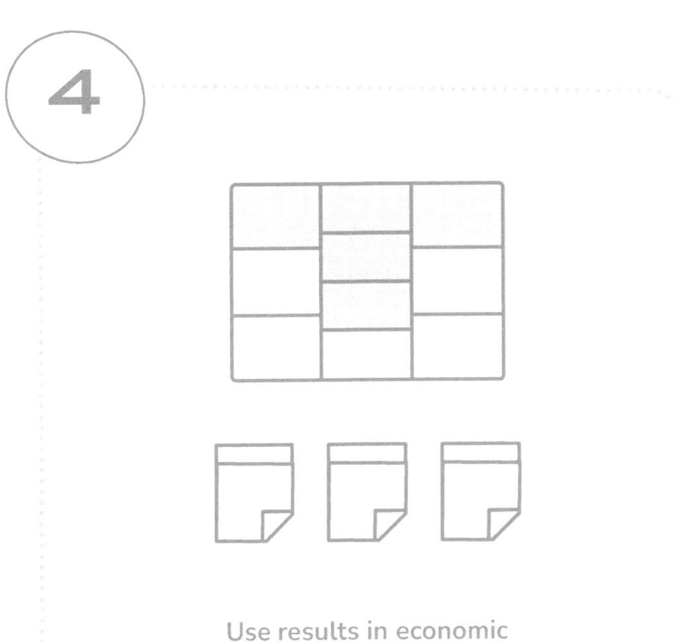

Use results in economic modeling & pricing

Adjust the structure of your cards to best reflect the **customer segments** you're serving.

Expensive B2C and most B2B solutions will be strongly influenced by tangible dimensions.

Inexpensive B2C and many B2P tools are strongly influenced by intangible dimensions.

We choose mobile games for fun!

Many professionals choose older solutions based on familiarity.

Customer Benefit Analysis and Systems Thinking

To understand your system of value, draw relationships between **dimension and magnitude of benefit cards.**

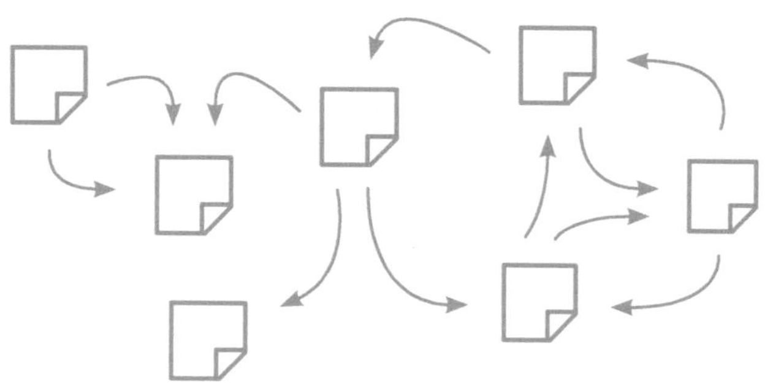

Whenever a dimension has an effect on another dimension, connect them with an arrow.

There are two kinds of causal links...

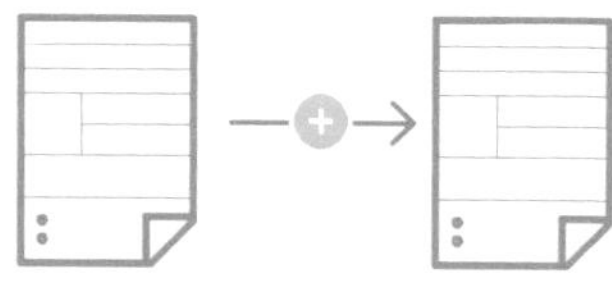

A plus sign means that the two benefits move in the same direction.

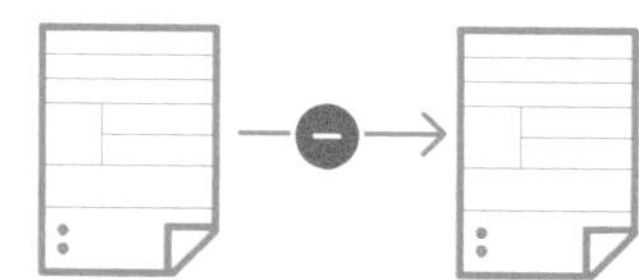

A minus sign means that the two benefits move in the opposite direction.

To illustrate a **Value System**, consider a solution designed to help trucking companies manage their fleet.

The desirability of a solution that reduces vehicle maintenance costs can only by assessed by understanding its effect on other dimensions of value. Most trucking company executives will drive away from a solution that decreases driver safety and satisfaction in order to reduce vehicle maintenance costs.

Trucking company executives will drive towards solutions that maximize the value of the system.

Reduce Fuel Costs

Increase On-time Delivery

Increase Driver Safety

Increase Customer Satisfaction

Reduce Maintenance Costs

Increase Driver Satisfaction

Use + − signs to capture positive / negative relationships associated with value.

Plotting the minimum value required helps you identify when your value system may have problems.

Maximum value obtainable

Point at which customer doesn't care... (harder to determine)

We will use this in Solution Design to ensure our solution is creating a positive economic impact

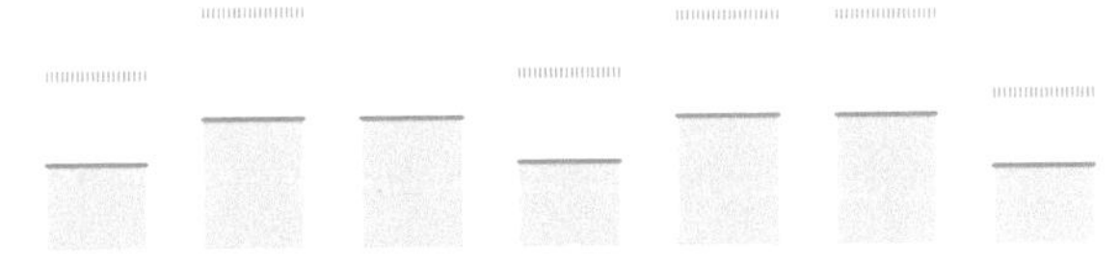

Patterns of minimum value are unique to market segments and customers.

Minimum value required

This combination results in an unacceptable solution.

While the patterns of relationships in a Value System tend to be similar for all customers in the same segment, each discrete customer will have **a unique attribution of value.**

Customers of expensive solutions often expect a benefit analysis that is tailored exclusively for their unique circumstances.

Customers of inexpensive solutions do not share these expectations and may not even desire a benefit analysis.

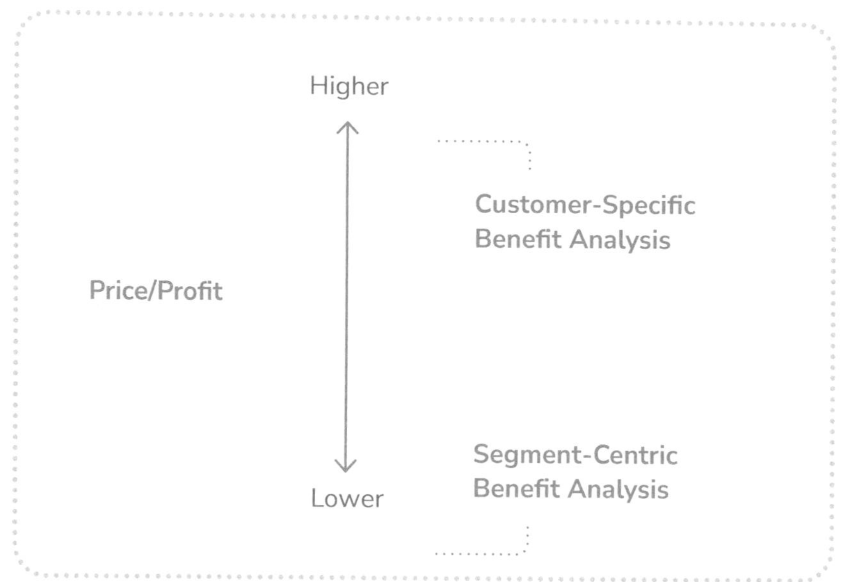

You will leverage your Benefit Analysis when designing your solution and creating your economic models.

 **You can use your Benefit Analysis in sales and marketing too!**

A model of tangible and intangible economic benefits creates a common means to identify potential value for all customers within a segment.

While both members of a couple considering the purchase of an EV will care about range and charging time, one person may not care about the styling or brand.

Direct benefits are those benefits that are recognized as valuable and materially influence a purchase decision.

Indirect benefits are those benefits that are not recognized as valuable.
This doesn't mean that the value is not there—it just means that the customer does not include this benefit as a material aspect of their decision making.

You can think of indirect and direct benefits as a customer-specific filter that overlays the value system.

One customer will identify some dimensions of value as direct, which another will classify those same dimensions of value as indirect.

Ultra-expensive, custom-created software-enabled solutions require a completely tailored model of tangible and intangible economic benefits that equate directly to the direct and indirect benefits desired by a single customer. Systems built for governmental, military, or proprietary applications within large companies are examples.

A trucking company focused on cost reduction will consider those dimensions of value that reduce cost as direct benefits.

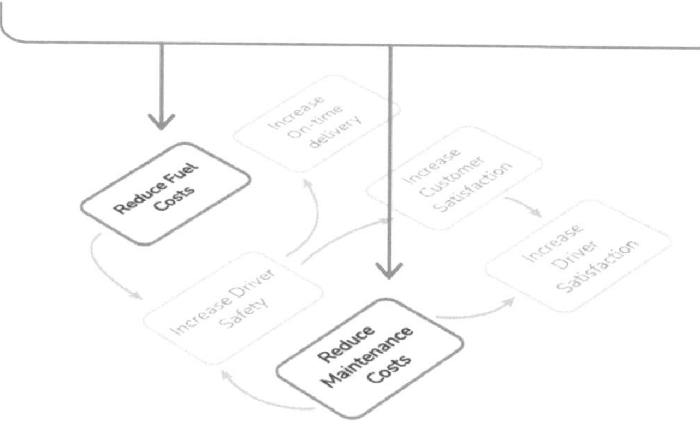

A trucking company focused on customer satisfaction would select a different set of dimensions as direct benefits.

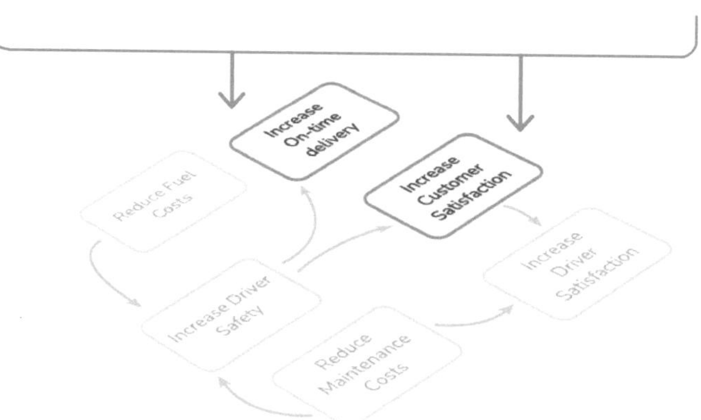

Customer Benefit Analysis can be performed at any time.

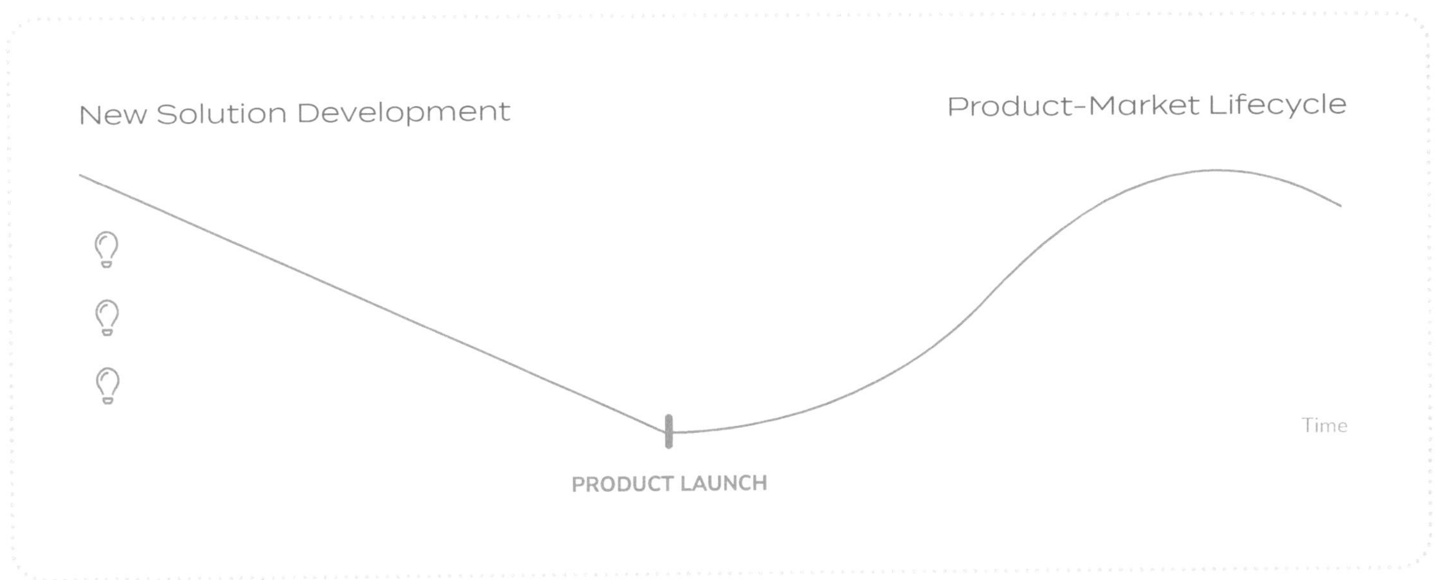

During New Solution Development, we can use Customer Benefit Analysis to:

- Identify the most promising ideas.
- Guide development to create profitable solutions.
- Create marketing and sales materials that promote the benefits customers will receive.

After the solution is launched, Customer Benefit Analysis helps with:

- Prioritize new and/or improved features.
- Adjust pricing choices to enhance profitability and respond to competition threats.

SOLUTION BLOCK

SOLUTION SUSTAINABILITY

SOLUTION FOCUS

Solution

The solution block defines how we provide value to our customers:

→ *How specific features are packaged to provide value to target customers*

→ *How features may evolve over time*

→ *The operating context of the solution*

→ *The manner in which solutions are provided*

Solutions

Solutions are the means by which we provide value to our customers.

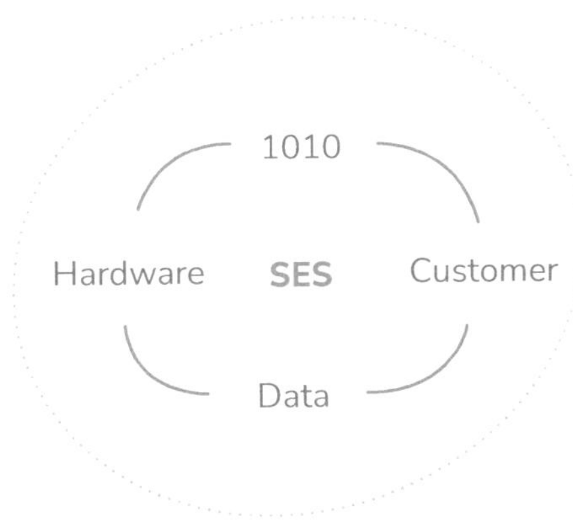

A Software-Enabled Solution always includes software.

A Software-Enabled Solution may include hardware, services, or data.

Solutions provide value through distinguishing characteristics called features.

Some features create tangible economic benefits

Payment Processing

Spell Checking

Service Reliability

Battery life

Data Accuracy

Some features create intangible economic benefits

Confidence

Aesthetics

Is a feature without economic benefits a feature?

NOPE

Providers differentiate their solutions through a unique mix of features:

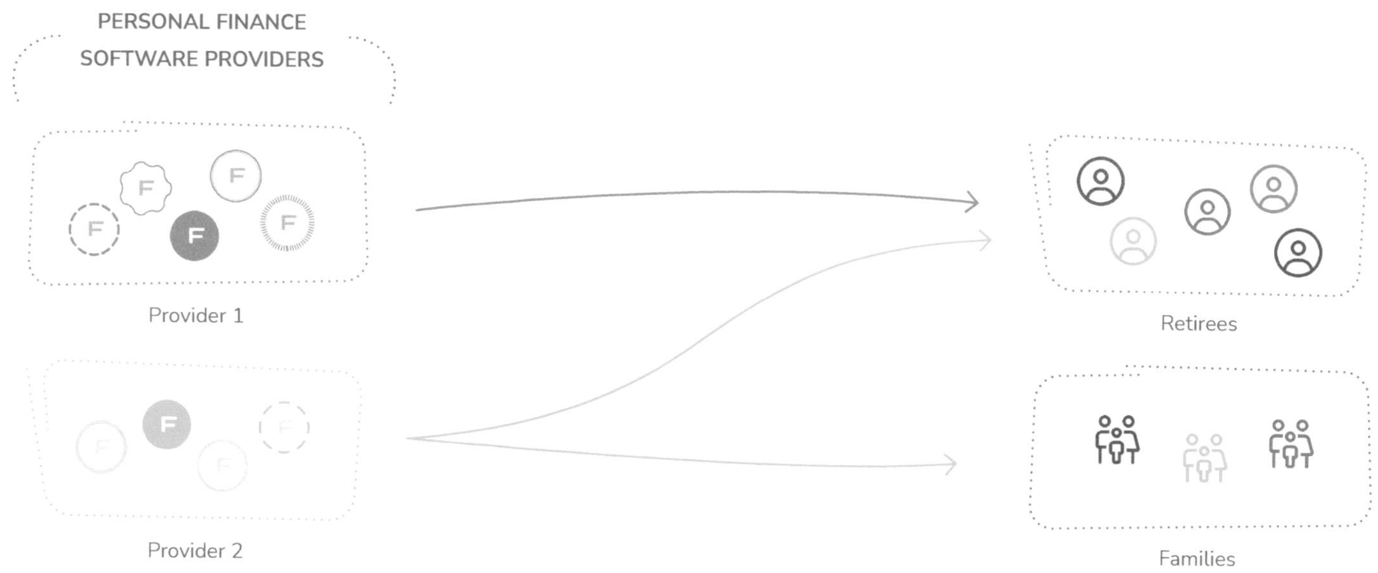

Customers reinforce segmentation boundaries because they ascribe different value to benefits created by different features.

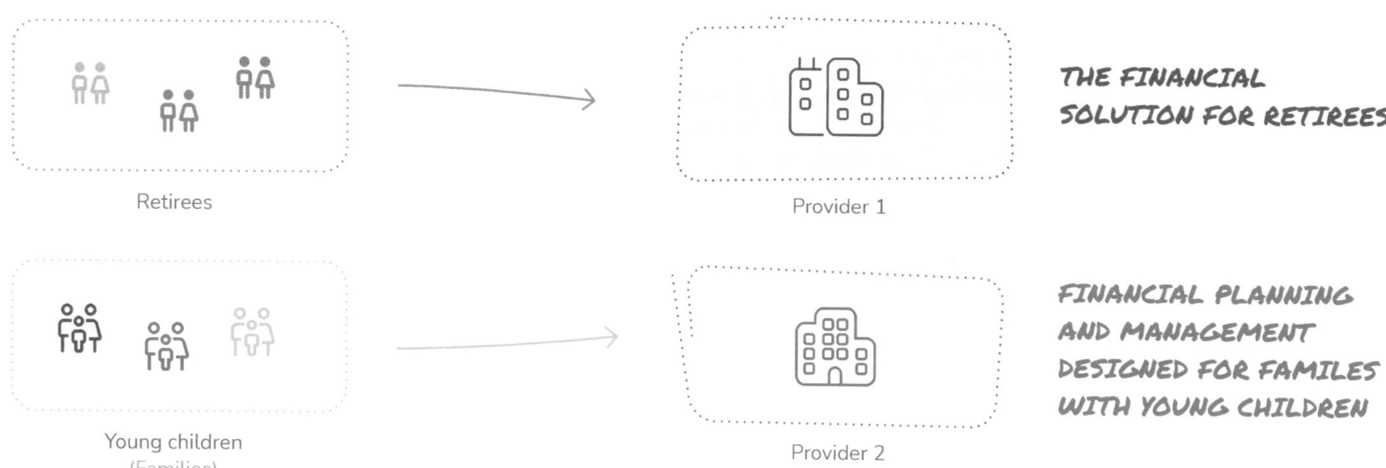

This pattern can be found in every industry:

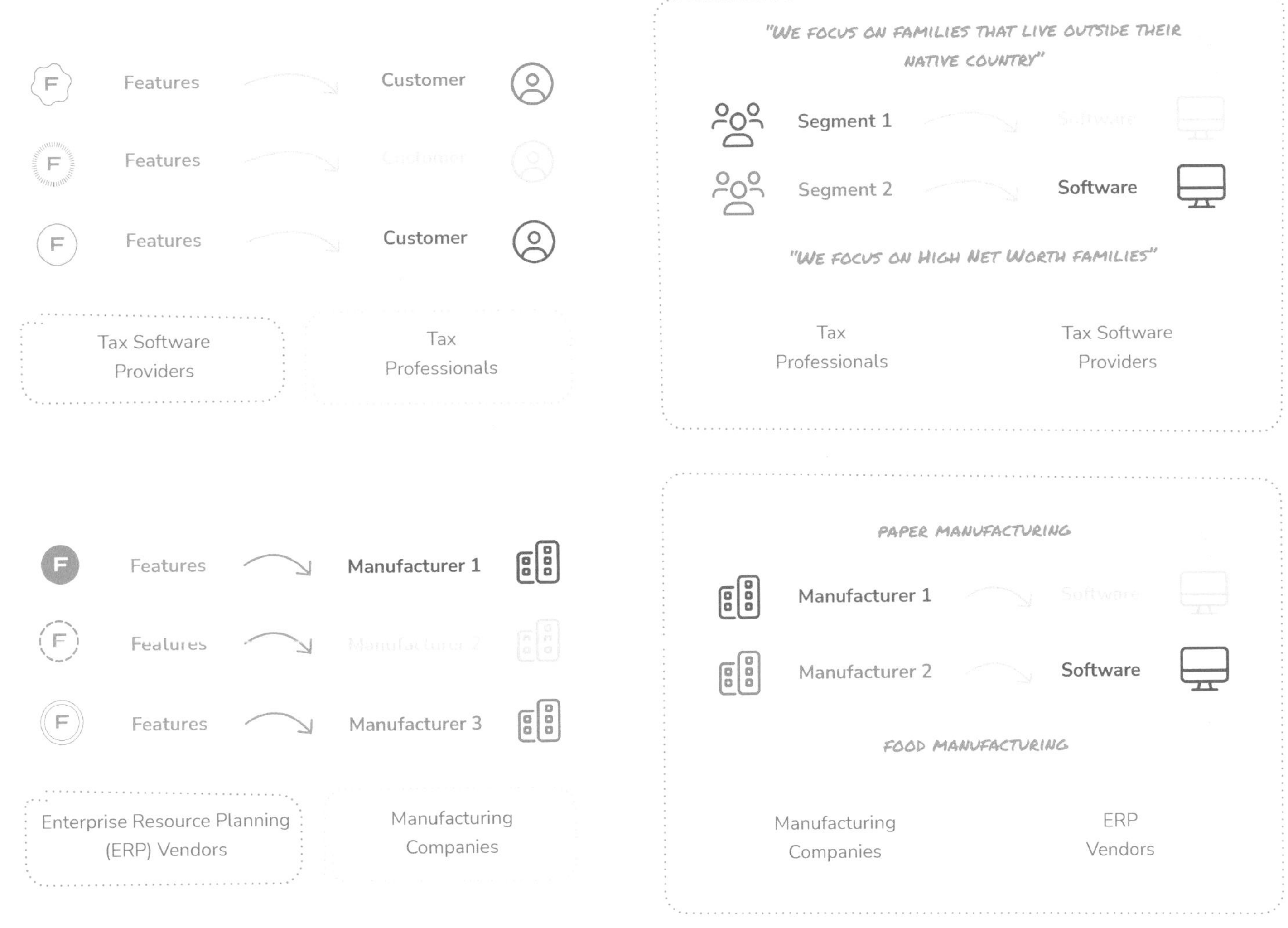

For a given provider, this pattern defines **which customers are most profitable.**

A **Solution Benefit Map** compares the results of a Customer Benefit Analysis against existing and future Features to identify those features with the greatest economic impact.

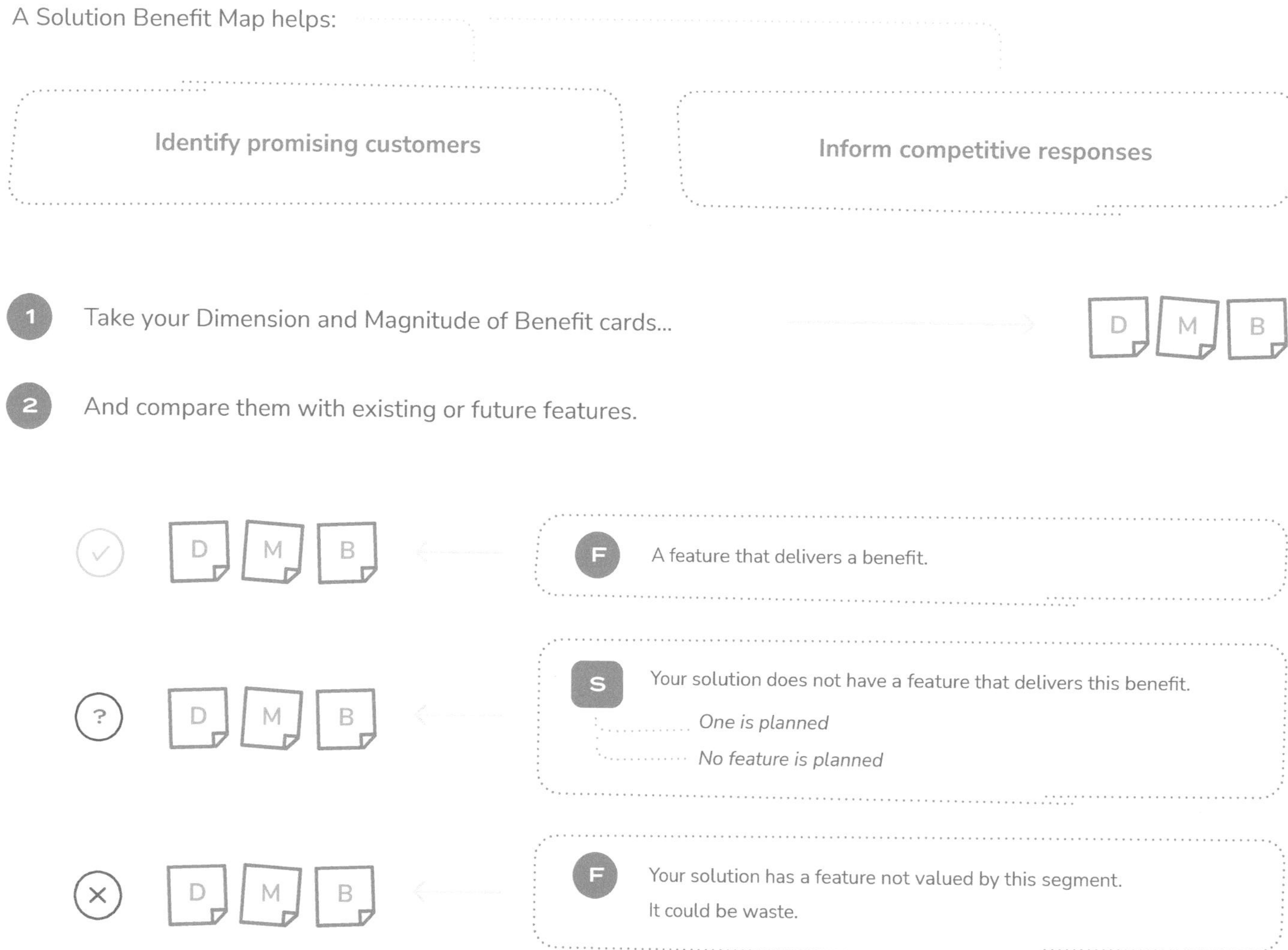

A Solution Benefit Map helps:
Identify promising customers
Inform competitive responses
1
Take your Dimension and Magnitude of Benefit cards...
D
M
B
2
And compare them with existing or future features.
D
M
B
F
A feature that delivers a benefit.
?
D
M
B
S
Your solution does not have a feature that delivers this benefit.
One is planned
No feature is planned
D
M
B
F
Your solution has a feature not valued by this segment.
It could be waste.

Example of a **Solution Benefit Map**

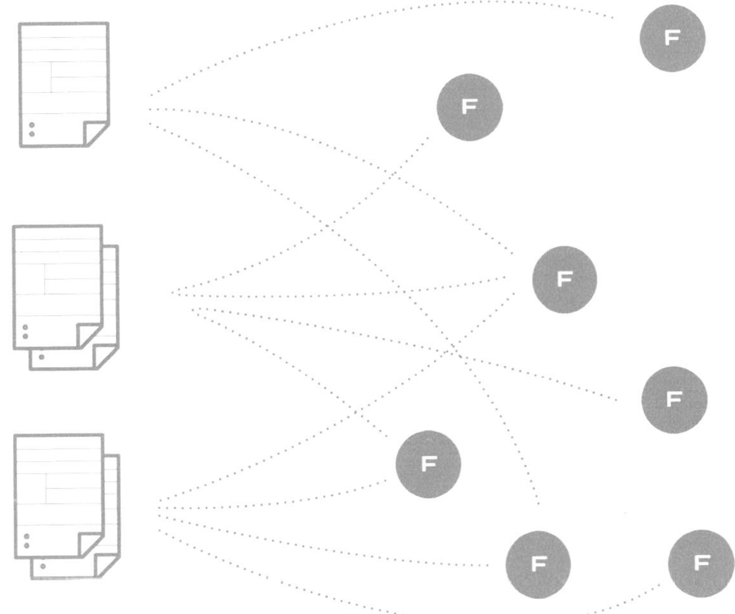

Feature name

Description

Tangible Benefit(s)

Intangible Benefit(s)

You have a collection of Dimension-Magnitude of benefit cards.

For each card, identify the feature or set of features that are needed to provide that benefit. If all features are required, mark the card with an 'S', which indicates that all features fo the Solution are needed.

Check your work by comparing the feature(s) to the Dimension and Magnitude cards. If the features cannot deliver the benefit defined in the cards, you're going to have to modify them or add new features. This may cause changes in your roadmap.

Use your **Solution Benefit Map** to identify promising opportunities and to eliminate features that no longer provide economic value.

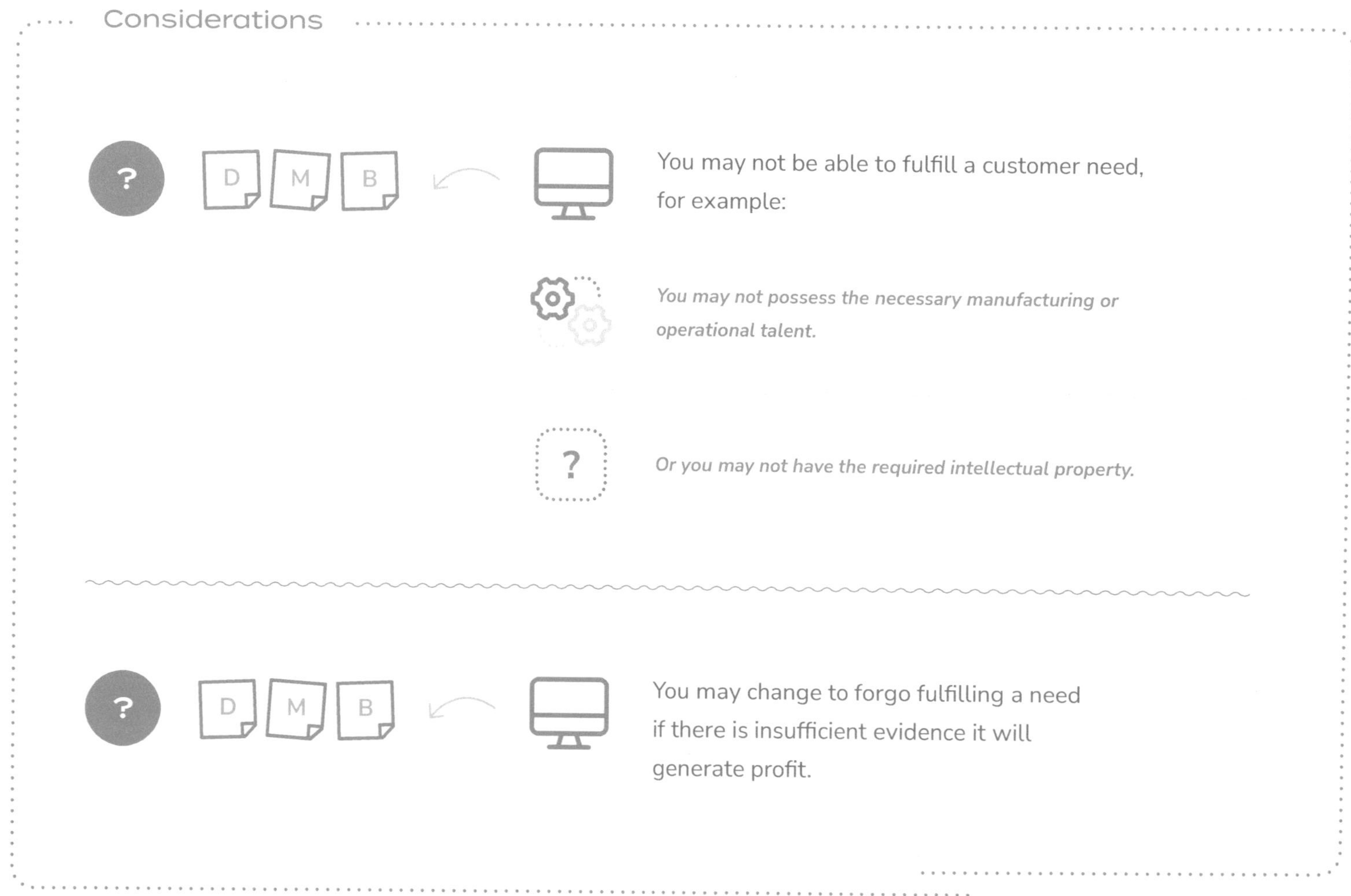

Considerations
?
D
M
B
You may not be able to fulfill a customer need, for example:
You may not possess the necessary manufacturing or operational talent.
?
Or you may not have the required intellectual property.
?
D
M
B
You may change to forgo fulfilling a need if there is insufficient evidence it will generate profit.

The Whole Product Framework

Originally developed by Theodore Levitt, the whole product framework is a useful tool for organizing the features and expected benefits for each customer segment.[3]

Levitt's use of the word 'product' is equivalent to our use of the word 'solution'.

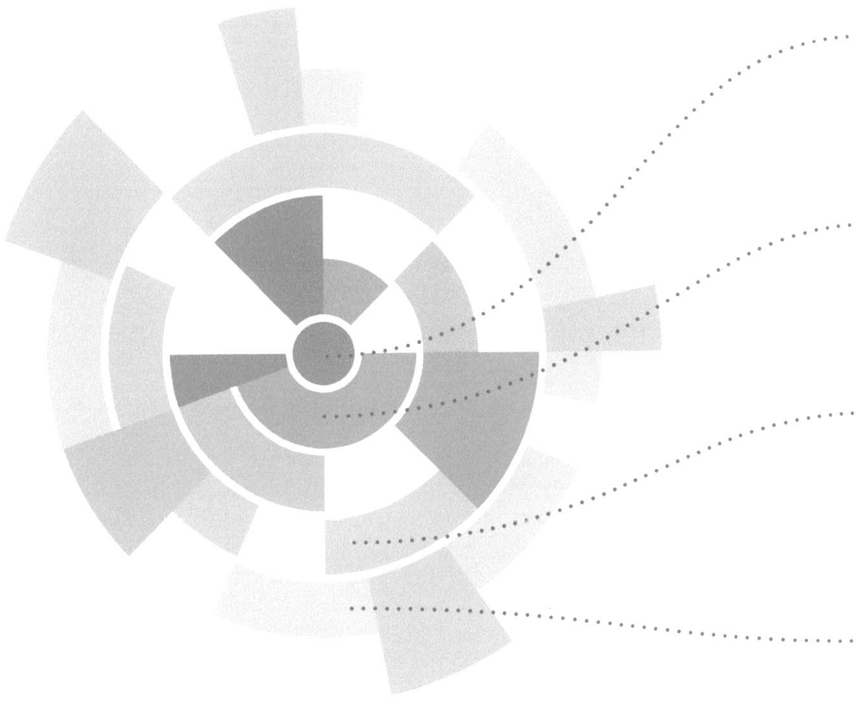

The Generic Product
The minimum set of features required to be able to satisfy a customer.

The Expected Product
The solution that is required to satisfy the customer's minimal purchase conditions.

The Augmented Product
Features that go beyond what customers expect that differentiate this specific solution from competitive or alternative solutions.

The Potential Product
Everything that might be done to attract and hold customers.

Whole Product Thinking helps **business leaders** design solutions that are both differentiated and lead to sustainability.

SUCCESSFUL SOLUTION DESIGN USES

Solution Benefit Maps and **Whole Product Thinking** to...

Change how customers perceive solutions and create economic opportunity.

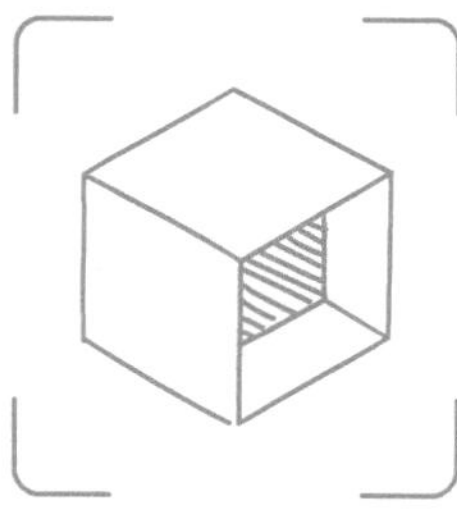

Example:

Reframe the expected solution by increasing quality:

Zoom took the expected features of video conferencing and made it an augmented solution by creating a vastly superior offering: the 'plain' feature was remarkably better in Zoom. Zoom added additional expected features such as chat and scheduling to highlight their augmented feature. Finally, Zoom created a novel pricing structure to drive adoption.

Example:

Neutralize a competitor by offering similar features

Lyft has successfully neutralized Uber's initial lead, enabling Lyft to emphasize its own unique set of features.

A **Killer Feature** is a single feature that provides the vast majority of a solution's economic value.

Uber's killer feature included a map and an integrated secure no-cash payment process. Lyft has neutralized this.

Figma's killer feature was design in the browser with integrated version control.

While killer features can be a goal of a solutions' designer, they more often emerge after a solution has been released.

Sometimes you get lucky and have two killer features!"

You can maximize the profit impact of killer features through the design choices you make in packaging, pricing, and licensing.

The Solution Context identifies critical aspects of a solution's operational environment*

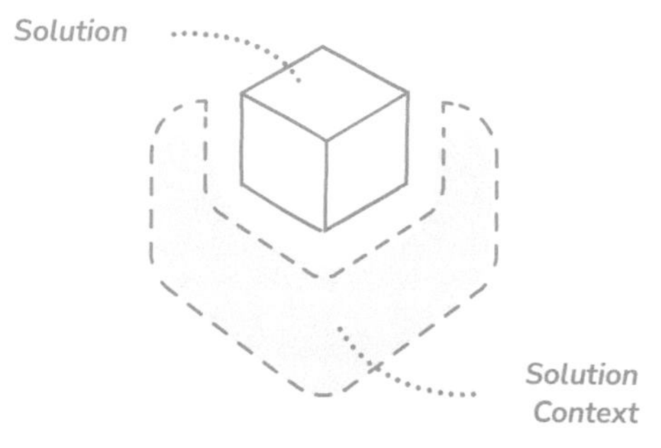

The Solution Context is inclusive of many factors: for a consumer using a ride-sharing service, the solution context includes such things as the app, their phone, their location, the weather, and payment methods. This Solution Context differs for that same user when they arrive home and watch a movie.

The Solution Context of an financial management system designed for large companies includes the customer's IT operating environment, the devices used to access the system, the applications to which it provides and/or consumes data, and so forth.

The boundary between the solution and the Solution Context provides a fertile ground for driving innovation.

Instead of providing a database as part of the solution, the provider might require customers to provide a compatible database. In both cases the customer must pay for the database - the boundary between the solution and the solution context defines how and when.

Moving part of the Solution Context into the solution can create value by reducing operational complexity.

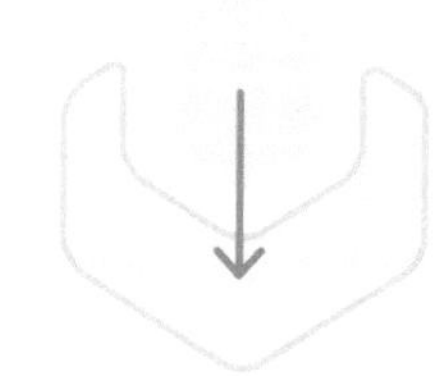

Moving part of the solution into the Solution Context can reduce provider costs and/or create more options and controls for customers.

A solution that helps restaurants manage reservations might require the owner to provide a payment processor. Extending the solution with payment processing moves payment processing from the solution context into the solution, lowering complexity and enabling more pricing options.

Solution Context is defined in the Scaled Agile Framework (SAFe®).

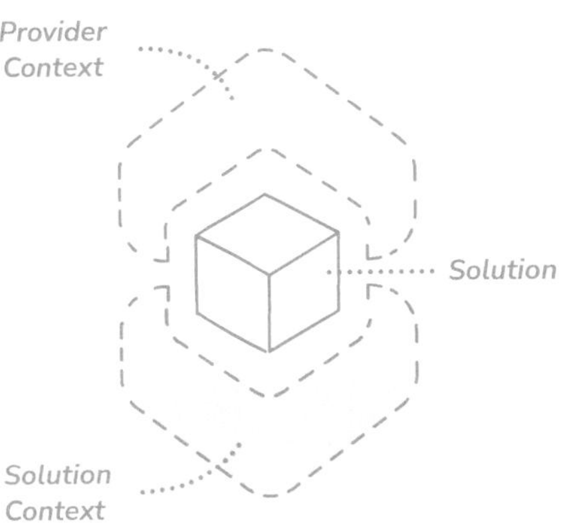

Solutions are offered to customers through a Provider Context, which identifies aspects of customer value that are not intrinsic to the solution and are integral to the solution's total economic benefit.

The Provider Context includes, but is not limited to, such things as brand, company mission, sales processes/ease of doing business, return policies, and customer care.

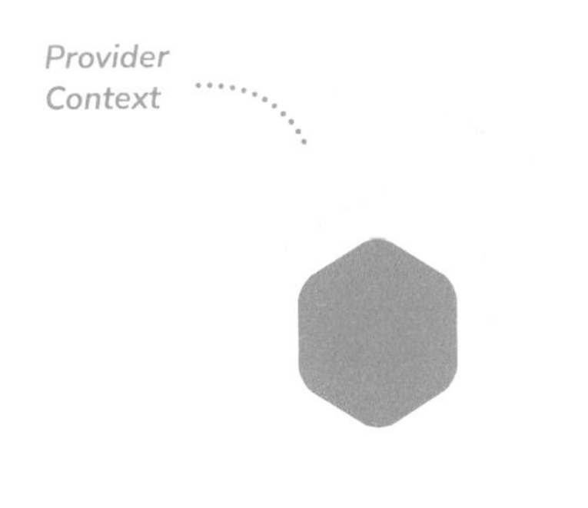

Changing or improving the Provider Context can improve overall solution profitability, often in a way that can be less costly than changing the solution itself.

Providing a self-service option for purchasing your solution can increase customer satisfaction and sales while lowering operational costs.

Value Exchange

The value exchange model block defines how a customer will exchange money for value. We explore:

- → *The seven value exchange models*
- → *How each value exchange model creates unique demands on your technical architecture*

Your value exchange model defines how you exchange solutions for money, forming the core of your business model.

Each value exchange model creates unique technical requirements, which means that changing your value exchange model often requires commensurate changes to your architecture.

A complex system may have multiple value exchange models.

The "base" system might be transaction-fee based while additional "optional" modules might be annually licensed. The central business model should be congruent with the core benefits received from the customer by the generic and expected solution. The augmented solution may benefit from different licensing models.

Additional ways in which you can design multiple value exchange models are covered in the profit engine block.

Each Value Exchange model has also developed a set of patterns regarding how the solution is managed over time. We'll explore these patterns and choices in this block and the Customer Licence block.

This means that Value Exchange Models are resistant to change, as they are a very deep part of your technical architecture and affect multiple corporate systems.

The Seven Value Exchange Models

TIME-BASED ACCESS

The provider grants the customer the right to use the solution for a defined period of time - even if the customer doesn't use the solution.

PERPETUAL

The customer is granted a license to use the software in perpetuity—that is, forever. Upgrades or updates are not usually included. Bug fixes or patches may be included as part of the original fee, or the customer may be required to pay a maintenance fee. Be very careful of perpetual licenses, as they often increase total support and maintenance costs - unless you're careful, you may have to support every version—forever!

Despite the potential drawbacks of perpetual licenses, they are surprisingly common and often required in many markets. Consumer software, productivity tools, operating systems, and some enterprise applications are based on them. Perpetual licenses may be required if you're providing a system or technology designed to be embedded within other systems. Examples range from the runtime libraries provided by programming language vendors to solutions that may become components of hardware devices or information appliances.

A subtle challenge with perpetual licenses + maintenance agreements is that customers may 'skip' the maintenance agreement for a few years, then try and pay to acquire the latest functionality. Your Profit Stream should account for how to make lapsed customers current if they decide they need the latest updates.

DEFINED TERM: MONTHLY, QUARTERLY, ANNUALLY, OR MULTI-TERM

The solution can be accessed for a defined period of time.

The effective date can start when the license is granted, the time the solution is installed, or the time the solution is first used. The term can end when defined - at the end of the month or the end of one calendar year after the start. The most common terms are month and annual licenses. In a hosted environment, the solution typically includes automatic upgrades. When the solution is executed on hardware supplied by the customer, updates may or may not be included. Renewal may be automatic and may be priced differently from the original annual license.

The difference between a perpetual license with an annual maintenance fee and an annual license is subtle, but important. In the case of a perpetual license, the maintenance fees are added on as a way of enticing the customer to pay for additional services, such as bug fixes or new releases. In the case of an annual license, if the customer hasn't paid and continues to use the solution, it is in breach of the license.

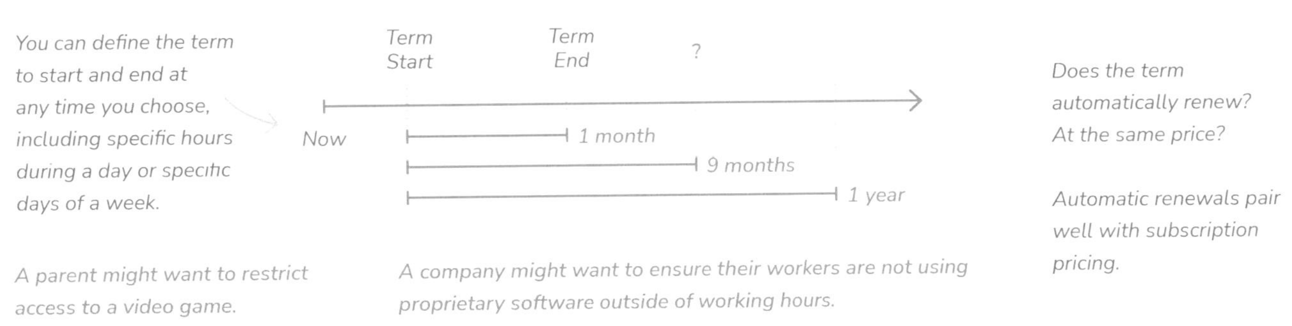

You can define the term to start and end at any time you choose, including specific hours during a day or specific days of a week.
Term Start
Term End
?
Now
1 month
9 months
1 year
Does the term automatically renew? At the same price?
Automatic renewals pair well with subscription pricing.
A parent might want to restrict access to a video game.
A company might want to ensure their workers are not using proprietary software outside of working hours.

Although monthly and annual licenses are the most common predefined time periods, there is nothing that prevents you from defining other periods (e.g., nine months) or a collection of times when the software can be accessed (e.g., Monday through Friday from 8 to 5). The hard part is defining one that works best for your target market and making certain you can appropriately enforce the business model and license terms (which market segment would find sensible a nine-month period or only accessing software Monday through Friday from 8 to 5?).

The Seven Value Exchange Models

PAY-AFTER-USE

An interesting question arises in any time-based usage model: What happens when the user accesses the application after the approved period of time? How you answer this question can make or break your relationship with your customer—and your bank account.

At one end of the spectrum is absolute enforcement of a business model with no grace period: When the term is finished, the software becomes inoperable. This severe choice is simply inappropriate for most target markets. For example, suppose a monthly user had a credit card expire. Should there be some grace period?

One option is to charge your customer after they have used the software by keeping track of how long it was used. This model places some demands on your technical architecture, but it does help ensure that your customer can use your solution and that you'll get paid.

An analogy is a car rental. You're typically charged for each day you rent the car, with strict definitions as to what constitutes a day. If you go beyond the original contract, the car company continues to charge you (they have your credit card on file, and the rate that you'll be charged is predefined in the contract).

ARCHITECTURE

Time-Based Access

Requirement: Identify when the Solution is being used outside of the license agreement term and respond accordingly.

Responses must be defined. For example, a hosted service could disallow login or implement a paywall. An on-premise solution might show a 'nag screen' reminding the user they are out of compliance, it might slow down, it might disable certain features, or it might simply stop working.

Ensure appropriate data management and retention policies. For example, GDPR compliance may require deletion of data when the license expires.

The Seven Value Exchange Models

TRANSACTION

A transaction is a defined and measurable unit of work.

The exchange of money is tied to the successful completion of the transaction, but customer value (and typically price) is often associated with an attribute of the transaction.

Transaction processing speed can be fast (like a credit card), or moderate (like mining a block on a blockchain), or slow (like computing a stress analysis on the structural plans of a building).

There is nothing about a transaction-based model that requires all transactions to perform the same amount of work. This means that you can tailor the kinds of transactions you're offering to meet the needs of specific segments—and design pricing models that ensure sustainable profitability.

Transactions give business leaders a lot of creative freedom in designing *pricing and billing models.* Variations include:

- Paying on a per-transaction basis
- Partial payments based on transaction progress
- Bulk purchase of a number pre-defined of transactions
- Sliding prices based on translation volumes

stripe 2.9% + 30¢

per successful card charge

Many credit card processors charge a flat fee and a percentage of the total dollar amount on each transaction.

Transaction Fees may be calculated in many different ways. Examples include:

FLAT FEES (a fixed cost per transaction)

PERCENTAGE FEES (a percentage of some calculated or defined amount)

SLIDING FEES (the cost per transaction decreases as certain volumes are realized)

PROCESSING FEES in which the work to perform the transaction is measured and the customer is billed accordingly (e.g., a simple transaction that could be computed with few resources costs less than a complex transaction that requires many resources).

Consider the impact of when customers use fewer transactions than expected, as this may severely impact your profitability. Combining monthly/term minimums in addition to transaction fees ensures that you have a floor for how far revenue can fall.

Building a transaction processor capable of thousands of transactions a month for a customers who only use dozens of transactions a month is unlikely to create a sustainable profit.

ARCHITECTURE

Transaction

Ensure the architecture implements the legal definition of the transaction.

Define and manage the entire transaction lifecycle

Define and manage reporting, audit, invoice, and remittance policies.

Ensure support, sales, and service organizations have the tools required for their job—for example, researching Customer inquiries, or correcting and/or adjusting invalid transactions.

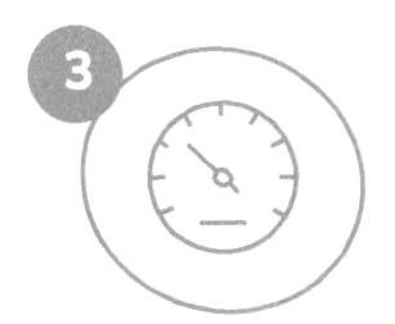

METER

Metering is a value exchange model based on constraining or consuming a well-defined resource or something that the solution processes.

A constraint model limits access to the solution to a specific set of predefined resources. A consumptive model creates a "pool" of possible resources that are consumed. The consumption can be based on concurrency, as when two or more resources simultaneously access or use the solution, or on an absolute value that is consumed as the solution is used. When all of the available resources are temporarily or permanently consumed, the solution typically becomes inoperable or otherwise unable to provide value.

CONCURRENT RESOURCE MANAGEMENT

Commonly used in the B2C and B2P markets, this meter controls the number of resources concurrently accessing the solution, with the most common resource either a user or a session. The business model is usually designed to constrain the resource ("a license for up to 10 concurrent users"). Both user and session must be defined, because in many solutions a single user can have multiple sessions. The specific definition of a resource always has technical implications; managing concurrent users is quite different from managing concurrent sessions, and both are different from managing concurrent threads or processes. Like transaction fees, concurrent resource business models have a variety of pricing schemes. You may pay less for more resources, and you may pay a different amount for a different resource.

IDENTIFIED RESOURCE MANAGEMENT

In this variant, specific resources are identified to the application and are allowed to access the solution when they have been properly authenticated. The constraint is the defined resources, the most common of which is a named user, that is, a specifically identified user allowed to access the application. Identified resource business models are often combined with concurrent (consumptive) resource business models for performance or business reasons. Thus, you may create a business model based on any 10 out of 35 named users concurrently accessing the system or any 3 out of 5 plug-ins concurrently used to extend the application.

The Seven Value Exchange Models

CONSUMPTIVE RESOURCE MANAGEMENT

In this variant, you create a specified amount of a resource that is consumed by the solution as it is running. Unlike a concurrent model, in which consumption varies based on the specific resources simultaneously accessing the solution, a purely consumptive model expends resources that are not returned.

Consider time as a consumptive resource. In this approach, you define a period of time (e.g., 100 hours of super computer time) and provide the customer with a license for it. As the solution is used, it keeps track of the time, "consuming" the designated value from the license. When all of the allotted time has been used the solution becomes inoperable. Key issues that must be resolved in this approach include the definition of time (actual CPU time, system-elapsed time, or other), the manner in which the solution will track resource consumption (locally, remotely, or distributed), and the granularity of the time-based license (milliseconds, seconds, days, weeks, months, and so forth).

It is possible to define and meter an abstract resource. Suppose you have a hosted solution for video publishing with two killer features: the ability to automatically correct background noise and the ability to automatically correct background lighting. You could define that any time the user invokes the background noise correction feature they are consuming one computing unit while any time they invoke the background lighting correction feature they are consuming three computing units. You could then provide a license for 20 computing units that your customer could spend as they deem appropriate.

Consumptive resource models can underlie subscription-based service models— during each billing period (e.g., monthly), for a set fee, you get a predefined number of resources; when the resources are consumed, you can purchase more or stop using the solution, and any resources that are not consumed are either carried over to the next billing period (possibly with a maximum limit) or lost forever. This is similar to the access-based subscriptions, except that you are metering and consuming a resource. The difference may be fine-grained, but it is worth exploring the potential benefits of each type because you may be able to access a new market or increase your market share in a given market with the right one.

Consumptive models have another critical requirement often overlooked—reporting and replenishment. It must be extremely easy for a user/administrator to predict how much an operation will "cost" before she decides to spend, the rate at which spending is occurring, and when the rate of spending will exceed the allotment for the month or a resource budget is nearing depletion. Because customers will often overspend, it should be painless to buy more. No one will blame you if they run out of a critical resource on Friday afternoon at 6 PM Eastern time, just before a critical big push weekend—especially if you warned them yesterday that it would happen. But they will never, ever forgive you if they can't buy more until Monday at 9 AM Pacific time.

ARCHITECTURE

Meter

Ensure that the architecture can count the item being metered.

When consumptive, ensure the architecture provides audit processes and can manage the replenishment of the resources.

When constrained, ensure the architecture prevents improper sharing, for example sharing login or access credentials.

The Seven Value Exchange Models

4

HARDWARE

The customer purchases hardware and the hardware comes preinstalled with a software creating a software-enabled solution. In most cases the software is so intimately tied to the hardware that the hardware is effectively useless without the software! Establishing the value of the hardware can be quite challenging, as many times the software portion of the solution is perceived as 'free' because it is part of the hardware. Designers can design their solution so that the software cannot be changed, or they can design their solution so that it can evolve over time. The solution can also be designed as a platform ecosystem, in which third party application providers create additional software solutions.

Home appliances, such as microwave ovens

Consumer electronics, such as 'smart' TVs, personal computers, and phones

Dedicated appliances such as network security solutions used by businesses

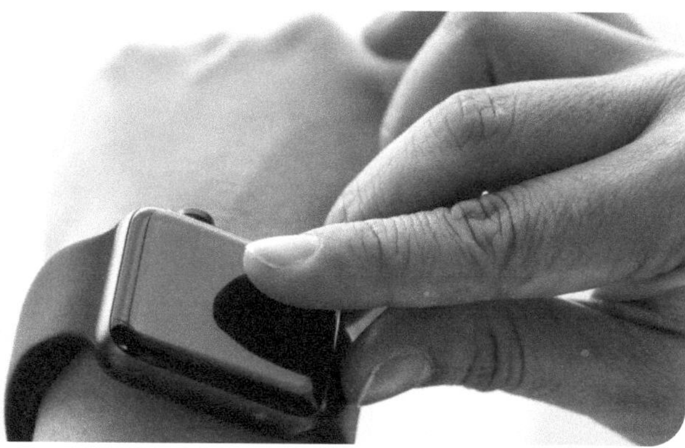

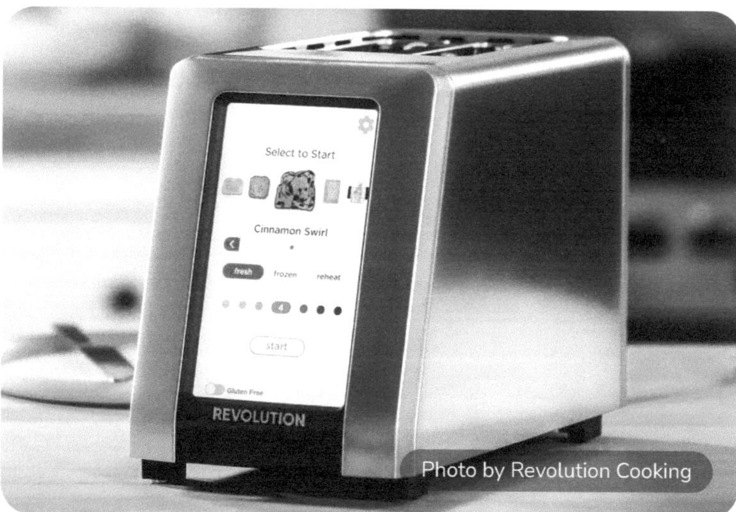

Photo by Revolution Cooking

The Revolution InstaGLO touchscreen toaster offers 63 precise toast settings, 7 browning levels, an automatic raising and lowering mechanism, and a countdown timer with an adjustable cheerful finishing chime—all powered by software.

ARCHITECTURE

Hardware

Identify if the hardware should support remote updates.

Determine if the software needs to identify or prevent tampering—you don't want hackers burning your toast!

Identify and support data rights, including compliance with emerging data privacy laws.

The Seven Value Exchange Models

SERVICE

The software-enabled solution requires human labor to deliver the value customers associate with the solution.

What is different from Software-as-a-Service (SaaS) and a Service Value Exchange?

SaaS is a deployment strategy in which the provider operates some or all of the Solution in a hosted environment, providing the software 'as a service' to the customer. SaaS solutions are most often time-based access value exchanges because the customer is paying for access to the solution for a defined period of time.

To help determine if you have a Service Value Exchange, ask the following questions:

What happens if the provider removes the human associated with the solution? If your solution is incapable of delivering value to your customer without a human involved, it is almost certainly a Service value exchange model.

Is the quality of the result partly determined by a human? If the answer is yes, it is a Service. If the amount you charge is based on the quality of the delivered result, then your Service value exchange has a structure that is similar to the Performance value exchange model.

Instacart is a solution that allows you to select grocery items from your preferred supermarket and offers same day delivery.

Fiverr is a solution which allows businesses and professionals to complete project-based work by leveraging the skills of freelancers anywhere in the world,

ARCHITECTURE

Service

Ensure the architecture can support any necessary content and/or workflow sharing that may be required between users.

Consider the impact of roles and access rights.

Because a service value exchange model is based on a relationship between humans and software, the specific responsibilities of the humans involved and the underlying software must be clearly defined. These responsibilities will evolve over time as software capabilities evolve.

The Seven Value Exchange Models

PERFORMANCE

The provider is compensated a percentage of the revenue gained by the customer's use of the solution or a percentage of the savings the customer realizes from the use of the solution.

Similar to transaction, in that the value exchange is based on a "transaction"—different from transaction, in that the revenue obtained is based on an outcome.

In essence, providers take a cut of the action when customers use the solution. However, this model is different than transaction because the customer must receive a positive benefit—*an increase in revenue or a cost savings*—in order for value to be exchanged.

Vendavo has created a software-enabled solution to provide customers advice on the optimal price point for solutions in a variety of domains ranging from aerospace to health care.

And since the product managers at Vendavo have selected Performance as their value exchange model, Vendavo only receives payment if their price recommendations result in positive revenue increase for the customer. If not, Vendavo receives zero compensation.

ARCHITECTURE

Performance

The architecture needs to keep track of the baseline result and the changed result so that the performance improvement can be determined.

Ensure capability for the customer and provider to agree that the solution is materially contributing the performance improvement.

The architecture may need to limit performance improvements if the projected or actual performance improvements exceed the terms of the agreement.

The Seven Value Exchange Models

DATA

The software-enabled solution creates unique data or content that the customer wishes to access.

Attributes often determine the value of data. Consider financial data:

TIMELINESS
Data that is delivered faster is generally more valuable

BREADTH
Data that includes related data may be more valuable

ACCURACY
More accurate data is generally more valuable

PRECISION
Data that is more precise is generally more valuable

SCARCITY
Unique and/or scarce data may be more valuable

Examples: Credit scores, stock quotes, patent data, digital goods in video games.

Carfax is a solution which offers, for a fee of about $40 USD, the complete history of a used vehicle. If you are buying a used car, this information could be quite valuable.

Or perhaps you would like the fly around the galaxy in a personal starship? This Jedi defender-class cruiser can be purchased for use in an online game, but it will cost you 2400 cartel coins, the equivalent of $20 USD.

ARCHITECTURE

Data

Define data management, use, and retention.

- Can your customers repackage or resell the data you are licensing?
- Can a digital good be transferred to another entity?

Consider automation and distribution.

Do you need to support the GPDR rights, such as the right to erasure or right to data portability? (See the Compliance block for more details)

Ensure operations can manage scope, complexity, volume, and speed.

Just because you can...

Doesn't mean you should.

Business leaders need to keep in mind that the type of value exchange influences customer behavior in ways that could backfire!

Per-User metering may reduce usage, thereby lowering perceived value.

The trick is to associate the type of value exchanged with the value derived.

Instead of per-user metering, consider "per device under management" metering.

PRICING BLOCK

SOLUTION + ECONOMIC SUSTAINABILITY

MONETIZATION FOCUS

Pricing

The price is much more than a number. The pricing block explores the Profit Stream pricing model:

- → *The overriding strategy that guides specific price choices*
- → *The structure of pricing metrics and fences*
- → *The specifics of price levels*
- → *How customer and market research can help inform the price*
- → *The policies that may adjust the price*
- → *The influence of different buyer types in setting the price*

The Profit Stream Pricing Model...

....uses systems thinking to identify and manage all aspects of a value-based approach to pricing that maximizes profit over time.

Price Strategy defines how you intend to compete and position your solution.

STRATEGY

Price Structure drives pricing by different segments and different solution attributes.

STRUCTURE

SPECIFICS

Price Specifics identify the actual price levels offered to different customer segments including all the details related to the chosen value exchange model.

POLICIES

Price Policies establish the processes and procedures needed to ensure the integrity of the price structure under pressure from customers and competition.

PRICING

Price Strategy

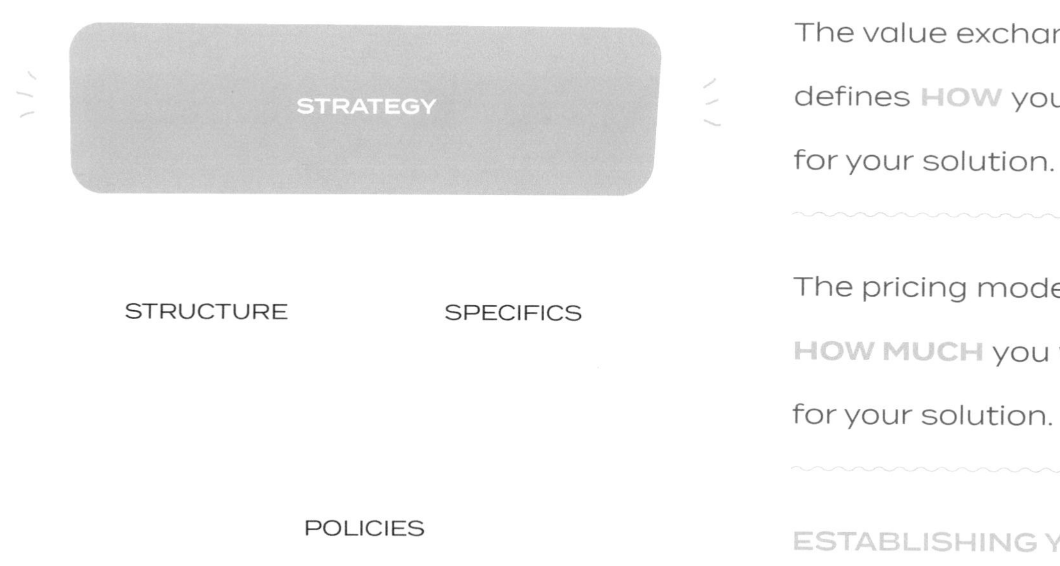

The value exchange model you choose defines **HOW** you will charge a customer for your solution.

The pricing model you select defines **HOW MUCH** you will charge customers for your solution.

ESTABLISHING YOUR PRICE STRATEGY IS THE FIRST STEP.

Constructing a pricing model is a difficult job. Charge too much and you may price yourself out of the market or leave yourself vulnerable to competitors. Charge too little and you give up profit. Between the extremes of "too high" and "too low", there are a number of complex options to explore, ranging from the impact of pricing on perceptions of quality to understanding when to use, and why you should mostly avoid, discounts.

An effective approach to pricing that maximizes profitability is a mix of art and science that integrates the following factors:

Choices about what to offer to customers

Where and how to compete

How to communicate value and price

How prices may vary across customer segments

Management of customer price expectations and incentives

Ongoing, active price management

Every product leader wants to create the perfect pricing model—the model that maximizes sustainable profits. This complex task is harder when we realize that leaders work with, and within, complex systems that impose their own, sometimes harsh, realities on pricing.

Here are few of these realities:

ROI HURDLES

As companies grow and offer more products and services, they typically develop a set of policies that establish the minimum profit margin that must exist for an offering to be considered successful. For example, a corporation will reject a solution with a 23% profit margin if the hurdle for profit margin is sel at 30%. While a solution may be profitable at 25%, it won't meet the minimum profit margin target and will be rejected from consideration.

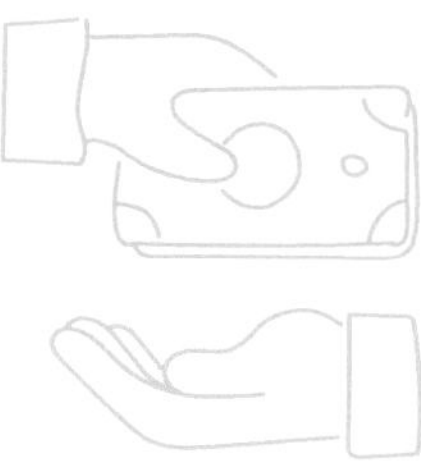

FIXED/VARIABLE COSTS FOR COMPONENTS

Product Managers of software enabled solutions and services always have suppliers, ranging from the low-level technical libraries that power the code to the cloud service providers that host their customers' software solutions and provide storage and compute services.

A unique challenge in managing price are the fees charged by suppliers and how the fees impact the resulting price charged to the end customer. The relationship is simple: more fees paid to suppliers creates greater risk to sustainable profits.

Potential new tariffs, which should be on your roadmap, can impact your costs and profits as well.

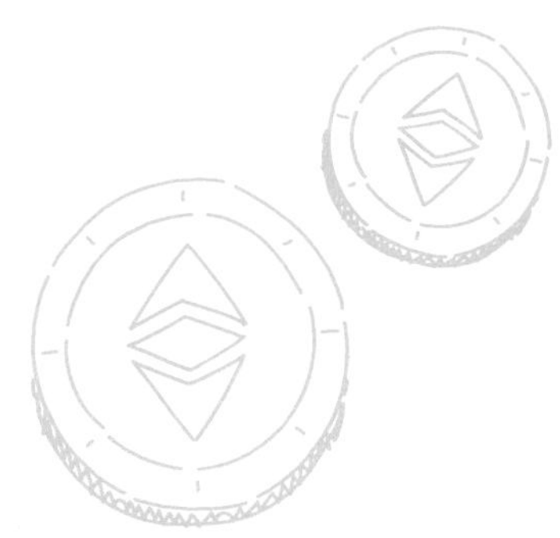

One example of the negative impact of sharply rising supplier fees is the Ethereum ecosystem.

When Ethereum was created, several financial applications were created on top of Ethereum because transactions, known as gas fees, were fractions of a penny. As more of these applications were released, gas fees increased from fractions of a penny to as much as several hundred dollars, creating havoc for the business models of many startups. This example illustrates why business leaders must remain vigilant about the fees their suppliers charge.

To correct this problem, Ethereum completely overhauled their infrastructure, moving from 'Proof of Work' to 'Proof of Stake', dramatically lowering transaction fees - and saving several solutions in the process!

Profitable pricing requires that you understand and manage the perceptions of monetary and psychological value that drive purchase decisions.

WHAT

Customer benefit analysis directly informs pricing by aligning the price metric, the unit to which price is applied, to the value metric, the unit of consumption that provides customer value.

WHY

When you've mastered customer benefit analysis, you can better communicate the value offered to customers, price by customer segment to reflect differences in value and price, and create pricing policies to manage sales issues fairly and consistently.

HOW

We'll first consider what influences price, identify approaches to avoid, describe common pricing strategies, build pricing structure then define price levels and policy.

PRICE STRATEGY

What influences price?

PRICE STRATEGY

MARKET

COMPETITORS

Analyze competitor pricing. How will you compete? Will you position your solution as a premium offering and price higher than competitors? Or will you position your solution as an economy offering and price lower to gain volume? Even a solution perceived as a commodity can be priced higher than competitors by positioning the attributes that differentiate your solution like awesome support, quality training, reliable solution information. Be creative and stand out!

REFERENCE PRICING

Customers use a reference price when making purchase decisions. They think about what they paid previously for the same or a similar solution. For innovative solutions, customers mentally search for some other solution as a reference to evaluate the price. Think like a customer and consider reference prices as you set your price.

SUBSTITUTES

What could a customer substitute for your solution? Customers can choose a different solution other than your competition. They could create their own solution or they could choose to do nothing. Any option has a cost. Substitutes influence the reference price for your solution.

BRAND

Customers assess brand when deciding whether to purchase. Well-known, well-respected brands achieve higher price points. Brand dramatically affects highly expensive purchases. Consider the strength of your brand relative to purchase size as a factor to set your price. And keep building your brand.

UNIQUENESS

Customers associate higher value with unique intellectual property (IP) or unique data. Digimarc, a developer of embedded digital identification technologies emerged as a small company with patented digital watermarking. Digimarc now provides product digitization to brands around the world. Evaluate the unique IP of your solution. If no one else can provide a similar solution to what you have developed ***without*** your IP, then you can set a higher price.

BUYER POWER

The degree to which your buyers can influence your price. Low buyer power means that you're immune to your customers' demands. High buyer power means that your customers have one or more ways to force you to lower your prices. For example, customers might demand better payment terms or design a bidding war in which multiple vendors must compete for a large customer purchase.

Barganing Leverage from High Volume and/or Frequency of Purchase + Price Sensitivity = BUYER POWER

CHANNEL STRATEGY

Your channel partners expect a reasonable margin for selling your solution at a price that also generates profit for you. If you also sell directly to customers, the direct price cannot be lower than the channel's price or the relationship with the channel will be damaged. Decide what tradeoffs in volume and profit you will make when you consider pricing and your channel strategy.

PRICE ELASTICITY

Price elasticity of demand is the change in consumption of a solution in relation to a change in the solution's price. A solution's price is elastic if a price change causes a substantial change in demand. A solution's price is inelastic if a price change does not cause demand to change significantly. One way to identify the price elasticity of your solution is the market research technique known as the Van Westendorp price sensitivity meter described on page 182. Your goal is to create a solution with a relatively inelastic price.

01. PERFECTLY ELASTIC
Any change in price would cause an extreme change in demand.

02. PERFECTLY INELASTIC
Demand doesn't change when price is changed.

03. UNITARY ELASTIC
Any price change results in equal change in demand.

04. RELATIVELY ELASTIC
Small changes in price cause large changes in demand

05. RELATIVELY INELASTIC
Large changes in price cause small changes in demand.

PRICE STRATEGY

STRATEGY

PENETRATION

PRICE LOW FOR GROWTH

A penetration strategy focuses on growth in a competitive market by setting a low price to provide customers with exceptional value. This strategy can quickly attract many customers to a new solution. Several entertainment streaming services leveraged a penetration strategy to quickly attract new customers. A penetration strategy is often changed to increase prices as solution adoption increases. While this strategy drives demand, there are risks to consider.

- Customers may expect continued low prices...forever.
- Competitors may respond by lowering prices.
- Price sensitive customers may leave if you attempt to raise prices.

These risks mean that a penetration strategy should be used until you've achieved your target market share, at which time you should consider adopting a different strategy.

PREMIUM

HIGH PREMIUM PRICE

A premium strategy establishes a higher price relative to competitors through a combination of positioning, brand, quality, and key dimensions of value. Setting a high price establishes value and increases profit to fuel investment in additional innovation.

A premium strategy establishes a high reference price point and boldly communicates value to the market. Superior solution performance, great customer service and/or delivery of additional value over time is needed to maintain high prices. The Apple iPhone has consistently succeeded with a premium strategy for its latest, most advanced models.

COMPETITIVE

FOLLOW THE MARKET

A competitive strategy concentrates on setting price based on competitor prices and cost of substitutes. The price may be set higher or lower than competitors to maximize profitability. A dominant input is an external variable such as economic conditions. For example, a solution that optimizes expense management typically performs better during an economic downturn when companies seek to control costs. For example, streaming services like Hulu, Paramount Plus, Netflix and Disney+ all offer a basic solution at roughly the same price.

STABLE

A stable strategy sets a price that removes variability in use or purchasing. This strategy can be a significant benefit for customers who experience substantial variation in consumption. For example, if you live in a cold climate, you'll typically spend more money on heating costs in the winter. Budgeting for this kind of variability can be extremely burdensome, particularly for low-income families who benefit greatly from consistency in pricing. Accordingly, many utilities use stable pricing strategies by charging the same amount per month to create a consistent cost for energy expenditures.

HIGH-LOW

A high-low pricing strategy is designed for solutions with a limited time of attractiveness. The price is set high initially when the solution is most desired. The price is lowered, often dramatically, as interest or relevance declines. Sports-related video games employ this strategy to maximize profit.

DYNAMIC

Dynamic pricing strategy adjusts prices based on changes in customer demand. The pricing algorithm may also incorcporate other features like competitor pricing.

The objective of this strategy is to maximize profit while matching what customers will pay at the moment they are ready to purchase. The strategy works for increasing price as demand increases and also for decreasing price as more people purchase. Airlines and ride sharing applications leverage dynamic pricing strategies.

ECONOMY

This strategy positions a similar solution at a lower price than the competition to gain volume. A "no-frills" solution that meets the basic needs of the consumer is the definition of a budget pricing strategy. A cost conscious customer segment benefits from this strategy. A solution with an economy pricing strategy can complement more expensive solutions in a portfolio.

PRICE STRATEGY

STRATEGY

SKIMMING

PROGRESSIVE

A skimming strategy focuses on maintaining the highest price possible over time. As competition and other forces drive prices lower, revenue and profit are continuously skimmed. Many high definition TV makers use price skimming by setting high initial prices for their new models with the latest technology.

Prices are carefully and progressively lowered over time as the market for similar TVs matures. This strategy differs from High-Low because prices are progressively lowered only as needed.

LOSS LEADER

ATTRACTION

A loss leader strategy offers one highly discounted solution along with other more expensive related solutions. The cheap solution is typically sold at a loss to generate sales of the more expensive solutions. Printers are often sold as loss leaders funded by sales of replacement ink cartridges. While this strategy can be effective when creating bundled offerings, the risk may outweigh the benefits: SaaS companies that offer freemium subscriptions often find that their users never convert to customers, resulting in significant costs and depressed profits. Many times the company would be healthier by simply not offering the freemium option.

VALUE-BASED

CUSTOMER-FOCUSED

The value-based pricing strategy is customer-driven and profit-oriented by aligning price to the customer's perception of value derived from the solution. A value strategy is "outside-in" by focusing on customers, their needs, and perceptions first. This strategy often allows for pricing higher than competitors who cannot make or effectively communicate the value provided.

Lifecycle

The maturity of your solution in the adoption lifecycle affects how you make pricing decisions.

ADOPTION

As adoption increases, adjust prices for different customer segments. One segment may pay more for additional value like dedicated customer support. Another segment of experienced buyers who carefully evaluate alternatives may choose to pay less.

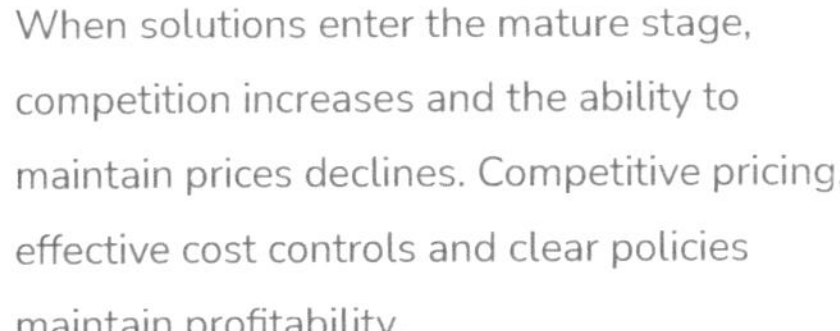

When solutions enter the mature stage, competition increases and the ability to maintain prices declines. Competitive pricing, effective cost controls and clear policies maintain profitability.

TIME

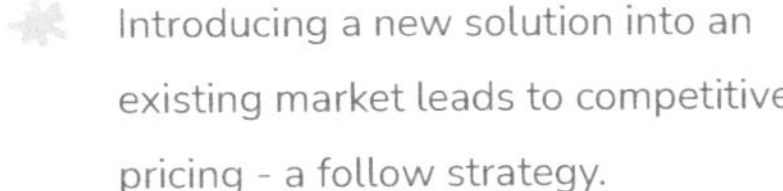

Introducing a new solution into an existing market leads to competitive pricing - a follow strategy.

OR

An innovative solution that creates a new market may be offered at a premium price.

Pricing Strategies to Avoid

PRODUCT MANAGER:
"I DON'T GET IT... I DID MY RESEARCH AND THEY TOLD ME WHAT THEY WOULD PAY"

Customer-Driven Pricing

Customer-driven pricing is setting price primarily based on basic research of customer willingness to pay while ignoring other factors. While a higher sales volume may result from this approach, one downside to this approach is that the price may be set less than the real value of the solution, which decreases profitability. Another issue is that buyers are not always honest about what they are willing to pay. Further, customers do not always have sufficient knowledge or experience to evaluate product value to determine what they would pay when asked.

CUSTOMER:
"THANKS FOR THE GREAT DEAL! I WOULD HAVE PAID TWICE AS MUCH"

Cost-Plus Pricing

Cost-plus pricing is setting a price based on the costs to build, maintain and sell a solution plus a desired margin for profit. In markets with weak demand, cost-plus pricing may lead to overpricing while cost-plus pricing leads to underpricing in markets with strong demand. Both outcomes are undesirable.

PRODUCT MANAGER:
"LET'S GAIN LOTS OF CUSTOMERS. IF WE GENERATE PROFIT QUICK, WE WIN!"

Market Share-Driven Pricing

Market share-driven pricing is a risky competitive strategy to set a low price to rapidly gain market share through sales volume. Market share can be a distracting vanity metric. Share is relevant only as a driver of profitability. While Apple could set a lower price for the next iPhone, the company deliberately maintains premium pricing for profit with relatively lower market share. Penetration is a better strategy to enter a market and deliberately plan to achieve profitability and adjust strategy over time.

STRUCTURE

Price Structure

Price structure is a consistent and planned approach to pricing software-enabled solutions that helps to achieve your organizational goals in a manner that is congruent with your pricing strategy.

Knowledge of customers and what they value drives the development of a price structure that stimulates unique pricing for different segments.

While more detailed segments generally increase profitability, organizations encounter limits in their ability to manage pricing complexity across multiple segments and to enforce the price structure at a reasonable cost.

Benefits of this approach...

Aligns with differences in economic value across segments

Accomodates variability of costs to serve each segment

Generates higher revenue from sales when value and / or cost to serve is higher while accepting lower revenue for additional profit from sales when value and / or cost to serve is lower.

Price Structure is a result of a set of intentional design choices

Recording the rationale behind each choice will help you improve positioning, messaging, and related marketing activities to effectively communicate value to different segments.

PRICE STRUCTURE

Price Metrics

Price Metrics are the units to which the price is applied and define the terms of value exchange.

The price metric for a cheeseburger or veggieburger at your favorite restaurant is the quantity of cheeseburgers or veggieburgers ordered. The price metric for Zoom's basic corporate videoconferencing service is the quantity of named users with access to the service.

To maximize value delivery and profit, multiple price metrics may apply to the same product or service.

A golf course charges a monthly membership fee (time-based access) for access to the course plus an additional fee for renting a cart for each round of golf (transaction). The price metrics: memberships + car rental.

Price metrics are intrinsically linked to your chosen value exchange model or models. Effective price metrics align to <u>how</u> customers receive value from the product or service.

PRICE STRUCTURE

5 criteria to create... PRICE METRICS that drive PROFIT

01

Choose a price metric that is...

* Easy to implement
* Easy to measure
* Easy to enforce, and...
* Easy to audit.

When customers purchase the solution, the metric must be absolutely clear including how it will be objectively measured.

Some customers will *demand* an auditable metric.

02

Ensure your price metric supports your competitive differentiation.

When customers are evaluating your solution before buying, ensure your price metric aligns to the perception you desire for your solution.

A company launching an innovative webinar platform sees that competitors use number of webinar hosts as the price metric.

To gain an advantage, the company chooses number of webinars hosted as the price metric to increase the attractiveness of their new solution for customers who may produce a limited number of webinars each year.

Ensure the metric functions effectively across segments.

Using different price metrics for different segments creates confusion for potential customers (and for your internal teams like finance).

While Zoom could introduce a per user price metric for small businesses and a minutes used price metric for large enterprises, several questions arise...

- *What is the criteria that a customer will use to decide if they are a small business or a large enterprise?*
- *How will customers determine if they are getting a good deal?*
- *How will we build the solution to handle two price metrics and interact with other systems like billing?*

04

Ensure the metric aligns to any differences in cost to serve different customer segments.

For a software company based in the United States, the cost to provide customer support to customers in North America during business hours is reasonable.

The cost to provide the same service to customers in Asia could be significantly higher. Choose a price metric that aligns to different costs to serve. In this case, a percentage of purchase price may work for the company and for customers.

Additional criteria may be added based on your context such as regulatory requirements, legal needs, partner relationships, in-licensing and considerations related to other solutions in the portfolio.

05

Ensure the metric aligns to how buyers experience value from using the product or service.

The magnitude of the purchase combined with WHEN and HOW buyers use the solution affect the selection of the price metric.

If a customer needs access to a critical research report to make an important one-time decision, then a logical metric might be a per report fee (Data). Alternatively, if a customer needs repeated access to research reports throughout the year, a price metric could be based on:

- Quantity of reports (Meter)
- Monthly subscription (Time-based access)
- Custom report prepared by analysts (Service)

PRICE STRUCTURE

Fences

A set of features that is highly valued by one segment may be irrelevant to another. Such differences in perceptions of value are natural and are used to create different offers at different price points. Perceptions of value are driven by factors such as:

- *How the solution is used*
- *Different customer financial models*
- *Unique alternatives to achieve value*
- *Different psycological benefits*
- *Geographic location*
- *State of customer organization*

Price fences are policies designed to prohibit customers in one segment from purchasing lower-priced solutions designed for another segment. They are usually expressed as fixed criteria that qualify customers for a different, typically lower-priced, solution.

Example of Fences:

One price for teachers, a different price for military service members, reduced pricing for high volume and standard pricing for all other customers.

All four types of customers have the same need for the solution and similar costs to serve, however they often have different perceptions of value before buying.

Price fences provide a mechanism to charge different prices to align to different levels of value and customer context. Controls ensure the feasibility and stability of the fences.

Price fences can increase profitability however they can also create dissatisfaction and cause customers to attempt to overcome the fences to pay a lower price.

As a result, developing Price Fences requires careful consideration and creativity. The following fences are a solid starting set to consider for your solution.

PRICE STRUCTURE

Designing effective price fences requires creativity. Here are some options to help you get started.

4 Types of **Price Fences**

BUYER IDENTIFICATION

Buyer Identification price fences are based on customers self-identifying their membership in a segment, with informal to formal verification processes to confirm membership This fence appeals to price-sensitive buyers who are likely to provide information to identify them. While this fence works extremely well for consumer products, it also works for business products by creating different price levels for commercial, government, education and other segments.

PURCHASE LOCATION

Different price levels may be established for customers purchasing the same solution in different geographic locations. The seller must be aware of the impact of exchange rate variability, taxes or other tariffs that may impact profitability. Buying power varies across countries, which may require the same solution to be offered at a lower price in a country with a weak economy. Be prepared to create a fence for a multi-national company that attempts to purchase a solution at a low price in one country, then uses the solution in other countries with higher prices.*

** See Custom Licenses and Compliance*

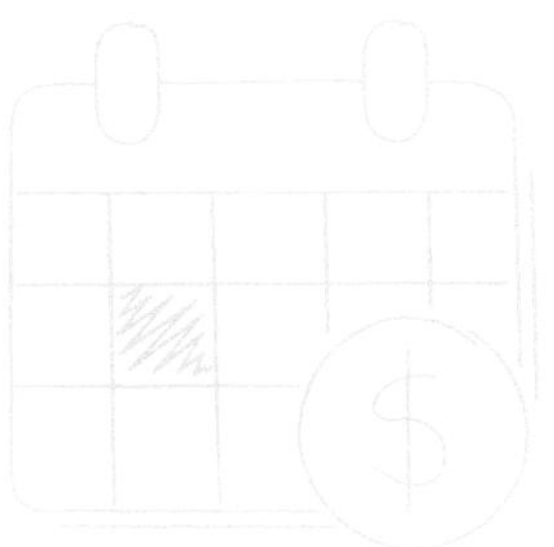

TIME-OF-PURCHASE

Time-of-purchase price fences are based on when a customer purchases the solution. An example is a limited duration price fence for hardware that promotes early purchases.

Offering a special low price to an initial, fixed number of customers is another approach to a time-of-purchase fence. Consider creating a condition to qualify for the special price like requiring buyers to provide a review after using the solution. A periodic and predictable discount is another time-of-purchase fence. This offer attracts educated buyers who expect and plan for the discount. An end of year special offer for companies to spend remaining budgets and short duration "flash sales" are popular tactics.

Create the biggest impact with time-of-purchase fences by correlating these offers with market events and market rhythms.

PURCHASE QUANTITY

Purchase quantity price fences provide discounts to customers who purchase in large volumes. These fences are common in B2B environments, where corporate buyers are paid to reduce costs. Small unit cost savings for large purchases create significant impact.
In general, the cost to serve buyers of large quantities is not proportionally higher than the cost to serve buyers of small quantities which make these fences attractive for profitability.

The next section explores the four types of fences in greater detail.

PURCHASE QUANTITY FENCES

Volume discounts, order discounts, step discounts and two-part prices are methods to create purchase quantity fences.

→ Order discounts apply to the size of a buyer's purchase. These discounts make sense when the costs of processing an order are unrelated to the size of the order.

→ Volume discounts apply to a buyer's total purchases over a period of time instead of the quantity purchased at any one time. The discount may also be calculated based on the volume of all purchases for individual solutions.

Volume and order discounts may be offered to the same segment. The volume discount helps retain large customers while the order discount encourages large orders.

→ Step discounts apply to purchases beyond specified amounts. This approach drives buyers to purchase more of a solution without lowering the price on smaller quantities. Step discounts segment different customers and different purchases by the same customers.

For example, a software solution may be offered at $100 per user for the first 10 users, then $75 per user for the next 50 users and $50 per user for any other users beyond 50.

→ Two-part pricing applies in situations when selling to a new customer incurs an incremental cost while selling more to an existing customer incurs low or no cost. Usage-based or metered solutions may benefit from two-part pricing.

New customers may be charged a one-time setup fee to get started using the solution then pay one rate for an initial volume or usage then a lower rate for a higher volume of usage. Existing customers would pay the same rate for their initial volume of usage then a lower rate for a higher volume.

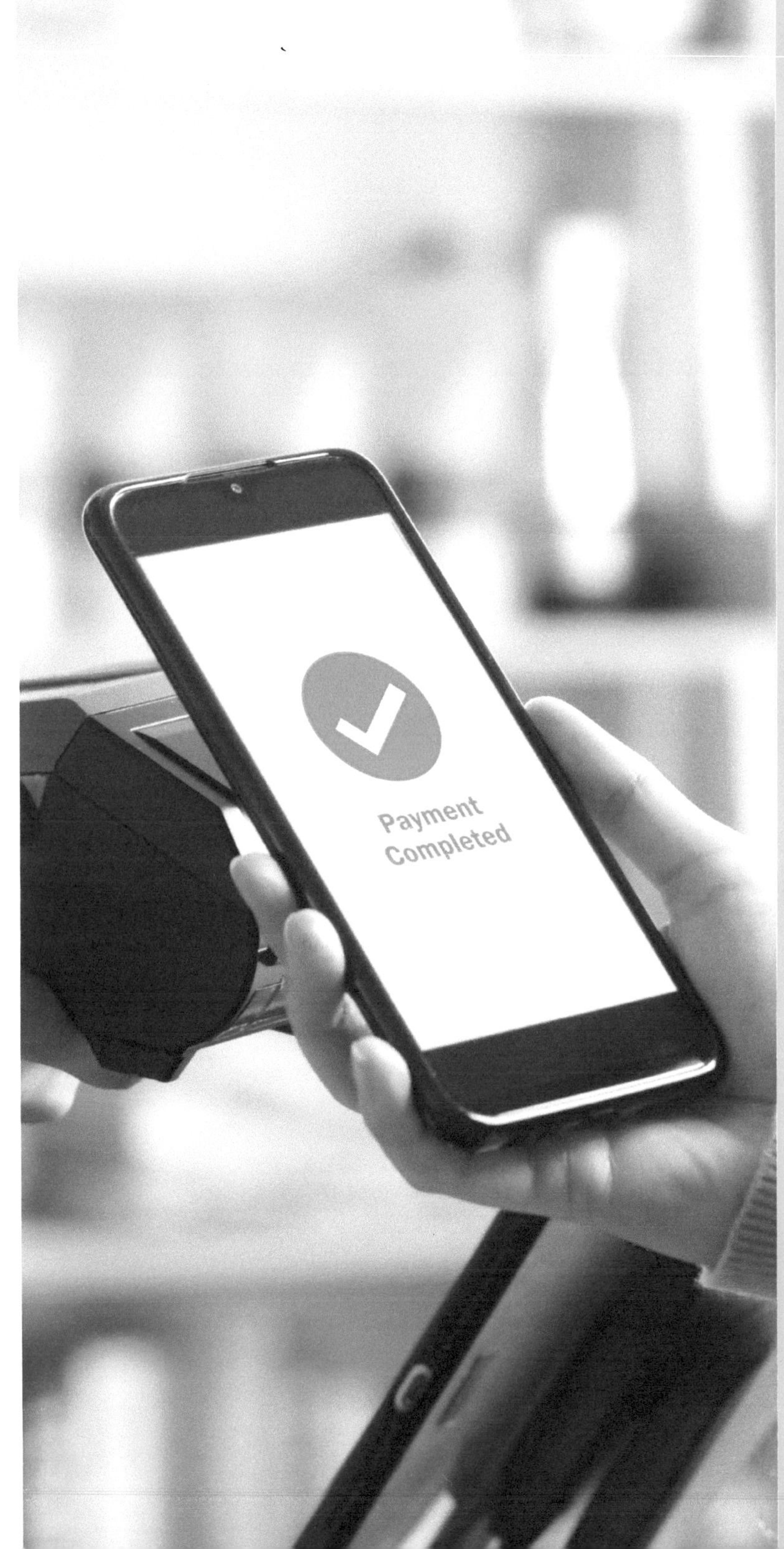

Price Levels

8 Principles for setting the price.

01

Price reflects value to the customer.

Focus first on what the solution is worth to the customer, not on the costs to produce, distribute and support the solution.

02

Price supports sustainability.

Set the price to support maintaining and improving the solution. The solution must be profitable to be sustainable. If not, either the solution doesn't provide enough value to customers or the value the solution provides costs too much to create.

03

Price reinforces positioning.

A premium solution warrants a high price.

04

Price addresses the competitive landscape.

Understanding the business models of competitors will help you make the right initial choices. Ongoing competitor research will help quickly correct poor choices.

05

Price clarity, not price complexity.

Create clear pricing for your customers. Reduce friction for customers even when the solution has many options. Remove complexity in the presentation and explanation of price for the solution. Clarity increases speed of decision making by customers. If removing complexity is difficult, evaluate how to simplify the offer.

06

Price reflects market maturity.

In a new market, try different price levels to discover what works best. Adjust price levels for different segments as the solution matures.

07

Price higher over lower.

Raising prices is harder than lowering prices. If the initial price is set too low and needs to be raised, the offering may need to be split or modularized to effectively communicate the value associated with the price increase.

08

Price aligns to market segment.

Use fences to create different price levels for different segments to maximize profitability.

PRICE SPECIFICS

Price Levels

5 Steps to set the price

Define Potential Price Range	Apply Chosen Strategy	Assess Sensitivity	Analyze Potential Revenue	Validate Price and Profitability

This iterative process integrates strategy, segmentation and market research to set price levels. While you might successfully set price levels after one pass through the process, be prepared to revisit steps as you converge on the price.

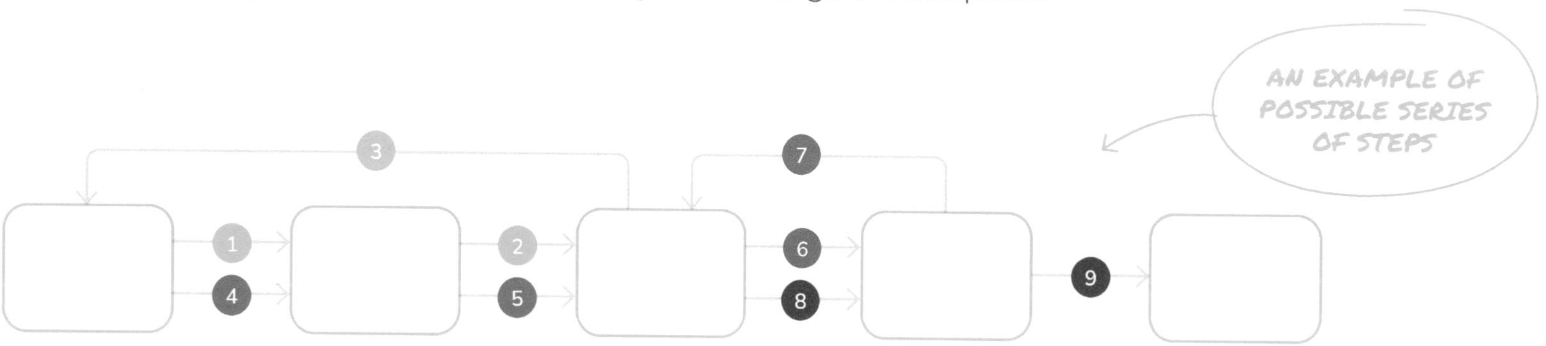

SYSTEMS THINKING ASSISTS THE PROCESS OF SETTING PRICE LEVELS.

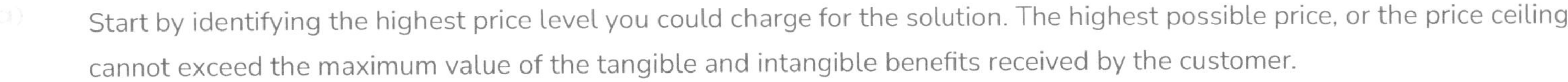

01. DEFINE POTENTIAL PRICE RANGE

a) Start by identifying the highest price level you could charge for the solution. The highest possible price, or the price ceiling, cannot exceed the maximum value of the tangible and intangible benefits received by the customer.

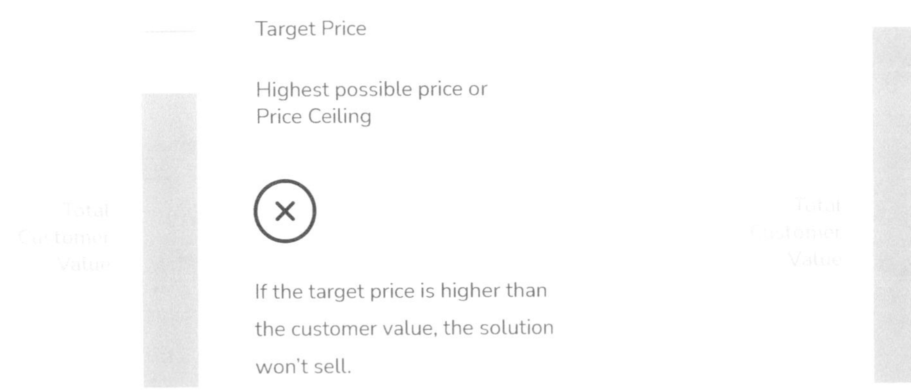

Price Ceiling = Target Price

Total Customer Value

If the price matches customer value, the solution still may not sell because the seller would receive all the benefit of the value exchange

Example: The solution enables customers to grow revenue by 20%. If the customer's current revenue is $1,000,000, then the total customer value is $200,000. But the customer likely won't pay $200,000 for the solution because the cost is equal to the benefit.

b) Check your estimated cost to provide the solution.

Solution Cost

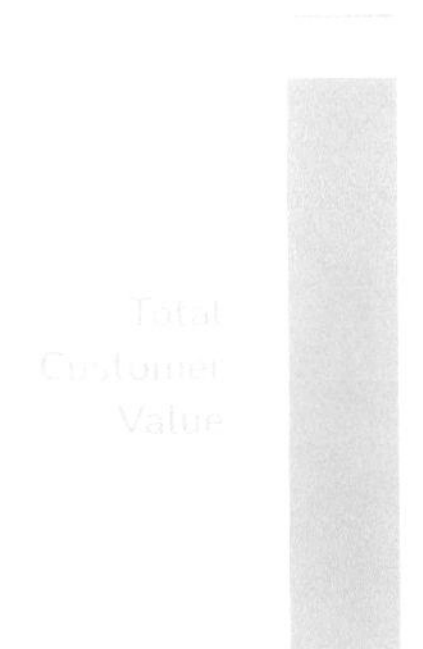

If the cost to deliver the solution exceeds the value, then the solution concept isn't viable and must be refactored or terminated.

Dyson invested $500 million to develop an electric car.

The company calculated the cost per car at $182,000 and killed the concept.

01. DEFINE POTENTIAL PRICE RANGE

c) Identify the lowest price, or floor. This is the cost of the solution plus the minimum required profit.

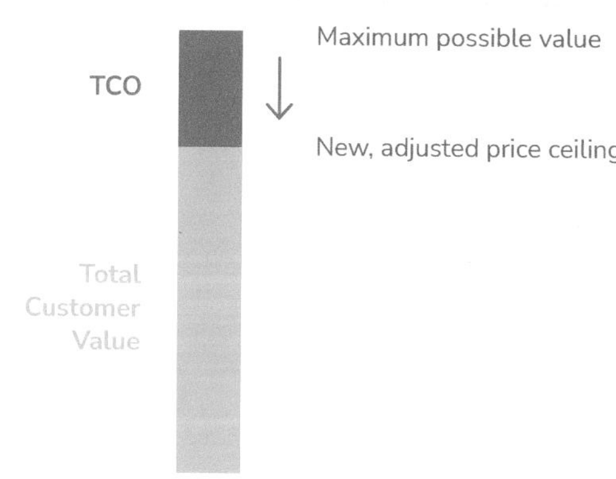

d) Estimate customer total cost of ownership (TCO). The customer may incur additional costs beyond the purchase price. TCO includes costs to configure, manage and learn how to use the solution. TCO lowers the ceiling.

e) Identify the price range of competitive solutions (typically 2 - 5). While any competitor pricing above your floor is winnable through a lower price, focus on winning through superior economic value.

02. APPLY CHOSEN STRATEGY

Identify a possible range of prices based on the price strategy you chose.

PENETRATION STRATEGY

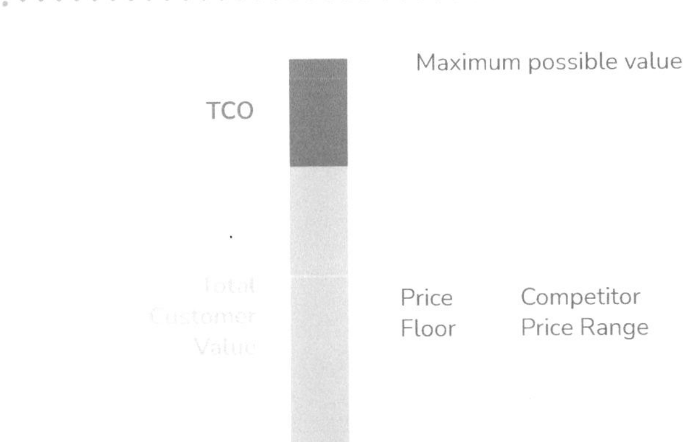

WHAT IF THE FLOOR IS TOO HIGH?

Consider these actions if you find that your price floor is in the middle of your competitors' pricing:

1) Choose a premium strategy and deliver a superior solution
2) Choose a competitive strategy and ensure sufficient differentiation of value to elevate your price level to the top of the competitor price range.

03. ASSESS SENSITIVITY

Consider the following factors that influence price sensitivity. Adjust the price level within the potential price range accordingly.

a) What is the magnitude of customer switching costs?

If customer switching costs are low, set a higher price. If customer switching costs are high, set price lower to compensate.

b) How easily can customers compare your solution to other solutions?

Set a higher price for an innovative solution that is difficult to compare to alternatives. Set a lower price for a solution that is easy to compare to alternatives.

Your Solution

Low **EASE OF COMPARISON** High

c) What is the perceived quality of your solution?

Higher quality solutions achieve higher price levels. Higher priced solutions are perceived as higher quality. Set price higher or lower based on the quality level of your solution relative to alternatives.

03. ASSESS SENSITIVITY

Your Solution

Low VALUE OF BENEFITS High

d) How valuable are the benefits obtained by customers from the solution?

Set prices higher when the value of benefits are high. Consider a lower price when the value of benefits is lower.

e) How large is the purchase relative to customer budget?

A large purchase requires customers to thoroughly evaluate their purchase decision. As a result, the price level must be set carefully. If the relative purchase size if low, consider a higher price level. If the relative purchase size is high, set an appropriate price level aligned to customer value perception.

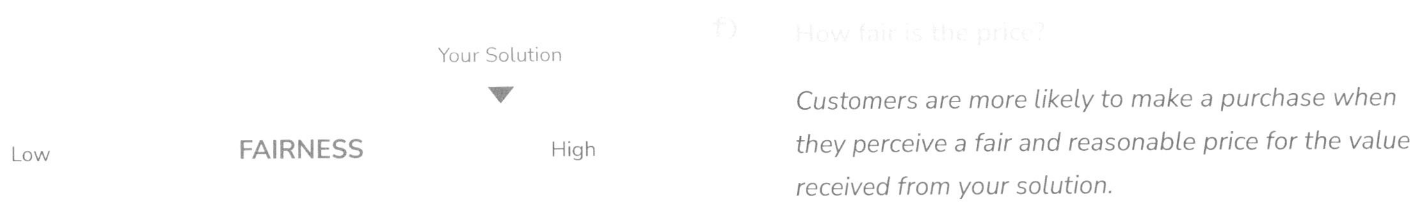

f) How fair is the price?

Customers are more likely to make a purchase when they perceive a fair and reasonable price for the value received from your solution.

Based on your assessment, refine your potential price range.

04. ASSESS POTENTIAL REVENUE

So far we have considered setting the price level for one unit of the solution for one customer. Now we need to assess potential revenue within the refined potential price range you identified.

Example: The potential price range is $10 to $50

Price Level	Forcasted Quantity Purchased	Potential Revenue
$10	**10,000**	$100,000
$20	**7,500**	$150,000
$30	**5,000**	$150,000
$40	**4,000**	$160,000
$50	**2,500**	$125,000

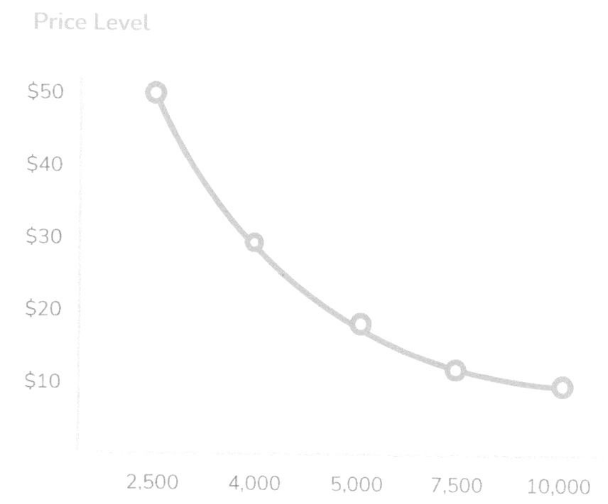

Forecasting the quantities purchased at different price levels is a result of various inputs.

A detailed conjoint analysis, covered soon, provides sophisticated quantitative data to extrapolate quantities based on the total addressable market.

Competitor price levels and market share provide an alternative, reasonably accurate insight into possible quantities. Any qualitative research also supports estimated quantities. The objective is to gather sufficient data to support a confident decision to set the price level.

REMEMBER, THE LEVEL OF ACCURACY OF THE FORECAST IS DRIVEN BY AVAILABLE TIME AND BUDGET FOR RESEARCH.

3 PRICING RESEARCH TECHNIQUES FOR MORE ACCURATE PRICE LEVEL ESTIMATION.

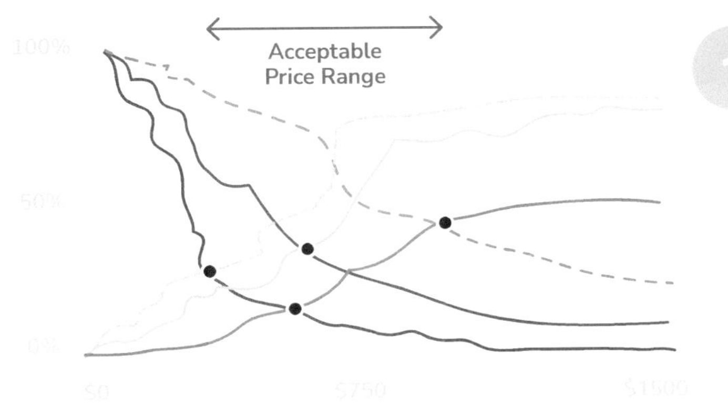

1

The Van Westendorp Price Sensitivity Meter identifies potential price ranges by asking respondents to rate the perceived value of a solution at discrete price points.

At the beginning of the chapter, we advocated against customer-driven pricing, specifically, don't simply ask "what would you pay for my solution?". Instead, use the Van Westendorp Price Sensitivity Meter to ask four different questions.

What price for the solution is too low, where you would doubt its quality and not buy it?

At what price would you consider the solution a bargain?

What price is expensive for you but you would still buy the solution?

At what price is the solution too expensive for you to purchase?

The Gabor-Granger Pricing Method identifies the price elasticity and revenue-optimizing price points for a solution. Each respondent answers a series of nearly identical questions like, "would you buy solution X at price Y?" In each of the series of questions, the price is changed based on the respondent's previous answer. The objective is to find the maximum price each respondent is willing to pay for the solution.

2

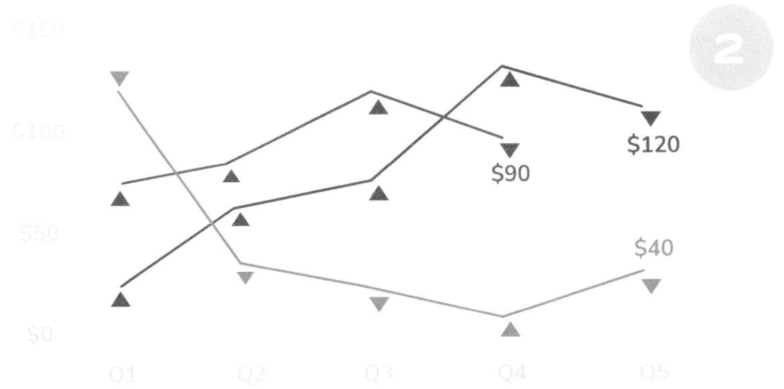

3

Conjoint Analysis identifies customer preferences and uses the research to select features, access price sensitivity, predict adoption of a solution and forecast sales volume.

EXAMPLE CONJOINT CHOICE QUESTION

BRAND	X	Y	Z
SPEED	200	300	250
DATA	100TB	50TB	100TB
SUPPORT	Live 24/7	Online 24/7	Live 24/7
PRICE	$250,000	$200,000	$175,000
	Choose	Choose	Choose

ATTRIBUTES

PRODUCT CONCEPTS TO SELECT

LEVELS OF EACH ATTRIBUTE

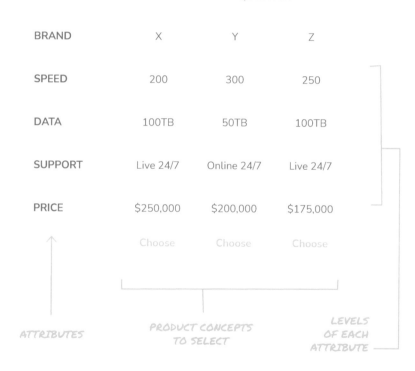

Conjoint Analysis decomposes the solution into its components referred to as attributes and levels. Then different combinations of attributes and levels are tested to identify consumer preferences.

05. VALIDATE PRICE AND PROFITABILITY

Next, calculate potential profitability based on your costs to deliver, support and maintain the solution. Although larger quantities of customers may lead to lower cost to serve each customer, the total cost to serve will likely be higher that smaller quantities of customers.

Price Level	Forecasted Quantity Purchased	Revenue	Projected Annual Cost to Serve	Potential Profit	
$10	10,000	$100,000	$50,000	$50,000	Competitor Price Range
$20	7,500	$150,000	$40,000	$110,000	
$30	5,000	$150,000	$30,000	$120,000	
$40	4,000	$160,000	$25,000	$135,000	Optimal Price Level
$50	2,500	$125,000	$15,000	$110,000	

Select the price level based on highest potential profit and your chosen strategy. In the example above, if you chose a premium strategy, then a price level of $40 provides the highest potential profit and aligns to the strategy.

Validate the feasibility of the price level with various stakeholders:

- **SALES LEADERS** have a sense of their ability to sell the solution at the price level you determined.
- **MARKETING LEADERS** may have broader awareness of the market including additional insights from analysts, industry trends and other market information.
- **FINANCE LEADERS** can validate your analysis and help improve your financial model.
- Other stakeholders like executive leaders, external analysts and advisors or others can also offer useful insights.

Validate the alignment of your selected price level to the price levels of other solutions in your portfolio if your solution is in a portfolio of other solutions. Following the process through to this final step results in more clarity for the positioning of the solutions value to customers and drives profitability.

Repeat the steps to determine the price level for each segment to identify appropriate price fences.

PRICING

Price Policies

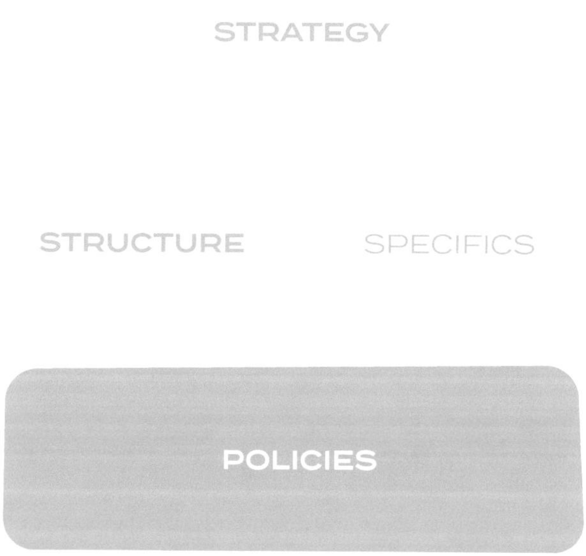

STRATEGY

STRUCTURE SPECIFICS

POLICIES

Price policies define the rules and conditions for price discounts and additional charges that could be applied to a specific business transaction within a customer segment.

The **goal** of price policies is to influence customer behavior through **consistent** and **transparent** communication that aligns differences in price paid with differences in cost to serve and value received.

A pricing policy is a rule that is consistently applied which defines the criteria for a seller to change a price for an individual customer for one or more specific transactions or for a limited time. Effective pricing policies can positively influence expectations and prevent customer behavior that could impact the difference between the value received and the price paid, which decreases profit.

For example, many sellers establish a discount approval process as a price policy.

The company defines discount levels and identifies who can approve discounts at each level. Once customers understand the discount approval process, they exploit the process to achieve the best discount.

Designing price policies provides an opportunity to reevaluate how to segment customers for different solutions at different price levels without undermining perceived value. Price policies drive consideration of current pricing for each segment and for continued pricing power in the future for all customers in the segment.

Price policies cover more than discounts. Policies should integrate how to adjust for changing variable costs such as transaction costs, third party costs, third party components, or fees for delivery of the service, like hosting fees. Policies should also address trial usage of the solution during the sales cycle and how the company will respond to competitor offers at lower prices.

PRICE POLICIES

Let's consider two effective price policies to address typical negotiation strategies used by customers:

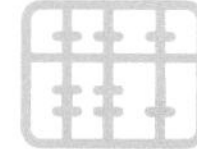

Competitive Bidding

Customers often issue requests for proposals or RFPs describing their required specifications. These documents typically provide no opportunity for sellers to clearly differentiate their solutions from competitors. This process is typically exploited by buyers seeking the lowest bidder. If you choose to compete in this process, consider how to reduce costs to meet the specifications without exceeding them. Options include reducing service levels, disabling specifics features of the solution, and removing any services like training. Calculate the lowest price to justify winning the business based on your reduced costs and do NOT bid any lower.

Volume Discounting

Customers often seek a discount for purchasing additional volume. Unless the seller carefully constructs the discount to apply only to the incremental volume, the customer will achieve a discount on the entire purchase and will expect the same discount in the future

For example, a customer is considering a $100,000 purchase. The customer offers to buy 20% more in exchange for a 5% discount. The customer will be increasing the purchase by $20,000 in exchange for a $6,000 discount for a final purchase of $114,000.

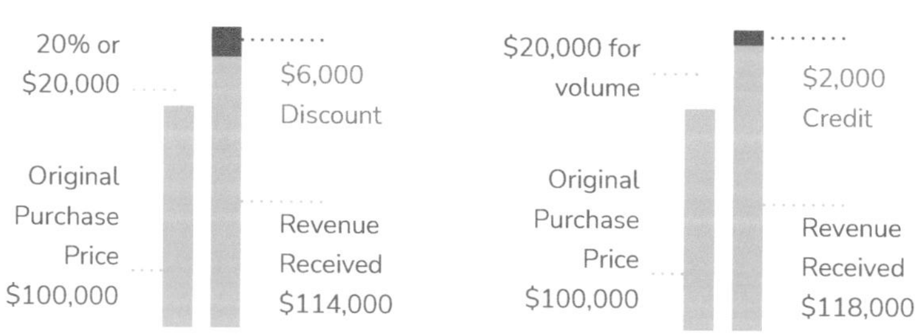

Approving this type of discount repeatedly for different customers will severely impact profitability. A policy to address this situation is to provide a credit or rebate for only the increase in volume. Using the same example, offer a credit at the end of the year of 10% on the additional 20% volume or $2,000. The customer only receives the credit if they actually increase their volume.

Creating Price Policies

Proactive pricing policies protect profitability through pre-approved trade-offs and discounts.

The highest impact policies promote trade-offs based on value, reframing negotiations from price to customer benefits. Policies may be created for the general buyer types to the right based on the importance of differentiation and the cost to compare offerings from multiple sellers.

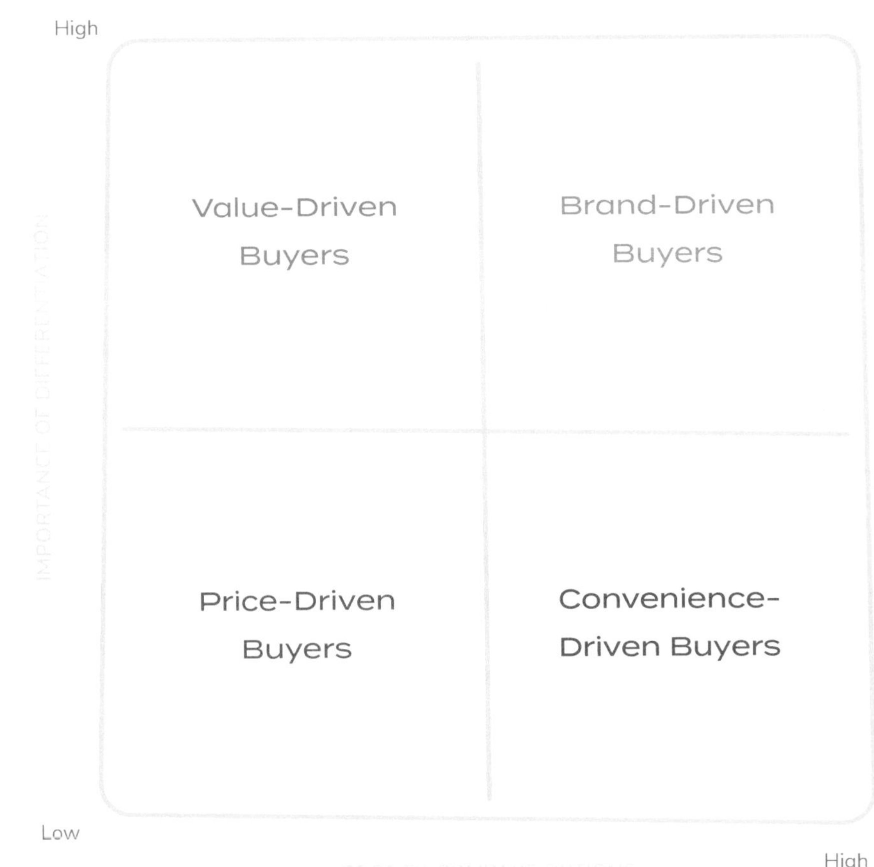

The placement of a customer within a quadrant is based on the unique relationship of that customer to a specific solution. For example, consider a specialized manufacturing company buying a new 3D printer. They are likely to be value-driven because they want to purchase a durable 3D printer that has many software capabilities. This CFO of the same company may be price-driven when considering software to manage business operations and payroll. The marketing team may be convenience or brand-driven when considering a solution to manage the website and marketing promotions.

PRICE POLICIES

Value-Driven Buyers

Value-Driven Buyers want as many features and benefits as possible at the lowest possible price.

Construct value-based price policies by listing all the ways your solution adds more value for the customer relative to competitive offerings.

Then consider every way that a customer could add or reduce value for you to create a set of pre-approved trade-offs.

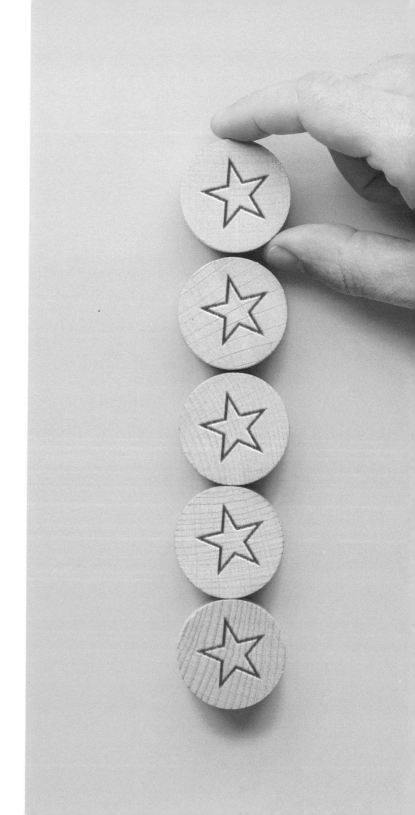

Ways to add more value to your solution:

TRAINING
Teaching a group of customers how to configure, manage and/or how to use the solution.

SUPPORT
Providing different levels of end user and technical support.

INSTALLATION
Offering additional services to install the solution for the customer.

UPGRADES
Including access to solution upgrade.

MAINTENANCE
Ongoing maintenance of the solution.

For example, a company offers a solution with superior training. If a customer highly values training but needs a lower price to fit their budget, one policy could pre-approve a salesperson to offer a small discount for the solution in exchange for pre-paid training for a defined number of end users to offset the discount. Be careful of this approach, as you are replacing recurring revenue with non-recurring revenue, which is not as valuable over the life of the solution.

Alternatively, if a different customer does not value training, another policy could pre-approve a salesperrson to remove training to close the sale at a lower cost for the customer without discounting the solution.

Never make a price concession that does not involve getting something from the customer.

Any concession should eliminate anything from the solution offering that a buyer does not value. Learning what buyers value results from offering trade-offs. Rejection of proposed trade-offs indicates that the price of the offering may be too high. Implementing value-based price policies for value-based buyers protects price integrity and profit by aligning the solution offering to what the buyers value at an acceptable price.

PRICE POLICIES

Brand-Driven Buyers

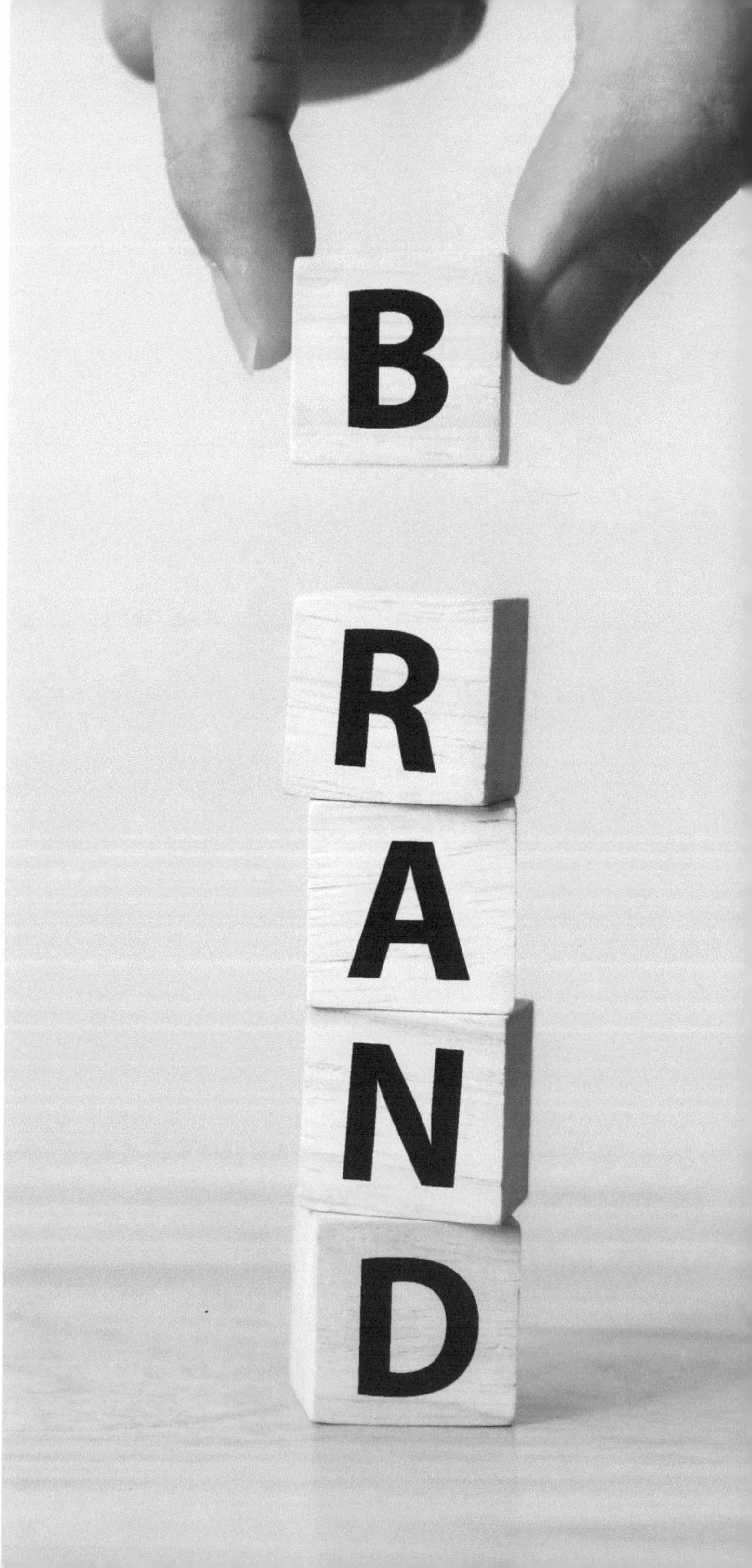

Brand-Driven Buyers value differentiation through brand when challenged by comparison of options prior to purchase.

As a result, brand-driven buyers rely on reputation for a great solution without seeking a less expensive provider.

Pricing for the first sale to brand-driven buyers is ***not*** the same as pricing for subsequent sales.

Most brand-driven buyers do not seek concessions. In the event that a brand-driven buyer asks for a discount on the first sale, consider a policy of simply saying no.

Brand-driven consumers are typically willing to spend a premium to acquire their preferred solution. Discounting a premium brand can create significant, irrecoverable erosion of the brand. In the long run, foregoing a sale can be better than discounting the solution.

A price objection from an existing brand-driven buyer indicates either a lack of performance by the seller's solution to meet expectations, or that the buyer acquired information that the price is too high relative to alternatives.

If the objection is based on lost confidence, establish a policy to correct the issue by adding value while protecting price. Identify what caused dissatisfaction and offer a solution that meets or exceeds the value.

Example:

An existing customer has hired new employees to use and maintain the solution. The new employees are struggling to effectively use the solution to do their jobs.

A policy could pre-approve a salesperson to offer a fixed number of additional training sessions included at no additional cost with a renewal at full price.

If the buyer believes the price is too high, establish a policy to ensure pricing aligns to value received.

Identify and quantify all value-added services provided to the customer. Illustrate to the buyer that the price includes all the additional value received by the buyer.

Example:

A customer purchased the solution one year ago. The customer has grown and needs to make an additional purchase, however the customer wants a discount based on their research of your competition.

The policy is to not offer a discount. Instead the salesperson reviews with the customer all of the additional services, features, and capabilities included with the solution. In many cases, the customer has not taken advantage of the full range of benefits included with the solution to justify the price.

PRICE POLICIES

Price-Driven Buyers

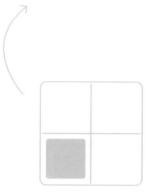

The opposite of Brand-Driven Buyers, Price-Driven Buyers only focus on getting the best price for what they specify as their needs.

B2B Price-Driven buyers typically send a Request For Proposal (RFP) to multiple solution providers. The RFP usually identifies specific requirements with explicit instructions for how to respond.

The policy for these buyers is to meet the minimum expectations stated in the RFP. Remove anything from the solution offering not specifically identified in the RFP when responding. If the customer did not identify training, do not include training in the response.

The resulting offer may be a "stripped-down" solution that will not likely be attractive to other customers.

If an RFP does not clearly define minimum expectations, ask for more detail or do not respond to the RFP. Further, in each response to a Price-Driven Customer clearly state what you are omitting in exchange for a lower price and what the buyer will pay for any additional services requested in the future.

Enforce a policy to not offer any special or promotional pricing to Price-Driven Buyers like a one-time low price that includes additional value. While you may win the sale, the buyer will expect more special pricing in the future.

PRICE POLICIES

Convenience-Driven Buyers

Convenience-Driven Buyers are generally price insensitive and do not invest time and energy to research competitive prices.

They look for the easiest way to satisfy their needs.

The recommended policy is no policy:
CONVENIENCE BUYERS DON'T NEED ONE!

PRICE POLICIES

Discounts

A DISCOUNT IS AN OFFER TO SELL THE SOLUTION AT A PRICE LOWER THAN THE REGULAR PRICE.

Indiscriminate use of discounts must be avoided to prevent creating a perception that customers can probably get a discount.

Customers look for information about what other customers paid for the solution.

For example, consistent discounts at end of a time period, month, quarter, or year, conditions buyers to wait until the end of the next time period.

Regardless of the attraction of these discounts to achieve revenue goals, avoid the temptation to use this tactic because it decreases profitability.

WHAT TO DO ABOUT DISCOUNT POLICIES?

By proactively setting price policies, you establish expectations for how your sales force should behave when negotiating with buyers. When a buyer requests a discount that is NOT already addressed by a policy, the salesperson must notify leaders—sales, product, marketing- for discussion.

The leaders select one of three options:

- Define a new policy
- Modify an existing policy
- Reject the request

If salespeople must consistently offer discounts to sell the solution, either the solution does not provide enough value to match the price, your price fails to account for the buyer's actual TCO (total cost of ownership), or both.

Discount analysis

LEVERAGE DISCOUNT ANALYSIS TO DETERMINE WHETHER...

- What policies are abused or over-used
- Additional stronger policies are needed
- The Price Level is too high

1. Review sales in the previous periods. The chart below illustrates individual sales for the previous 12 months. The period you select may sales by hour, day, month or quarter depending on your context.
2. Compare the List Price to the actual Sales Price
3. Calculate the percentage of List Price achieved for each sale
4. Plot each sale on a scatter chart

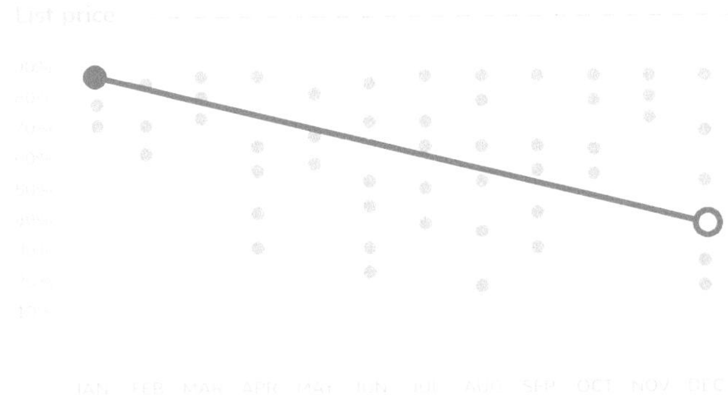

Visit www.profit-streams.com/discount-analysis for more examples of discount analysis and how to respond.

5. Identify the best fit line through the data
6. The larger the discount from List Price that must be offered to close sales, the greater the perceived gap between value and price.
7. Interview salespeople to review why requests for discounts were accommodated
8. Interview customers to understand their perspective of Total Cost of Ownership and how they perceive the value they receive from using your product or solution
9. Based on your analysis, take action:
   + Consider lowering the Price Level
   + Evaluate the positioning of the solution's value
   + Create or update policies to reduce excessive discounts

Intentional discounts that maintain profitability.

Temporary, well-planned and designed discounts that align to market events and rhythms maintain profitability.

Examples:

A solution nearing end of life...

I need a new phone but I want a good deal!

Promotion associated with a special milestone...

10% off for 10 days to celebrate our 10 year anniversary!

Offers that leverage seasonal opportunities...

I'm thrilled with my Cyber Monday purchase!

An alternative to discounts: **Policies that create purchase options and protect profit**

Some customers have cash to spend and will purchase a solution at full price.

Other customers are cash-constrained and can't afford to pay full price now. Instead of discounting, create an option to purchase differently.

	CUSTOMER A Has cash to spend	CUSTOMER B Is Cash-Constrained
Term	5 years	5 years
Paid Now 1 year	$150,000	$50,000
Paid Annually 2-5 years	0	$30,000 x 4
	$150,000	**$170,000**

By creating an option to pay over time, Customer B is satisfied without discounting price.

Customer ROI

Customers purchase your solutions when the total economic value is greater than their total cost. The customer ROI block explores when and how to create tools to help your customers in making these financial decisions. It covers:

- *The meaning and use of various financial terms*
- *Total benefits and total costs of ownership*

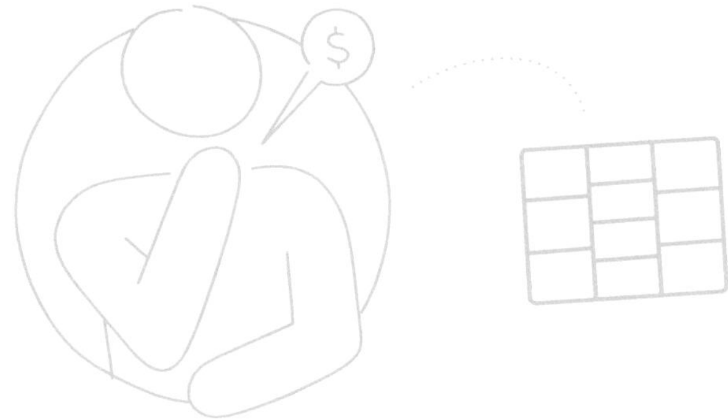

You must understand how your customers make financial decisions, and then help them make their decision-making process easier.

Customer ROI

How to make financial decisions easier for customers.

Every customer makes a financial decision when they purchase a solution. The speed and complexity of the decision varies based on the size of the purchase.

Small purchases by consumers are made quickly. Multimillion dollar purchases by companies may take weeks, require hours of financial analysis and the final decision may involve several people. Similarly, large consumer purchases, such as buying a home, or a car, may also take many weeks, require financial analysis, and involve several people.

Customers have many choices and make decisions based on a combination of rational and irrational factors. In this section we focus on the rational factors, which are based on agreed-upon criteria supported by reliable financial models. Customers use these models to assess the financial impact of their choices. Their analysis can range from a simple 'back of napkin' estimate of financial returns to a complex financial model that calculates such things as Return on Investment (ROI) and Internal Rate of Return (IRR). These techniques are used to answer questions such as:

- *Will I get back more than I spend?*
- *Is the price fair based on the expected benefits?*
- *Can I prove the expected return on investment to other stakeholders?*

Customer ROI modeling enables you to approach financial analysis objectively and accurately *from the customer's perspective* to provide customers with information required to make a decision.

Provide your prospects with an ROI calculator to help them justify expensive decisions.

Key Financial Terms

DEFINED

While the Profit Stream Canvas identifies Customer ROI as a key financial metric, other metrics may also be used by different customers to make decisions.

This section provides a brief overview of common metrics used for financial modeling.

KEY FINANCIAL TERMS DEFINED

Return on Investment (ROI)

ROI is a key metric customers use to evaluate and prioritize potential investments. ROI is the ratio of the net gain from an investment divided by its total costs.

$$ROI = \frac{\text{Benefits - Costs}}{\text{Costs}} \times 100\%$$

Imagine a baker who makes iced sugar cookies with airbrushed custom designs in liquid food coloring.

The baker ordered 50 different custom templates last year at an average cost of $20 per template or $1,000 per year.

She is considering the purchase of a cutting machine to make her own templates.

The machine costs $750 plus $1 for each plastic sheet to make one template.

The benefit is a cost saving of $1,000. Her costs for the first year are $800, $750 for the machine plus $50 for plastic sheets. Her one year ROI is:

$$\frac{\$1{,}000 - \$800}{\$800} \times 100\% = 25\%$$

ROI is often calculated based on the annual net return over three years as shown here:

$$\frac{(\text{Net Years } 1 + 2 + 3) \times 1/3}{\text{Initial Costs}} \times 100\%$$

The baker's three year ROI is:

$$\frac{((\$1{,}000-\$800)+(\$1{,}000-\$50)+(\$1{,}000-\$50)) \times 1/3}{\$800} \times 100\% = 87.5\%$$

ADVANTAGES OF ROI

- ROI is a familiar concept to people without financial expertise.
- Calculation of ROI is relatively easy.
- The ROI of potential investments may be compared when the same principles are applied to calculations.

DISADVANTAGES OF ROI

- ROI is calculated based on forecasted income, not periodic cash flows, which applies a more accurate discount rate.
- ROI calculations ignore the timing of benefits.

Net Present Value (NPV)

NPV is the value of the ongoing benefits of an investment discounted to the present year. NPV will quickly signal whether to stop an investment, however it's less useful to inform a decision to proceed with an investment.

NPV is the difference between the present value of future cash inflows and the present value (PV) of future cash outflows over a specific period of time.

NPV = PV of expected cash inflows - PV of expected cash outflows

NPV is typically calculated over three years using the following formula:

C_o = Initial investment, a negative number

C_n = Cash inflows minus cash outflows in $year_n$

V_n = Discount rate for $year_n$

$$NPV = C_o + \frac{C_1}{(1+V_1)} + \frac{C_2}{(1+V_2)^2} + \frac{C_3}{(1+V_3)^3}$$

Positive NPV shows that the forecasted earnings generated by an investment exceed anticipated costs. If a potential investment has a negative NPV, then the investment should be rejected.

The baker from the ROI example wants to be conservative and assumes stable sales of $5,000 per year and a discount rate of 7%

The ingredients - sugar, flour, butter, etc. - cost $1,000 per year.

Total yearly cash outflows will be $1,050 including the templates.

The 3 year NPV for the investment in the cutting machine is...

$$NPV = \$800 + \frac{(\$5{,}000-\$1{,}050)}{1.07} + \frac{(\$5{,}000-\$1{,}050)}{(1.07)} + \frac{(\$5{,}000-\$1{,}050)}{(1.07)} = \$8{,}940$$

Advantages of NPV

NPV provides a true representation of benefits over the entire period selected for analysis.

NPV correctly applies discounting to investments with extreme benefit projections.

NPV properly adjusts for investments with high upfront costs to accurately represent value.

NPV is useful for comparing two mutually exclusive investments with equivalent time horizons and equivalent initial investments.

Disadvantages of NPV

NPV does not identify the time required to achieve positive cash flow.

NPV only portrays the result of cash flows, not the ratio of costs to benefits.

The result of NPV analysis are very sensitive to changes in the assumed discount rate.

Payback Period (PP)

PP is the breakeven point or the time required for an investment to yield a positive accumulative cash flow. PP illustrates how quickly an investment will pay for itself. It is a vital measurement of risk. PP is calculated by dividing the investment amount by the annual cost flow.

$$PP = \frac{\text{Investment}}{\text{Annual Cash Flow}}$$

From the previous example, the baker's initial investment is $750. Annual cash flow is $5,000 less $1,000 for ingredients and $50 for templates.

$$PP = \frac{\$750}{\$5,000 - (\$1,000 + \$50)} = 0.2$$

OR ABOUT TWO AND A HALF MONTHS.

Advantages of PP

Calculating PP is relatively easy and provides an initial risk screening.

PP can be used to compare investments and assess risk.

Disadvantages of PP

PP disregards the time value of money.

PP does not reflect performance after payback occurs.

Total Cost of Ownership (TCO)

TCO is the purchase price of the solution plus the costs of operation and maintenance over the solutions lifespan. TCO for software-enabled solutions includes licensing, maintenance, infrastructure, labor and any other costs to use and maintain the solution. Accurate estimates of TCO improve the reliability of ROI calculations.

The baker expects the cutting machine will last ten years with maintenance service for $100 every two years. The TCO of the machine is:

$750 + ($50 * 10) + ($100 * 4) = $1,650

Advantages of TCO

TCO recognizes operational costs beyond the initial investment.

TCO provides complete input for effective, accurate customer benefit analysis.

TCO is useful for comparison of similar solutions.

Disadvantages of TCO

TCO does not recognize the benefits of investment.

TCO ignores the time value of money.

Internal Rate of Return (IRR)

IRR is the annual rate of growth that an investment is expected to generate. It is the discount rate necessary to drive the NPV to zero.

IRR is calculated by finding the discount rate where the present value of expected cash flows minus the present value of the cash investment is equal to zero. IRR may be expressed as the expected payoff divided by the initial investment minus one.

Most spreadsheet programs include a function that calculates IRR based on the initial investment and a stream of cash inflows.

The baker's IRR is:

$$\frac{\text{Template savings of \$1,000}}{\text{Cost of machine and templates of \$800}} - 1 = 25\%$$

Advantages of IRR

IRR is defined with mathematical precision

IRR illustrates the benefits of an investment in simple percentage terms.

Disadvantages of IRR

The initial investment amount between investment alternatives is not considered.

IRR ignores the actual dollar value of comparable investments.

Building the Customer ROI model

Now that we have defined the relevant financial terms commonly used by B2B customers, let's explore how to build a clear, data-driven, accurate, and believable ROI model to help customers make a purchase decision.

You may need to use less technical terms to share ROI in B2C segments.

DRIVERS OF CUSTOMER ROI

Breadth. How many people will the solution affect? How many assets or items are involved in the solution? *The greater the breadth, the higher the potential return.*

Repeatability. How frequently will people use the solution? *The greater the repeatability, the higher the potential return.*

Cost. How costly is the task to perform -without- the solution? *The greater the cost of the task, the higher the potential return.*

Collaboration. To what extent will people need to collaborate to benefit from the solution? *The greater the collaboration component of the task, the higher the potential return.*

Knowledge. What is the reuse of information created through use of the solution? *The greater the use of knowledge, the higher the potential return.*

1 Identify Total Benefits of Ownership (TBO)

Start with your Customer Benefit Analysis.

Use your Dimension and Magnitude of Benefit cards to identify the directly quantifiable benefits that customers receive from the solution. Then, identify any indirect benefits.

Linkwire observed a serious problem for thousands of small businesses in skilled trades—plumbers, electricians, builders, painters, and others. Business owners and managers spend several hours each week to plan how to dispatch skilled workers for service calls and to meet with new customers to provide estimates. Inefficient routing leads to fewer service calls and frequent delays to meet new customers. Most business owners use paper and pencil to schedule work and can't afford to purchase complex dispatching systems designed for large enterprises like trucking companies and big retailers.

Linkwire's solution for the small businesses reduces planning time, increases route efficiency and accelerates engagement with new customers—all direct benefits. The solution also provides indirect benefits of reduced stress, increased manager and employee satisfaction, and more reliable scheduling.

DIRECT BENEFITS

REDUCED PLANNING TIME

More time to manage and grow the business

INCREASED ROUTE EFFICIENCY

More service calls

ACCELERATED ENGAGEMENT WITH NEW CUSTOMERS

More sales calls

INDIRECT BENEFITS

REDUCED STRESS

More effective and happier owners and managers

INCREASED SATISFACTION

Higher retention of skilled employees

MORE RELIABLE SCHEDULING

Higher confidence in business operations

Model the benefits

Once direct and indirect benefits are clear, create a model to input specific customer information to calculate benefits.

What is the name of your business?	**Smith Plumbing**	
How many employees provide service to customers?	**10**	*Drives magnitude of benefits*
What is the average number of service calls per day, per employee?	**5**	*The solution can increase number of service calls*
What is the average revenue per service call?	**$100**	*Drives magnitude of benefits*
What is the average number of sales calls per day?	**2**	*The solution can increase number of sales calls*
How much time is spent scheduling each day?	**3hrs**	*The solution reduces scheduling time*
What do you charge to provide an estimate during a sales call?	**$25**	*Many service providers charge a small estimation fee that is usually applied to the cost of the service.*

This input provides the current state...

10 employees x 5 service calls/day = 50 service calls

50 service calls x $100 = $5,000/day

2 sales calls/day x $25 = **$50 potential new revenue/day**

Linkwire asserts that using their solution results in at least one more service call per employee per day, at least one more sales call per day, and a 50% reduction in planning time, resulting in one additional service call per day.

For Smith Plumbing, the potential benefits are...

10 additional service calls	X	$100	=	$1,000
1 additional sales call	X	$25	=	$25
1 additional service call	X	$100	=	$100

$1,125 / day

About the inefficient transfer of time

Time saved does not always equal time worked. Saving time for repetitive work can result in more work.

A correction factor of 50% to 70% can be used to adjust estimated time savings to a reasonable estimate of value to the solution buyer.

In the case of Linkwire, saving scheduling time results in additional sales and service calls.

Identify Total Cost of Ownership (TCO)

Gather all one-time or recurring costs for your solution.
The believability for the ROI model depends on the complete transparency of the TCO. Costs may be expensed or depreciated over time.

TYPICAL COSTS FOR SOFTWARE-ENABLED SOLUTIONS

Expensed Costs

Software / Hardware / Consulting / Personnel / Training / Support / Maintenance / Other

Depreciated Costs

Software / Hardware

4 Model the costs

Once all the costs to the customer are clear, create a model to input specific customer information to calculate costs.

- *Linkwire selected a time-based access Value Exchange Model based on the number of people using the solution for scheduling.*
- *Linkwire's solution is cloud-based and requires no customer hardware.*
- *Linkwire offers monthly billing for access and a 5% discount for 12 months purchased in advance.*
- *Linkwire includes maintenance and basic online support in its basic solution.*
- *Linkwire provides training at a cost of $250 for each user.*

Smith Plumbing provides the following information:

How many people schedule service for your company?	2
Do you need 24/7 live support 365 days a year?	YES

Smith Plumbing will need licenses and training for two users and a premium support upgrade.

Add formulas to complete the model

Start by identifying ROI for the first year.

Smith Plumbing *could* realize a direct benefit of up to $1,200 per day. Linkwire assumes ten non-working days due to holidays each year resulting in 50 five-day work weeks or 250 working days per year. As a result, Smith Plumbing's total potential *benefit* is:

$1,125/day x 250 days = $281,250

To create a more believable ROI model, adjust the potential benefit. In this case, a more believable outcome may be one more service call each week for each employee and one more sales call for the company each week.

Why dampen the potential benefits?

- Service calls may be cancelled
- Service calls may take longer than expected
- Sales calls may not be requested
- Additional service calls may not be scheduled
- *Although huge benefits are possible, they are not believable*

For Smith Plumbing, the adjusted benefits are:

$100 *Revenue per service call*	x	10 *Number of employees*	x	50 *Work weeks*	= *$50,000*
$25 *Revenue per sales call*	x	50 *Work Weeks*			= *$1,250*
					$51,250

Smith Plumbing's costs are limited to software, support, and training.

Linkwire will display results for both monthly and annual payment plan options.

SOFTWARE	*Monthly*	**$600** / user / month x 12 months x 2 users	= $14,400
	Annual	**$540** / user / year x 1 year x 2 users	= $12,960
PREMIUM SUPPORT		**$200** / month x 12 months	= $2,400
TRAINING		**$500** / user x 2 users	= $1,000
TOTAL ANNUAL COSTS		**Monthly plan**	= **$17,800**
TOTAL ANNUAL COSTS		**Annual plan**	= **$16,360**

ROI for Smith Plumbing for year 1 is calculated as follows

$$\text{ROI Monthly plan} = \frac{\$51{,}250 - \$17{,}800}{\$17{,}800} \times 100 = 188\%$$

$$\text{ROI Anual plan} = \frac{\$51{,}250 - \$16{,}360}{\$16{,}360} \times 100 = 213\%$$

These are spectacular results! Linkwire would consider presenting a "worst case scenario" by stating: "Even if our solution is only half as effective as we expect, your ROI could still be 94% in the first year."

Next, calculate NPV, PP and IRR over a three year period...

$$\text{NPV} = -\$17{,}800 + \frac{\$51{,}250}{(1 + 7\%)} + \frac{(\$51{,}250 - \$17{,}800)}{(1 + 7\%)^2} + \frac{(\$51{,}250 - \$17{,}800)}{(1 + 7\%)^3} = \$104{,}419$$

$$\text{PP} \quad \frac{\$17{,}000}{\$51{,}250} = 0.347 \times 12 \text{ months} = \textit{About 4 months}$$

$$\text{IRR} = 256\%$$

Finally, present the results...

Based on the information you provided, Linkwire can help you add one more service call per employee per week and one more sales call each week. Assuming 50 work weeks in a year:

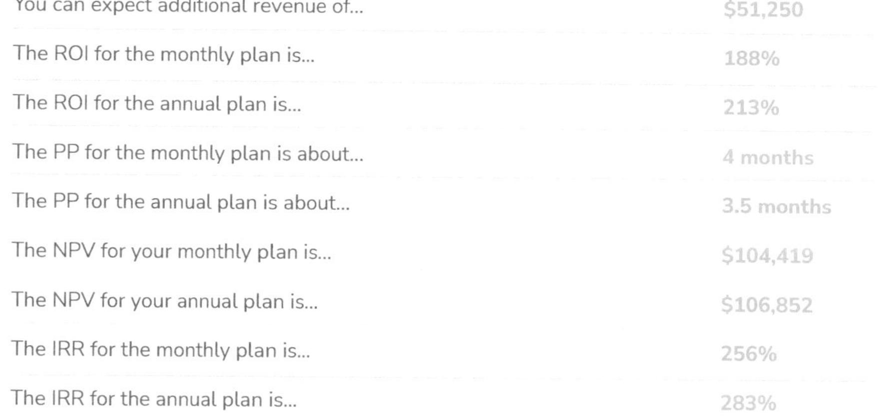

You can expect additional revenue of...	$51,250
The ROI for the monthly plan is...	188%
The ROI for the annual plan is...	213%
The PP for the monthly plan is about...	4 months
The PP for the annual plan is about...	3.5 months
The NPV for your monthly plan is...	$104,419
The NPV for your annual plan is...	$106,852
The IRR for the monthly plan is...	256%
The IRR for the annual plan is...	283%

Describe the indirect benefits to provide a complete explanation

You can also expect reduced stress from daily scheduling, as well as happier employees, lending to increased retention of your people.

5 Ways to Resolve Negative ROI

After you create your model, test it with multiple inputs. If the ROI is negative for any of the tests consider the following changes.

1. ADJUST THE PRICE. Revisit your price analysis and evaluate changing the price level.

2. CONSIDER RAMPING COSTS OVER TIME. Customer costs may be spread out to increase over years.

3. REDUCE INITIAL COSTS TO START USING THE PRODUCT. Training could be paid only when delivered. Support could be paid monthly instead of the beginning of the year.

4. EVALUATE EXPECTED BENEFITS. The correction factor to damper results may be too aggressive.

5. REVISIT CUSTOMER BENEFIT ANALYSIS. Identify any other believable benefits that can improve the Customer's ROI.

MEASURE, MEASURE, MEASURE!

Once you launch your solution, measure actual customer results. Gather as much data as possible to improve your ROI model. Create case studies based on actual customer results that support your ROI model and continue to research similar solutions and industry metrics that support the positioning of your solution.

If you have a SaaS platform, make sure you carefully track release dates for significant revenue generating features in the platform. Data before and after those key dates can provide valuable insights here, but only if you can look back over time to see when the solution changed.

SOLUTION ROI BLOCK

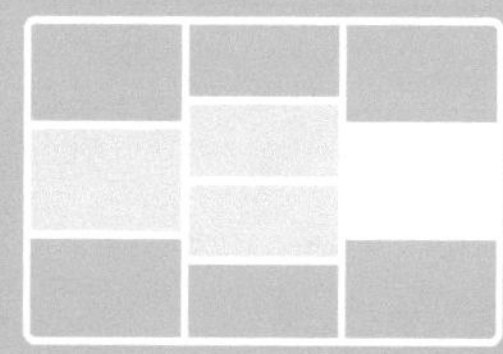

ECONOMIC SUSTAINABILITY

SOLUTION FOCUS

Solution ROI

Your Solution ROI is how you will model the economic value of your solution over time. We'll explore:

- → *Solution cost factors and how they vary over the solution lifecycle*
- → *How to model revenue*
- → *How to understand profit curves and when you should be profitable*

A sustainable solution generates a positive return on investment. Building and maintaining a financial model for the solution validates economic feasibility and enables business leaders to forecast the financial future of the **Profit Stream.**

Establishing a price asserts the value of the solution. When a customer purchases the solution for that price, the value is confirmed. When enough customers join and repeat this process, a **Profit Stream** is created - provided you set a profitable price (covered earlier!) and your cost model doesn't increase faster than your revenue.

SOLUTION COST FACTORS

There are three main cost factors for any solution.

1

Costs to create and sell first version

Design, Raw Materials, Tools, Development, Sales and Marketing

2

Costs to make and sell subsequent units

Raw Materials, Tools, Development, Sales and Marketing

3

Costs associated with ongoing use

Maintenance

Software and hardware have shared and distinct cost factors. Both incur costs to create the first version, however software does not bear the same unit cost as hardware.

Similarly, because software is updatable, software bears maintenance costs by the solution provider. The hardware owner assumes costs for ongoing use.

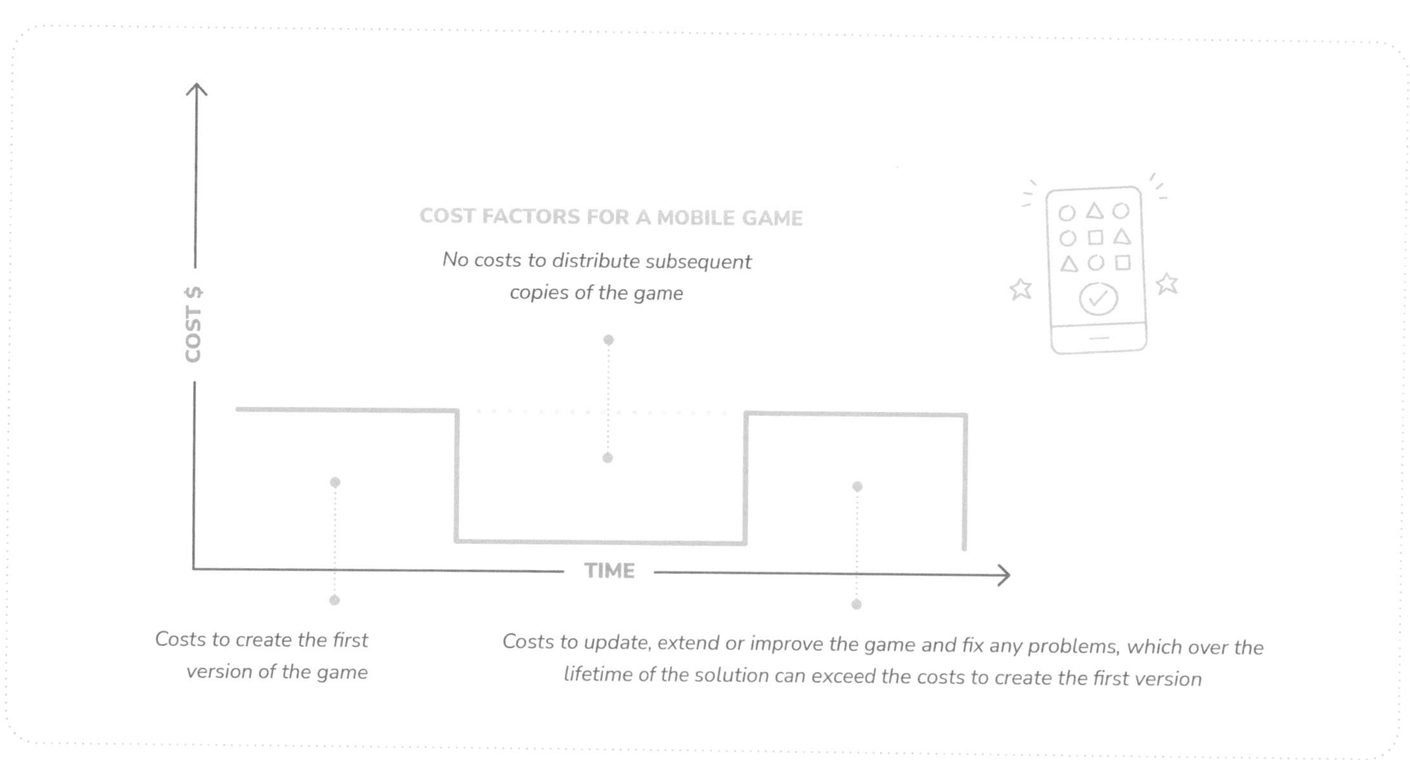

COST FACTORS FOR A MOBILE GAME
COST $
TIME
No costs to distribute subsequent copies of the game
Costs to create the first version of the game
Costs to update, extend or improve the game and fix any problems, which over the lifetime of the solution can exceed the costs to create the first version

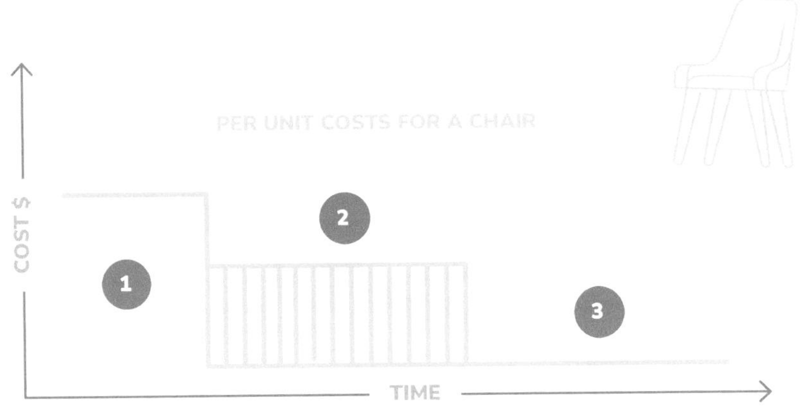

1. *Costs to create the first chair.*
2. *Costs to create each subsequent chair.*
3. *During the warranty period, manufacturers are responsible for some or all of the costs for resolving defects. After the warranty period, the owner assumes responsibility for these costs.*

Lifetime cost factors vary for different choices for software-enabled solutions.

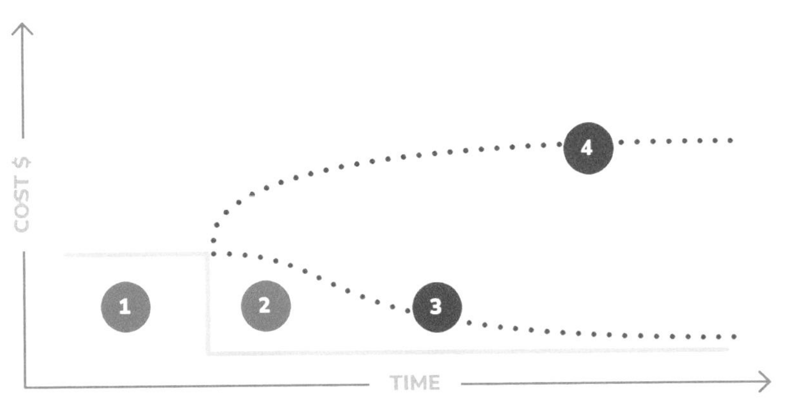

1. *All solutions bear costs to create first version.*
2. *Software that is embedded in hardware and NOT upgraded or extended (like software in a cheap microwave) has no ongoing costs.*
3. *Some SES costs decline rapidly for only limited maintenance and critical updates.*
4. *Some SES costs increase as functionality is added.*

In order to maintain, improve, extend or fix a solution, an ongoing investment is required.

Creating the Business Model for Solution ROI

Begin by capturing all costs

DEVELOPMENT COSTS

Development employee labor including benefits and overhead

Development subcontractor labor

Development resource costs

- Computers and servers
- Infrastructure
- Cloud Software
- Software for development and testing
- In-license costs
- Materials

SALES COSTS

Labor including benefit and overhead

Commissions

Software for sales customer relationship management

Any other sales costs

MARKETING COSTS

Labor including benefits and overhead

Any marketing subcontractor costs

Advertising

Promotions

Marketing software

Any other marketing costs

SERVICES COSTS

Support labor including benefits and overhead

Professional or field services including benefits and overhead

Software and infrastructure for customer support

Mobile hardware for professional or field services

ANY OTHER COSTS

While labor costs are a vital element of internal financial modeling, knowledge of individual compensation plans is not required. A financial leader can provide summary compensation costs.

Ask the financial leader if any other costs are allocated to the solution.

CREATING THE BUSINESS MODEL FOR SOLUTION ROI

These charts illustrate a pure-software solution. Solutions that rely on hardware or services will have slightly different curves.

Model costs over time

Costs will vary over the life of the solution as illustrated...

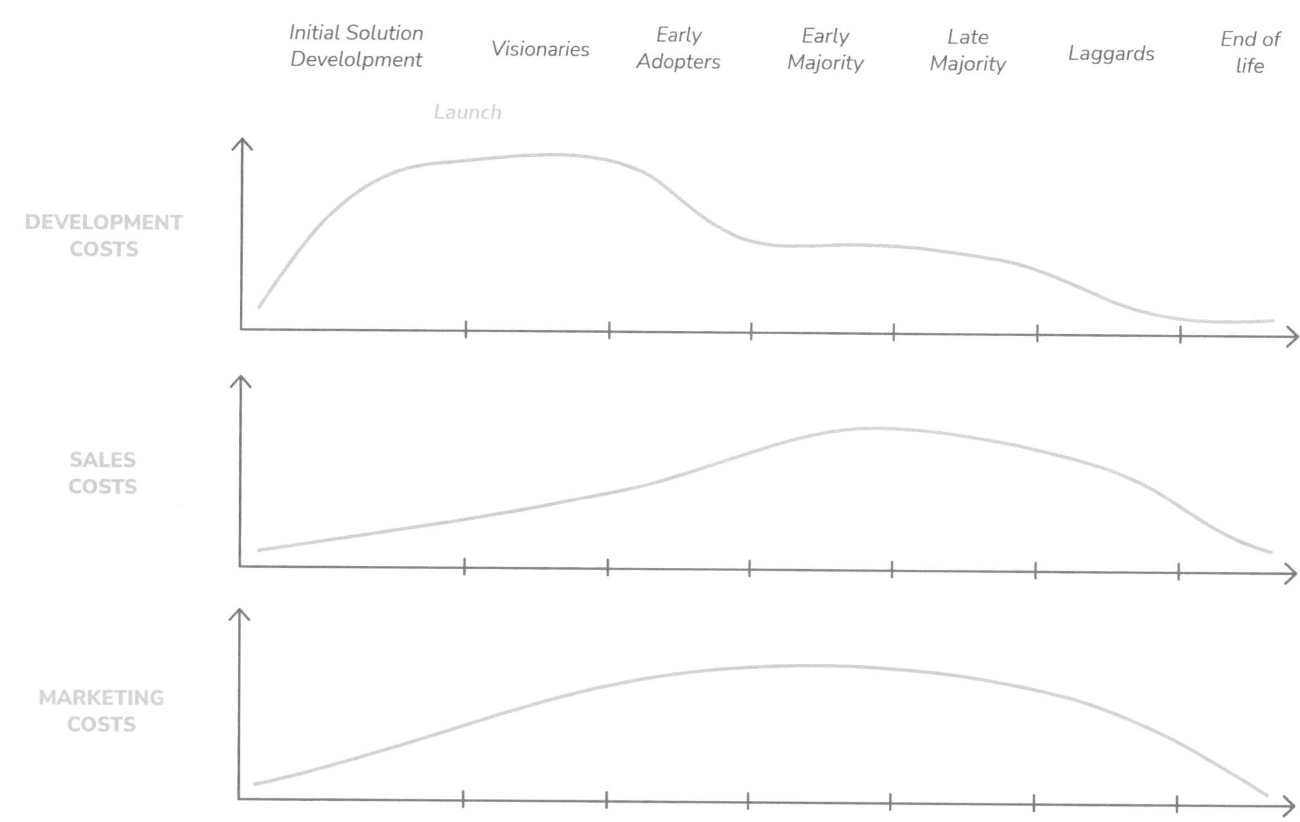

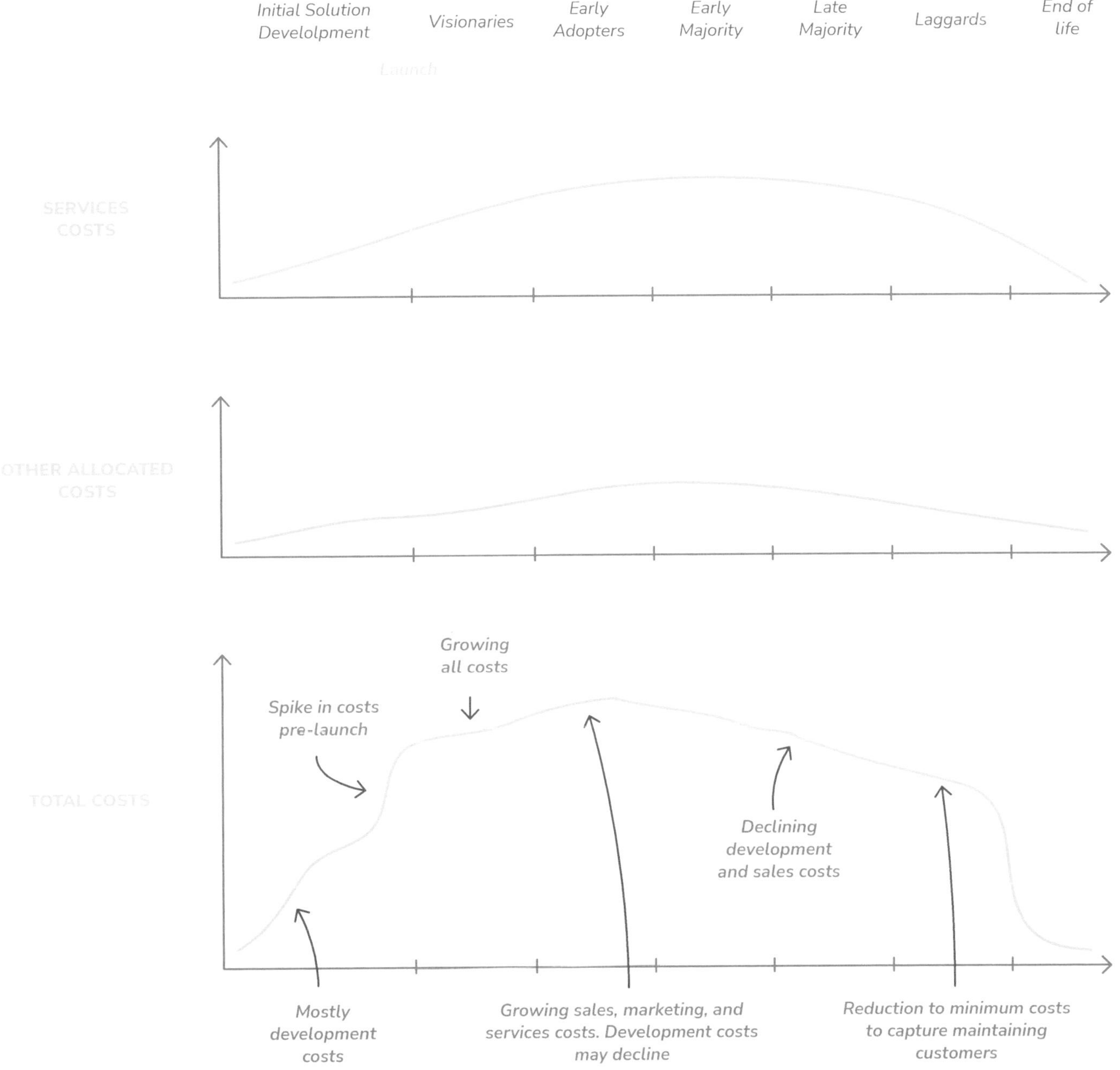

Initial Solution Develolpment
Visionaries
Early Adopters
Early Majority
Late Majority
Laggards
End of life
Launch
SERVICES COSTS
OTHER ALLOCATED COSTS
TOTAL COSTS
Growing all costs
Spike in costs pre-launch
Declining development and sales costs
Mostly development costs
Growing sales, marketing, and services costs. Development costs may decline
Reduction to minimum costs to capture maintaining customers

CREATING THE BUSINESS MODEL FOR SOLUTION ROI

Model Revenue and Costs

Create a pro-forma revenue forecast based on the selected Value Exchange Model, Pricing, and Sales projections for each segment throughout the life of the solution.

Revenue Inputs	
Total Addressable Market	500,000
Visionaries	3%
Early Adopters	12%
Early Majority	15%
Late Majority	35%
Laggards	35%
Conversion	25%
Monthly Retention	75%
Price	$59
Variable Costs	
Customer Acquisition (CAC)	$3
Blue Shaded Cells are Manual Input	
All other cells are calculated	

Schedule / Milestones >>	Development						Launch!	
Revenue	**Jan Year 1**	**Feb Year 1**	**Mar Year 1**	**Apr Year 1**	**May Year 1**	**Jun Year 1**	**Jul Year 1**	**Aug Year 1**
Potential Visionaries	0	0	0	0	0	0	1250	1250
Potential Early Adopters	0	0	0	0	0	0	0	0
Potential Early Majority	0	0	0	0	0	0	0	0
Potential Late Majority	0	0	0	0	0	0	0	0
Potential Laggards	0	0	0	0	0	0	0	0
New Customers	0	0	0	0	0	0	313	313
Retained Customers	0	0	0	0	0	0	0	234
Total Customers	0	0	0	0	0	0	313	547
Monthly Revenue	$0	$0	$0	$0	$0	$0	$18,438	$32,266
Cumulative Revenue	$0	$0	$0	$0	$0	$0	$18,438	$50,703
Costs								
Development	$102,500	$102,500	$102,500	$102,500	$102,500	$102,500	$102,500	$102,500
Services	$17,667	$17,667	$17,667	$17,667	$17,667	$17,667	$17,667	$17,667
Other Allocated Costs	$3,000	$3,000	$3,000	$3,000	$3,000	$3,000	$5,000	$5,000
CAC	0	0	0	0	0	$938	$938	$938
Monthly Costs	$123,167	$123,167	$123,167	$123,167	$123,167	$124,104	$126,104	$126,104
Monthly Profit/Loss	-$123,167	-$123,167	-$123,167	-$123,167	-$123,167	-$124,104	-$107,667	-$75,401
Cumulative Profit/Loss	-$123,167	-$246,333	-$369,500	-$492,667	-$615,833	-$739,938	-$847,604	-$923,005

Estimate conversion and retention

2 customer support and services employees with average loaded salary of $100K / year

Estimate market size and potential adoption based on your research.

8 person development team with average loaded salary of $150K / year

Begin solution marketing

For example, based on the total addressable market for each segment, how many customers are early adopters? Early majority? Based on your sales and marketing plans, how many customers can be realistically acquired in each stage of the Solution maturity?

Avoid constant growth projections such as 10% monthly growth. Let's assume 10 customers purchase in January, then we expect 11 more customers in February for a total of 21. Now expect 23 more customers in March, for a total of 44. If we continue this logic, we'll have over 35,000 customers in December! While that outcome would be great, it's highly unlikely.

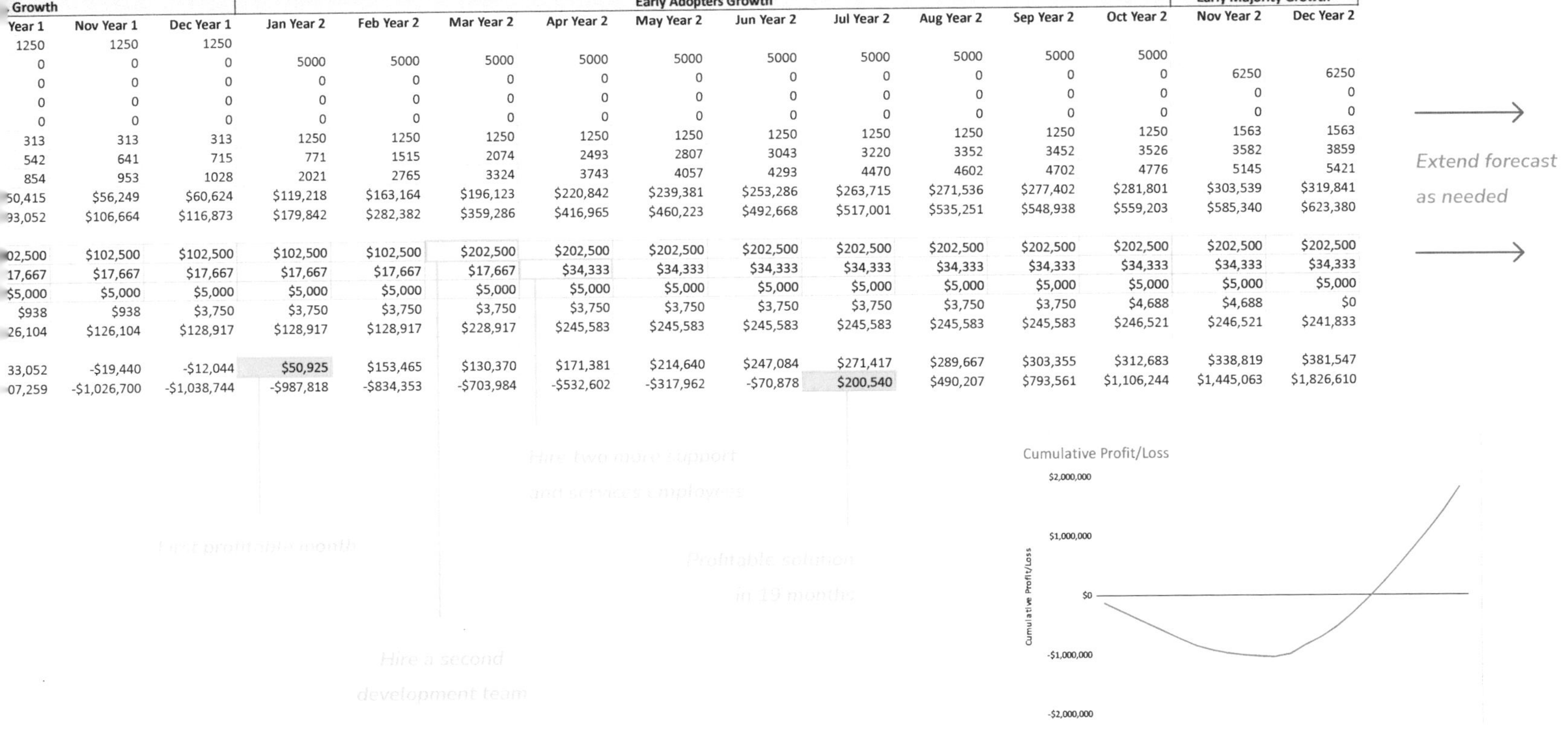

Growth						Early Adopters Growth							Early Majority Growth	
Year 1	Nov Year 1	Dec Year 1	Jan Year 2	Feb Year 2	Mar Year 2	Apr Year 2	May Year 2	Jun Year 2	Jul Year 2	Aug Year 2	Sep Year 2	Oct Year 2	Nov Year 2	Dec Year 2
1250	1250	1250												
0	0	0	5000	5000	5000	5000	5000	5000	5000	5000	5000	5000		
0	0	0	0	0	0	0	0	0	0	0	0	0	6250	6250
0	0	0	0	0	0	0	0	0	0	0	0	0	0	0
0	0	0	0	0	0	0	0	0	0	0	0	0	0	0
313	313	313	1250	1250	1250	1250	1250	1250	1250	1250	1250	1250	1563	1563
542	641	715	771	1515	2074	2493	2807	3043	3220	3352	3452	3526	3582	3859
854	953	1028	2021	2765	3324	3743	4057	4293	4470	4602	4702	4776	5145	5421
50,415	$56,249	$60,624	$119,218	$163,164	$196,123	$220,842	$239,381	$253,286	$263,715	$271,536	$277,402	$281,801	$303,539	$319,841
93,052	$106,664	$116,873	$179,842	$282,382	$359,286	$416,965	$460,223	$492,668	$517,001	$535,251	$548,938	$559,203	$585,340	$623,380
02,500	$102,500	$102,500	$102,500	$102,500	$202,500	$202,500	$202,500	$202,500	$202,500	$202,500	$202,500	$202,500	$202,500	$202,500
17,667	$17,667	$17,667	$17,667	$17,667	$17,667	$34,333	$34,333	$34,333	$34,333	$34,333	$34,333	$34,333	$34,333	$34,333
$5,000	$5,000	$5,000	$5,000	$5,000	$5,000	$5,000	$5,000	$5,000	$5,000	$5,000	$5,000	$5,000	$5,000	$5,000
$938	$938	$3,750	$3,750	$3,750	$3,750	$3,750	$3,750	$3,750	$3,750	$3,750	$3,750	$4,688	$4,688	$0
26,104	$126,104	$128,917	$128,917	$128,917	$228,917	$245,583	$245,583	$245,583	$245,583	$245,583	$245,583	$246,521	$246,521	$241,833
33,052	-$19,440	-$12,044	$50,925	$153,465	$130,370	$171,381	$214,640	$247,084	$271,417	$289,667	$303,355	$312,683	$338,819	$381,547
07,259	-$1,026,700	-$1,038,744	-$987,818	-$834,353	-$703,984	-$532,602	-$317,962	-$70,878	$200,540	$490,207	$793,561	$1,106,244	$1,445,063	$1,826,610

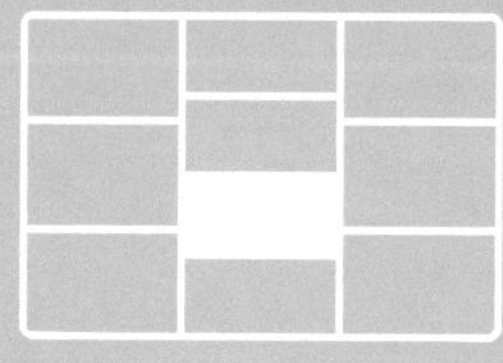

Profit Engine

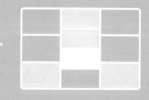

A value exchange model defines how you make money once.
A profit engine defines how you make money over time.

We'll explore five distinct profit engines, including the profit engine available to every software-enabled solution.

Profit Engines

How do you create a more profitable business?

How do you generate more profit from each customer?

How do you stimulate repeated value exchanges?

A Profit Engine is an underlying set of business model choices designed to create additional or repeated value exchanges or increase the profit of a single value exchange.

Visa's core value exchange model is Transaction—about 165 Billion transactions per year!

How could Visa generate more profit?

- *Visa could create the largest global network of credit card readers to drive more transactions*
- *Visa could offer travel protection and other services to reduce risk*
- *Visa could lower the costs to process each transaction*

All of these options are potential profit engines for Visa.

Visa 2021 Annual Report

5 COMMON PROFIT ENGINES FOR SOFTWARE-ENABLED SOLUTIONS

Leverage the Installed Base

There are four methods to leverage the installed base solution:

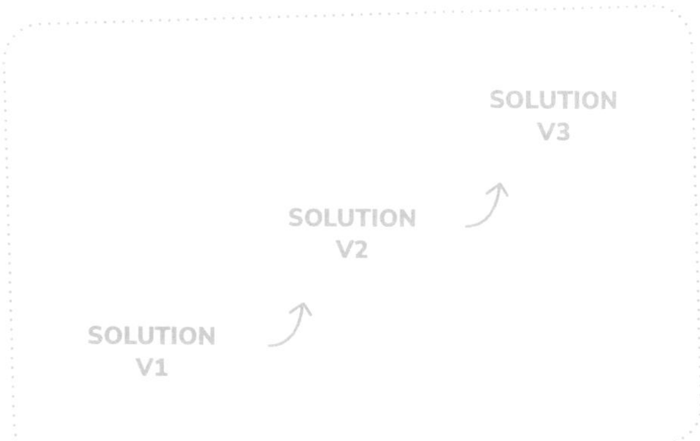

UPGRADE THE SOLUTION

Since each upgraded version adds more value for customers, price level may be increased for customers that select the upgrade.

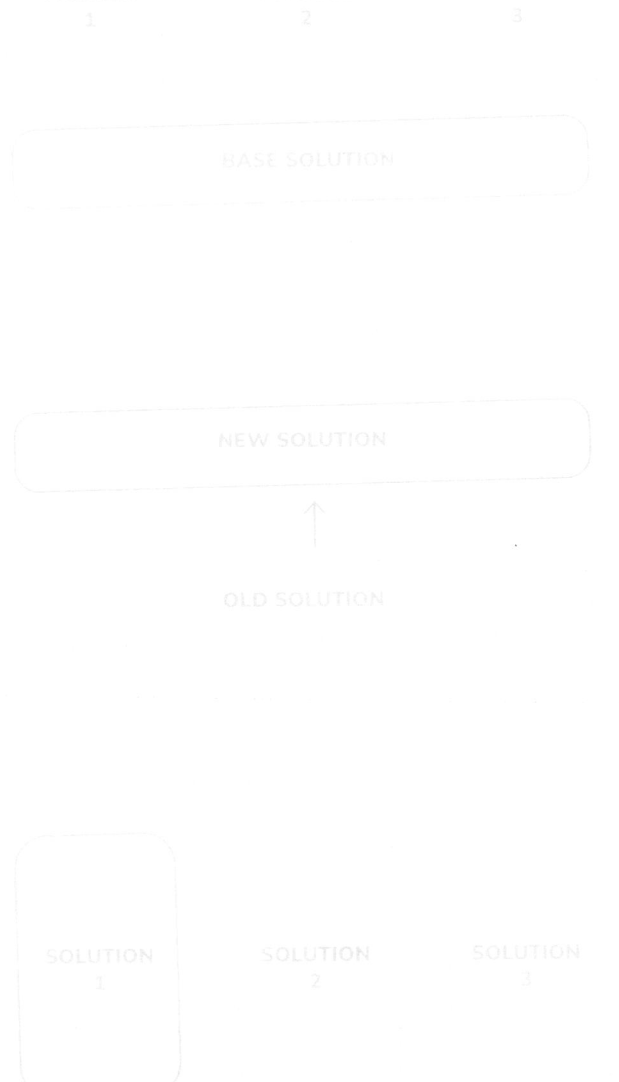

ADD MODULES

Adding modules with differentiated benefits enables customers to tailor their solution by only purchasing the modules they need. This can increase total revenue by ensuring the base solution is not offering 'too much value'. Collections of modules can be organized into bundles, creating even more packaging and pricing options for solution providers.

REPLACE THE SOLUTION

Significant improvement or expansion of the solution leads to complete replacement of the existing solution. While the goal is to migrate all customers to the new solution, in practice some customers will be lost. This loss must be accounted for in your financial modeling.

ADD RELATED SOLUTIONS

Instead of adding more features into an existing solution, create related, independent solutions that can be targeted to the installed base. These solutions may also attract new customers. We explore this in greater detail starting on page 365. This profit engine may be called a "Solution Line" or "Product Line".

5 COMMON **PROFIT ENGINES** FOR SOFTWARE-ENABLED SOLUTIONS

2 Product Pyramid

Create a Product Pyramid by identifying increasing functionality and benefits at increasing price levels and potentially increasing prestige for customers.

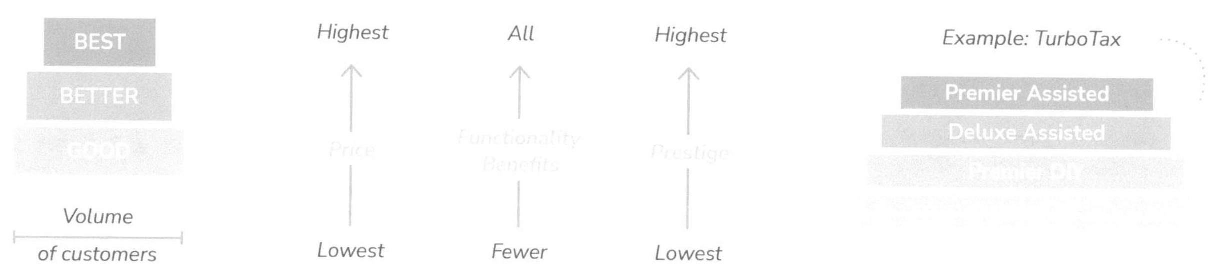

Product Pyramids can evolve over the life of the solution to offer more options to existing segments or to serve new segments.

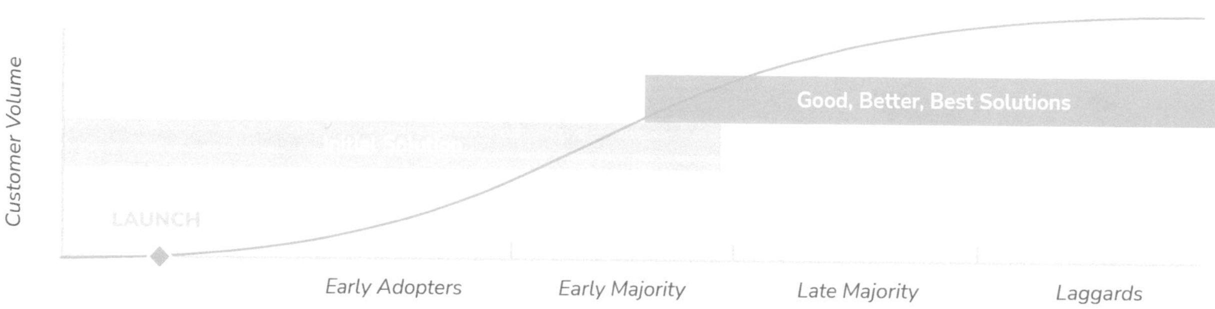

3 Platform Ecosystem

Build an entire ecosystem around the core solution as the platform for value creation.

Apple's iPhone serves as a platform for an enormous ecosystem of applications.

Amazon Web Services provides a platform for an ecosystem of businesses and application developers

The Salesforce.com platform enables customers to access multiple sales, marketing, and other cloud services AND promotes third-party solution providers who offer added value.

PLATFORM BOUNDARIES

Carefully defining the boundaries of your platform is essential to your long-term success.

- Will you certify participants in the ecosystem?
- Will you distribute other solutions through the ecosystem? If so, how? If not, what will you require from ecosystem participants?
- Will you sell other solutions provided by other participants in the ecosystem?
- Will you offer solutions that compete with other solutions in the ecosystem?
- How do any regulations or laws affect ecosystem governance?
- How will you make the platform interesting for participants to join? What value do they gain?

WHOLE SOLUTIONS

Leverage Whole Solution Thinking to maximize platform success.

- Provide training and reference materials to support adoption and usage
- Certify aspects of solutions in the ecosystem like security, performance and/or quality
- Seed the initial ecosystem through relationships with partners. Provide partners with added benefits from early participation
- Demonstrate qualitative and quantitative benefits resulting from engagement in the ecosystem

5 COMMON **PROFIT ENGINES**

FOR SOFTWARE-ENABLED SOLUTIONS

Single Package Solutions

Complex solutions are designed and built using modular components that are usually packaged and sold separately.

While all of the components can be up front, these solutions often grow over time as components are added. While this approach appeals to customers who value flexibility and may be dealing with an atypical solution context, it can also create challenges that can lower profits.

The inability to forecast the total cost of ownership may inhibit future sales, especially if the customer runs out of budget.

Customers may not have the skill and expertise needed to properly select and configure the components needed to solve their problem.

Even the smallest incompatibilities between components can create significant challenges, increasing costs and lowering quality.

B2B customers are often restricted in how they allocate their budgets. They might have enough budget to purchase hardware as a capital expense but not enough budget to commit to an ongoing operational expense.

A single package solution is a pre-designed solution of several components. By reducing flexibility, single package solutions can increase profits by:

Cisco FlexPods integrate solutions from Cisco, NetApp, and Oracle into a powerful computing platform.

Creating a more accurate and precise total cost of ownership that ensures the customer has the required budget for the full solution.

Increasing customer satisfaction and reducing the fear and anxiety associated with designing a solution.

Eliminating any incompatibilities between components.

Enabling B2B customers to select which portion of their budget is being allocated to specific aspects of the solution, giving them greater control over capital and operational expenses.

Some consumers prefer to pay for hardware and get "free" software updates, others prefer to get "free" hardware and pay a monthly software fee. Both can be profitable.

You don't have to limit yourself to either component-based or single-package solutions. Both can co-exist, enabling you to increase the size of your target markets.

5 COMMON **PROFIT ENGINES**
FOR SOFTWARE-ENABLED SOLUTIONS

5 Experience Curve

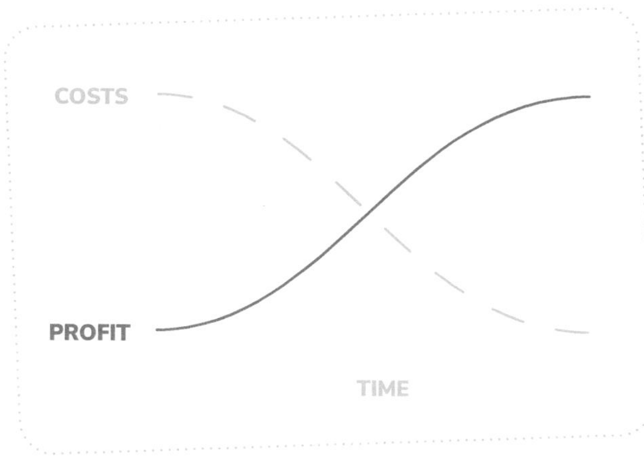

This profit engine is most common in hardware environments, where relentless focus on manufacturing process improvements create substantial financial benefits.

This profit engine results from experience accumulated by launching, selling, supporting, maintaining, and extending the solution. Focused, disciplined adaptation decreases costs to support existing and new customers.

Implement this profit engine for software-enabled solutions through...

- *Stable architecture*
- *Reusable components across solutions*
- *Software patterns and common standards*
- *Automation of testing, distribution, and onboarding*
- *Identification and implementation of self-service support opportunities*

Continuously optimize the flow of value to customers while lowering costs. Identify potential opportunities to modify the solution to create a new offering for a separate market segment.

REVVING THE PROFIT ENGINE

All other profit engines work in conjunction with the installed base.

The selection of profit engine is based on:

→ TECHNICAL ARCHITECTURE CAPABILITIES

→ CORE ORGANIZATIONAL COMPETENCIES

→ COMPETITIVE ENVIRONMENT

For your solution, consider options to create additional or repeated value exchanges or how to increase the profit of each value exchange.

CUSTOMER LICENSES BLOCK

RELATIONSHIP SUSTAINABILITY

CUSTOMER + MONETIZATION FOCUS

Customer Licenses

Customer licenses are the legal agreements that define and govern the **relationship between you and your customers.** We'll cover:

→ *The legal chain of rights*

→ *Common terms and their meaning*

→ *How to align license agreements with value exchange models*

→ *Privacy policies*

→ *How to manage and enforce your rights as a provider*

Customer licenses are the legal agreements, or contracts, that define and govern the relationship between a software-enabled solution provider and their customers.

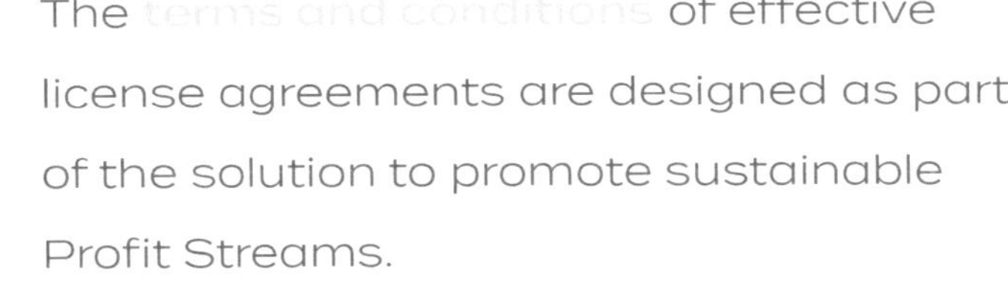

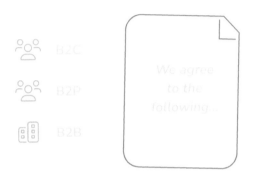

The terms and conditions of effective license agreements are designed as part of the solution to promote sustainable Profit Streams.

Sustainable solution licenses are...

FAIR

The license strives to promote an equitable relationship that balances present and future needs of both parties.

UNDERSTANDABLE

Customers can easily understand the license and its implications.

CONGRUENT

The license supports the value exchange model and promotes the profit engine.

ENFORCEABLE

Both parties can enforce their rights. Enforcement is covered in greater detail later in the book.

The information provided in this book does not, and is not intended to, constitute legal advice. Always review your Customer Licenses with appropriate legal counsel.

Customer licenses may exist within a legal chain of rights.

Design choices must be made with an awareness of the relationships between the entities.

A SES PROVIDER SERVES CUSTOMERS WHEN IT SELLS ITS SOLUTIONS.

These relationships are captured in the Customer Licenses section.

A SES PROVIDER IS A CUSTOMER WHEN IT IS LICENSING SOLUTIONS FROM OTHER PROVIDERS.

We explore these relationships in the Solution Licenses section.

The Solution Context has a significant impact on how licenses are stored, presented, and accepted.

The four most common patterns are:

Shrink-Wrapped License
A shrink-wrapped license asserts that the customer agrees to the license by opening the package or using the solution. It is most commonly used in B2C, B2P, and low-cost B2B markets.

Also known as an End-User License Agreement (EULA) because the customer is typically the end user. These agreements cannot be negotiated.

Negotiated License
Negotiated licenses are used in expensive B2B and/or bespoke solution development.

Terms of Service (TOS) defined by the provider
Typically associated with hosted solutions or Software-As-A-Service (SaaS), the TOS present the customer license on a website. A customer tacitly agrees to the T.O.S. by using the website and explicitly agrees to the TO.S. when performing certain actions, such as creating an account.

Terms of Service (TOS) defined by the Solution Context
Software-Enabled solutions that operate within a Solution Context may choose to use the TOS defined by the Solution Context.

Apps that run on an iphone can use Apple's Standard TOS. Apps that run in a Platform-As-Service can use the PAAS providers' standard TOS.

Related to the Customer License is the **Privacy Policy,** which defines how the Solution Provider gathers, uses, discloses, and manages a customer's data or their own data. Privacy Policies are covered here and again in the Compliance section.

Exploring the **Customer License**

Customer licenses define a set of rights and restrictions that govern the behavior of customers and providers.

Rights

What a given party can do with the solution and artifacts generated or manipulated by the solution.

Restrictions

What a given party cannot do with the solution and artifacts generated or manipulated by the solution.

Obligations

Obligations describe the duties of a given party to do or not do something with the solution.

High impact licenses differentiate as many rights and restrictions as possible, as each may provide differentiated value. Review the definitions that follow as you define the rights and restrictions relative to your solution.

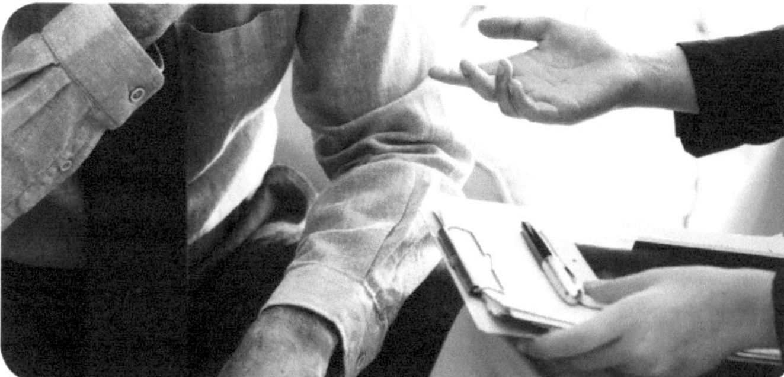

Developing a Customer License is a complex activity that must include representation from product management, legal, and engineering. Consider adding the wisdom of sales and finance.

Managing **License Agreements**

License agreements evolve with the solution. It is a best practice to store your license agreements in the same source code repository as your other source code so that you can recreate the specific version of the license agreement that was agreed upon by you and your customers.

This section does not cover all aspects of a customer license. It is designed to provide a guide to several terms and conditions that most affect your Profit Stream.

Definitions

Before the license can define rights, restrictions, and obligations, it must provide **precise, legal descriptions of all important items or terms referenced in the license agreement.** These are contained in the beginning of the agreement.

A provider of a game for a personal computer might define their solution as: "Software means the object code proprietary to the company and listed on the pricing schedule."

A SaaS provider of solutions to manage resumes and credentials for professionals might define their solution as: "These Terms of Use (the "Terms") apply to your use of websites and mobile applications (the "Service") operated by Company".

Because these definitions are referenced by subsequent terms, business leaders must carefully consider how solutions are defined to promote their Profit Stream.

SaaS providers may prefer a broad definition of a solution to make it easier to reserve the right to update the solution, while the provider of an on-premise solution, such as a game or professional productivity application, may provide a very narrow definition of the solution in order to more effectively limit support and/or updates to a specific version number or defined aspects of the solution context, such as supported operating systems.

The **Value Exchange Model** will influence the definitions.

Profit Streams based on **transactions** must define the transaction.

Profit Streams based on **performance** must define how performance will be measured.

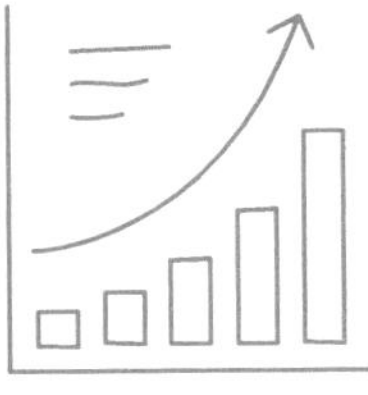

Profit Streams based on a **meter** must define what is being counted.

DEFINITIONS

Usage or grant

This section includes a set of generic rights and restrictions, starting with the essential right of providing a license to use the solution to the individuals and entities who are entitled to use it.

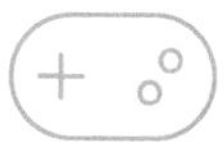

Anyone who has access to the cartridge and game console.

The user who created the account.

Any employee of the company who logs in via company's Single Sign-On (SSO) gateway.

Additional rights and/or restrictions may include...

Installation/Access

The number of instances, devices and people that may install and/or use the solution is usually specified in this section.

Clearly identified segments help define fences that are formally defined in the license agreement.

For example, Spotify defines specific plans for students, individuals, and families. These fences are precisely defined in the pricing pages for Spotify and enforced by the license agreement.

Exclusivity

Most SES licenses are non-exclusive, meaning the provider can license the solution to others.

Ownership

The provider will retain ownership of all intellectual property.

Renting, leasing, lending, or sharing:

Most solutions prohibit these activities. Most hardware solutions allow for the transfer of the software portion of the solution to another party when ownership of the hardware is transferred.

Reverse Engineering

Most providers prohibit reverse engineering.

Embed

Is the intent of the solution to be embedded or used within other solutions? If the solution can be embedded, can your customer's customer further embed the solution?

Some data solutions are designed to be included or integrated into other solutions.

Many APIs are designed to be integrated into a larger solution.

Hardware sub-assemblies may be integrated into larger solutions.

Modify

Is the intent of the provider to allow customers to modify some or all aspects of the solution? For example, is the customer allowed to modify aspects of the hardware or change the default processing of the solution, such as modifying the source code of a workflow management solution?

License agreement updates

This portion of the license agreement defines how the license agreement itself may be modified. SaaS providers typically retain the right to unilaterally modify license agreements. Negotiated agreements will define how the parties may modify the agreement.

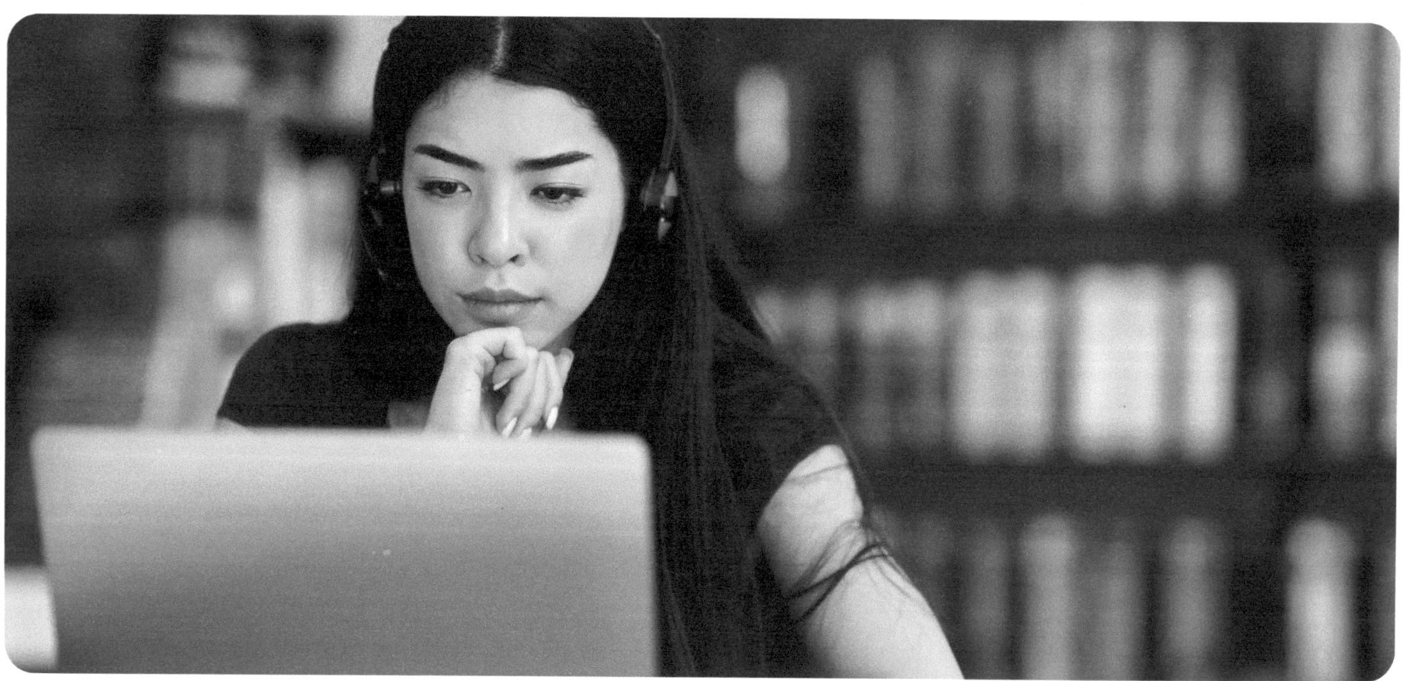

Business leaders can improve their choices by reviewing the license agreements of other solution providers. **Asking your legal team for clarity of unfamiliar terms is a way to accelerate your learning!**

Modifications, including bug fixes, enhancements, and upgrades

Business leaders must decide how they wish to manage modifications to the solution. Common choices include:

No updates.

The Customer is given the right to receive modifications and/or upgrades for a defined period of time or a defined set of versions. Modifications may be further defined by type, such as bug fixes or enhancements, with providers agreeing to different obligations to each of these types of modifications.

The Customer must use the version of the Solution chosen by the provider. This is common in SaaS solutions, in which the vendor determines which version of the solution is provided to customers. Customers sometimes worry that their hosted solution will either become obsolete or will change too quickly. SaaS providers must balance the rate of change to eliminate these concerns.

While there are a few common patterns, there are a significant number of variations in how modifications are designed and managed...

TIME-BASED ACCESS, RUN ON PREMISE

Solutions that are distributed and operate on customer-provided environments are precisely versioned with specific rules on the nature of modifications.

DATA SOLUTIONS

Data solutions that may be reasonably improved over a period of time acceptable to the provider, such as providing a credit report and one update to that credit report within 90 days.

DEFINITIONS

Duration or term and other key dates

The value exchange model dictates the content of this section, which defines when the agreement begins and ends. There are are two general cases:

01. Time-Based Access

Because time-based access motivates the exchange of money based on time, the agreement must clearly define the start and end of the term and what will happen when the term expires.

The agreement effective date defines when the agreement is considered in effect. A customer creating an account through a website may initiate the effective date. A highly negotiated license may have an effective date that is different from the date both parties execute the agreement.

The term start date is when the license begins. For online services, this can be the same date as when the customer established their account or it might be when a customer upgrades from a 'free account' to a 'paid account' in an online service. For negotiated contracts, this is the date explicitly agreed to by both parties.

The term end date is when access to the solution is terminated.
The term end date may be absolute, such as when a subscription ends, or calculated, such as adding a fixed amount of time to the term start date. This can range from a customer canceling or otherwise terminating their account to a specific date agreed upon by the parties in a negotiated agreement.

The expiration or termination date is when the agreement is terminated.
Because the rights and obligations of the parties may extend beyond the initial or immediate use of the solution, the termination date often exceeds the term end date. For example, a gamer who purchases a digital good in a video game may lose access to that possession when they terminate their account. A financial institution who purchases a credit report to process a loan request may be required to delete the report after a defined period of time.

The termination notice date defines the date or amount of time either party must provide to the other should they intend to terminate the license.
This is common in more complex and/or expensive solutions, in which the customer may need time to prepare and implement a change in solution providers.

All other Value Exchange Models

Most of the other value exchange models will have a license agreement that defines the same dates as time-based access, with slightly different meanings and slightly different purposes.

DEFINITIONS

Fees, pricing schedules, and payment terms

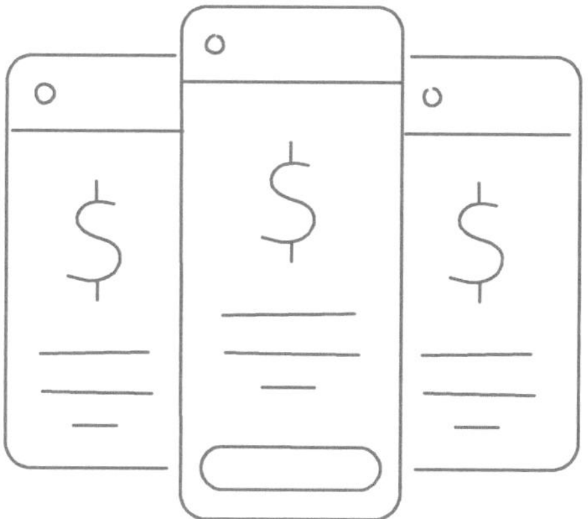

An integral element of every valid contract is the exchange of consideration between the parties to the contract - terms stating what each party to the contract is giving, or will give, to the other party to the contract. For most customer licenses, this section includes a description of the payment terms that support the chosen value exchange model.

The product manager must ensure the technical architecture supports the payment terms. Automatic renewal or subscription payments can be an essential element of the business model and may be specified in this section.

Returns and refunds

Return rights, including period for returns, and any applicable refunds, are defined here.

Audit rights

Audit rights define when and how the provider can audit how the solution is being used and how the customer can audit any responsibilities of the provider, such as compliance with data protection or privacy regulations.

Territory

This section identifies the applicable territory where the solution can be used or identifies any specific information related to various territories.

Territories influence the Profit Stream in a number of ways.

PRICING FENCES

It is common to vary prices in different geographies to account for the variations in exchange rates from the base currency of the solution provider.

A provider headquartered in Europe may choose the Euro as their base currency and define a set of pricing fences to normalize the price of the offering in different regions. These may be defined in the license agreement.

OPERATING RESTRICTIONS

Territory-based operating restrictions are common when the provider is operating under export limitations or when the provider has failed to secure rights from key suppliers.

A U.S.-based provider has integrated advanced cryptography in their solution.

Providers who operate globally may need to create entirely distinct license agreements for customers who reside in other countries.

DEFINITIONS

Consent to use of data

This section describes how the vendor records and uses customer data including any diagnostic or usage data collected in order to improve the solution.

The section is often strongly related to compliance, such as compliance with the European Union's General Data Protection Regulation or GDPR.

Privacy or confidentiality

The vendor may reiterate ownership and confidentiality of intellectual property. The vendor may also describe protection of the customer's confidential information, which must be part of the solution's technical architecture.

Support

This section describes how to access available support based on the terms and fees associated with the value exchange model. Providing options for different levels of support creates opportunities for unique offerings for different customer segments.

Warranty

This section describes whether the solution includes a warranty, the type and duration of the warranty, and how warranty claims will be remedied including refunds.

This section may also include disclaimers and limitations for any damages. Most pure-software solutions disclaim all warranties. Hardware-based SES may warrant various aspects of the hardware.

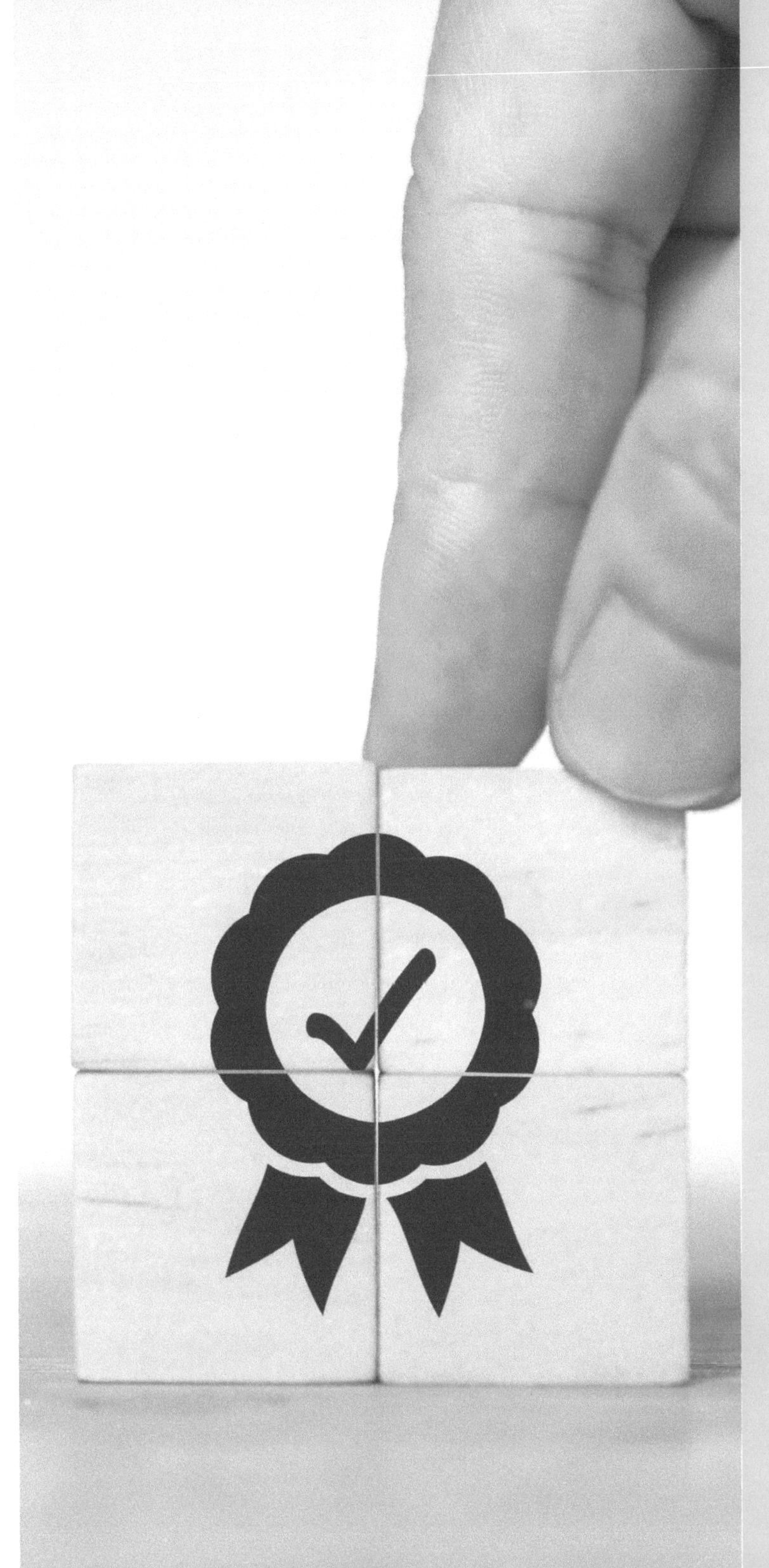

License agreements from SaaS providers, including games, consumer websites, professional apps, and hosted business critical apps, have a number of license terms that differ significantly from on-premise or embedded solutions.

Providers of on-premise solutions should review these terms as some of them may apply to their offering, especially if they have plans to add a SaaS offering or migrate an on-premise solution to a cloud solution.

Here are additional terms that are common in these agreements.

SERVICE ELIGIBILITY

This section defines who is eligible to use the service and is designed to support your target segments and/or price fences.

Common distinctions for service eligibility include:

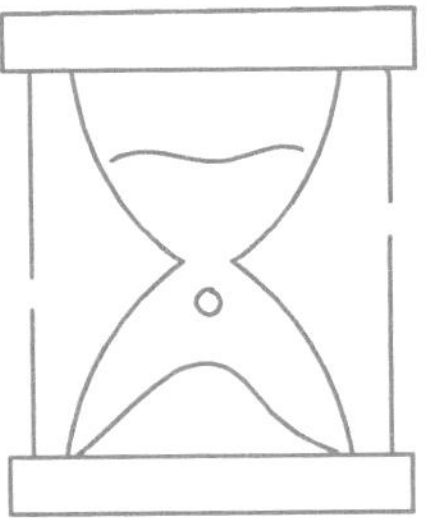

Age

The license agreement should make explicit the intended age of its users and any compliance with regulations governing use of online services by children, such as the Children's Online Privacy Protection Act (COPPA) in the United States or General Data Protection Regulation (GDPR) in Europe. Note that the age of a minor or child is defined differently in these regulations.

Human

You will need to determine if an account may be created and/or accessed by non-humans, including bots or other software applications.

Unique Accounts

You will need to determine if a party may create more than one account for themselves or on behalf of others.

This section will also include a description of the rights the provider reserves when in responding to any violations of eligibility requirements.

SERVICE AVAILABILITY

This section defines the obligations of the service provider in offering their services, including when the service will be unavailable, such as during maintenance.

USER GENERATED OR USER-UPLOADED CONTENT

Hosted services must define how they handle user-generated and/or user-uploaded content. Typical restrictions include prohibiting certain kinds of content and requiring that content respects intellectual property rights of others.

The terms defined here should cover the full set of activities associated with creating, editing, sharing, referencing, and deleting content.

It is also common to ensure that your service has the necessary legal right to use the content provided by your users and customers. Typical content clauses include this kind of language:

You agree that you own the content and information that you submit or post to the Services, and in doing so hereby grant Company and our affiliates the following non-exclusive license: A worldwide, transferable and sublicensable right to use, copy, modify, distribute, publish and process, information and content that you provide through our Services and the services of others, without any further consent, notice and/or compensation to you or others.

ADDITIONAL RIGHTS, RESTRICTIONS, AND OBLIGATIONS

should be designed to support your business model and drive your profit engine.

Account Management

Because the pricing structure of many SaaS solutions is based on the number of users, SaaS providers will typically add several restrictions on how a user will manage their account, such as requiring that passwords are maintained in a confidential manner or prohibiting the sharing of accounts with other users.

Linking Policy

This section describes guidelines for how users can incorporate or links to external websites and the rights the provider reserves on managing these links. For example, a website designed for children may prohibit the ability to link to websites containing adult content.

Acceptable Use Policies (AUP) / Behavioral Policies

Because many SaaS solutions promote interaction with other users, SaaS providers typically outline a set of obligations and restrictions on the acceptable use of their services. These can range from informal recommendations to specific terms that enable the provider to enforce behavior.

Service providers that provide access to their solution via an API often provide special terms that cover the use of that API.

These terms are designed to protect the provider from attacks and/or other forms of misuse while ensuring the quality of the service for others.

Third Party Solution Notice

Providing an API does not mean that the provider endorses solutions developed by third party developers or application providers that use the API. Most solution providers do not endorse third party solutions.

Astute business leaders are always on the prowl for ways they can create a more profitable solution. Providers of solutions with APIs may endorse 3rd party solutions for a certification fee!

Supported Versions

The specific versions of the API that are available and how they are supported, including any APIs in the process of being deprecated, must be defined in the license. Add clarity to the license with additional information that will allow API customers to manage their ongoing use of the API.

Pre-Release Access

API providers should consider how customers will gain access to future releases of the API to help them manage their development activities.

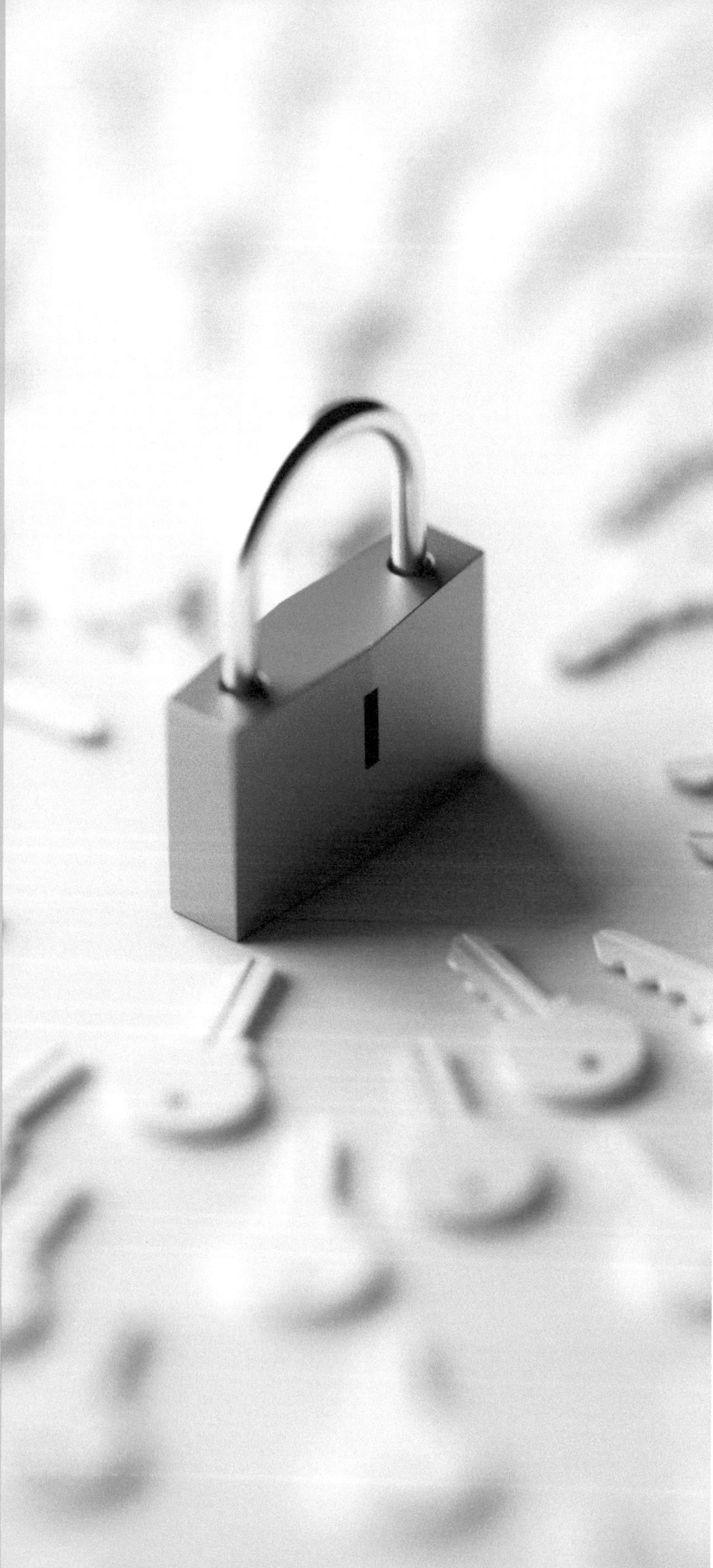

Privacy Policies

A privacy policy is a legal agreement that defines how and why a provider is collecting, using, and sharing user and/or customer information.

While the website of a small business may not need a privacy policy, companies that offer any solution, including their website, in jurisdictions covered by the European General Data Protection Regulation (GDPR), along with laws in states like California, Nevada, Delaware, Virginia, and Colorado, all require one.

Providers of solutions intended to be used by other providers as part of a supply chain of solutions may be required to disclose how they handle private data. Though this requirement partly anticipates privacy laws becoming stricter, the primary purpose of the privacy policy is to ensure there is a closed chain of protected data, from the vendors to end-users.

All Google or Apple software or apps require privacy policies from everyone in their ecosystems. Since analytics software can rely on personal information, using any kind of personal information means you need a privacy policy.

A basic privacy policy covers:

A list and description of information collected

Where you find that information

Why you collect it

How it is collected

Who can see it, whether it will be shared or sold

The rights that users have over their data

How users can use those rights

Your contact information

Other parts you may want to include:

How you store the data

Links to other policies on your website (cookie policy, terms of service)

How to access or remove data

This list will likely change soon because privacy law changes quickly to keep up with technology and other influences. Once you create a policy, you will have to closely monitor it to stay up to date with new or changed laws. Experts say our current privacy laws are still far from adequate, so expect that you will have to update your privacy policy frequently.

Enforcing License Agreements

Business leaders must decide how they will enforce their license agreements. **As with other aspects of Profit Stream design, this is a question of System Design.** The strength of enforcement and the nature and severity of the response must be weighed against the moral, ethical and financial goals of the business.

I'm going to share my account login with my friends

Lost revenue

Hey! You're stealing from me!

Provider

Our account monitoring has detected fraudulent use and has disabled your account.

I've been caught, what do I need to do to reset my account?

The essential activities are identifying and responding to the violation. The most common responses are:

Disabling some or all of the application

Slowing down the application

Automatically fixing the problem (i.e., charging the customer)

B2P and B2B markets have less incentive to steal as penalties for theft can exceed the costs of the solution.

PROVIDER BENEFITS

- *Increases revenue*
- *Reduces theft*
- *Lowers risks, specially for solutions subject to export controls*

CUSTOMER BENEFITS

- *Manages costs by encouraging customers to stay within license terms*
- *Creates opportunities to align usage with payment and pricing models*

There are two main enforcement strategies:

The Honor System

License managers, including monitoring

SaaS/Cloud based monitoring and access solutions

Business leaders use a mix of these techniques to balance enforcement of a given term with its impact to the business.

Any term of the license agreement is a candidate for enforcement:

- *Enforcing fences*
- *Enforcing the terms of time-based access*
- *Enforcing account eligibility for online services*
- *Enforcing geographic restrictions*
- *Preventing copying of on-premise software (such as a video game)*
- *Enforcing the specific set of features and/or processing capabilities in a defined package*

To help identify the most important terms to enforce, ask yourself which terms, when violated, cause direct or indirect financial loss.

Enforcing License Agreements

THE HONOR SYSTEM

The simplest and easiest way to enforce a license model is to expect that your customers will honor the terms of their license agreement. The provider is not giving up any rights, as they can still take action against the customer for breach of contract if violations are found.

LICENSE MANAGERS

A license manager is a part of the solution that monitors the terms of the license, enabling the solution to determine how to respond to violations.

License managers can be implemented in a variety of ways: you can write your own license management system or you can license technology from a third party provider. How you implement and use a license manager can be captured in the following process:

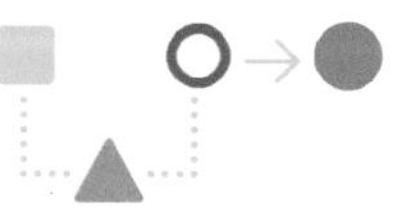

- *Review your customer license agreement/TOS to identify the terms and conditions you need to enforce*
- *Determine how to detect violations*
- *Decide on the appropriate response*
- *Implement these choices in your solution*

FellowNeko - stock.adobe.com

Netflix's license agreement prohibits the sharing of passwords between users as this directly affects profit. How Netflix has enforced this policy has changed, ranging from little to no enforcement to promote growth to stricter enforcement to capture profit.

CLOUD MONITORING

Cloud monitoring systems are special kinds of license monitoring solutions created for SaaS solutions. These license managers typically provide facilities for responding dynamically to customer and user changes, such as when a customer upgrades their account and is granted immediate access to new features. Cloud monitoring systems often promote multi-factor authentication as a means to improve compliance.

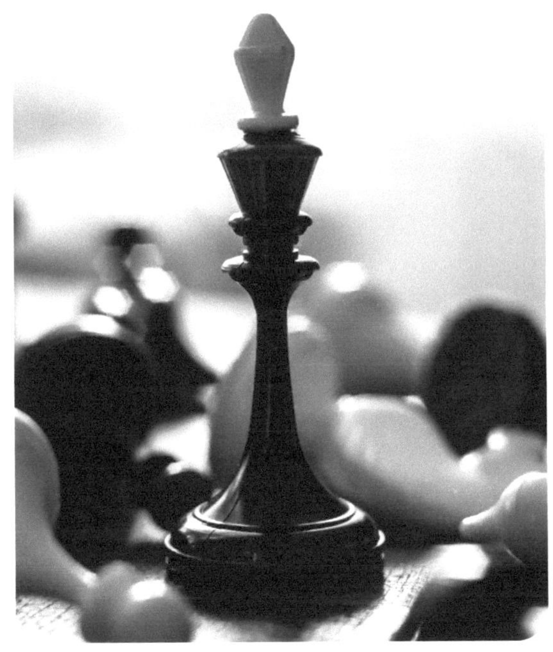

License enforcement can feel like an endless chess game, in which moves and countermoves are being made on a constantly changing board.

The more valuable your solution, the more you need to play this game to win.

SOLUTION LICENSES BLOCK

RELATIONSHIP SUSTAINABILITY

CUSTOMER + MONETIZATION FOCUS

Solution Licenses

Solution licenses are the **legal agreements that define and govern the relationship between the solutions and technologies** you acquire from suppliers and you. We'll cover:

→ *The risks and rewards of in-licensing*

→ *Key terms and conditions*

→ *How to manage differences in business models*

→ *Techniques for managing in-licensing, including open source licenses*

→ *Understanding and managing fees*

Solution Licenses

Every software-enabled solution is part **new code** and part **systems integration** with previously-written software — even if the software you are integrating with is nothing more than the runtime library that comes with your favorite compiler.

What you're integrating is a solution, typically from another company. And that solution comes to you based on a business and license model.

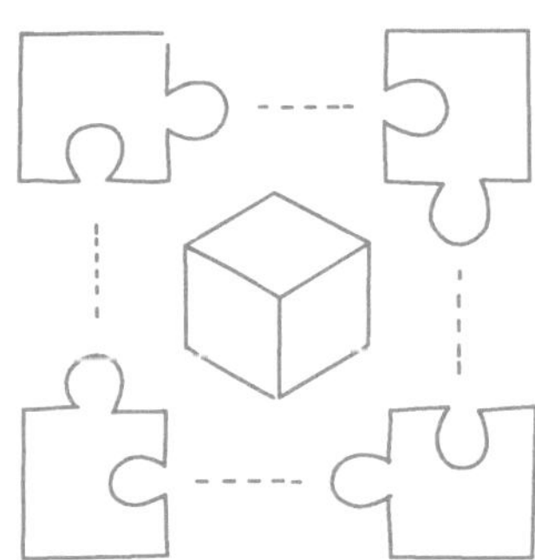

The process of incorporating a solution from another vendor into your solution is called **technology in-licensing.**

Which means that you're the customer and you should assume that the vendor you're using has read this book!

There are many motivations for licensing solutions from others. The most obvious reason is that **licensing solutions can be cheaper and faster than building them on your own.**

Sometimes licensing isn't a choice, but a requirement, because your company may have obtained a vital patent on a technology essential to your success.

An additional consideration is the skills and experience of your key staff.

You may not want them spending precious time and energy designing and building components that you can obtain via a license.

Of course, the converse is also true: licensing solutions can create unforeseen challenges that restrict your ability to operate or harm your profits.

Any, or all, of these factors mean that you are likely to be licensing one or more key solutions from another party. As a result, understanding basic concepts associated with in-license agreements and how they affect your technical architecture AND your profitability is vital for everyone on the team.

10 MOTIVATIONS - AND RISKS - OF IN-LICENSING

Remember the verb-based Customer Benefit Analysis? Use the same verbs to help guide your choices in selecting in-licenses. These ten motivations will help you get started.

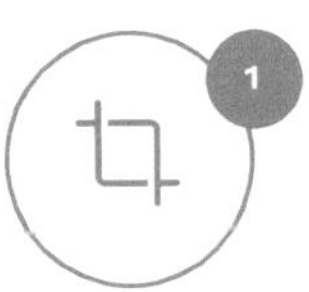

Reduce Complexity

You can reduce, manage, or otherwise eliminate complexity and risk by licensing technology from a third party. Presumably, the technology or provider is an expert in a given area that you deem important to success. By licensing their technology you gain the provider's expertise.

Risk

You may be able to shift complexity from your team to the technology provider, but in doing so you increase risk by increasing your reliance on third-party technology. If the technology evolves in a way that fails to match your needs, you could be in serious trouble.

A supplier might change focus, leaving you without an equivalent replacement. You may not even be able to find a suitable and compatible new supplier.

This almost happened to one of our teams when a search engine vendor whose technology we had licensed decided to reposition themselves as a portal vendor. They initially stopped development of their core technology (text indexing and searching). Fortunately, several customers, including us, managed to convince the vendor to maintain its investment in the core technology. Everything worked out, but the situation was very tense for several weeks as we explored several undesirable replacement scenarios.

A corollary is that you must make certain that you assess the viability of the technology provider. Given today's volatile corporate market, there is always the risk that a small technology provider may go out of business.

10 MOTIVATIONS - AND RISKS - OF IN-LICENSING

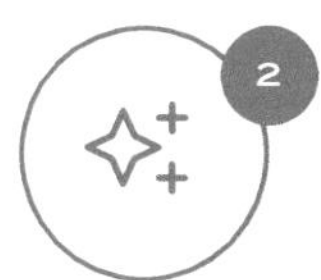

Focus on what makes you special

In-licensing technology makes your system easier to construct because you can focus on creating your unique technology.

Risk

Incompatible business models may make the use of certain kinds of technologies practically impossible. For example, you might want to sell your solution via a time-based access but your supplier wants you to pay a transaction fee for every API call.

Another issue is the restrictions that may come with various components. High-end cryptographic libraries are often subject to various forms of export restrictions, which means your solution may be export-restricted if you leverage them. Improperly integrating open source software may force you into open sourcing your own solution.

All of these factors complicate your ability to make a profit.

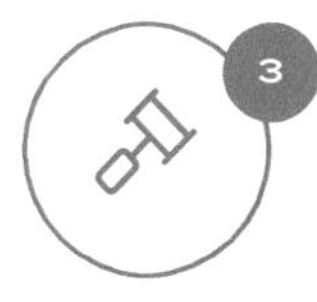

Secure legal protection

You can obtain *legal* protection by licensing technology protected by a patent.

Risk

Indemnity - legal protection from the penalties or liabilities incurred for using the component - is hard to secure. Suppose you license a component from company A because it has a patent on a key technology. Unless Company A agrees to indemnify you, this license is not likely to protect you from being sued by company B, who may claim that you're infringing on their rights. Be sure to acknowledge IP protection in your analysis and decisions for in-licensing.

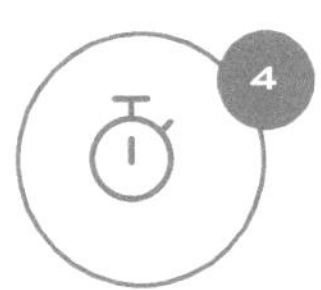

Reduce time-to-market

You can reduce time-to-market by using existing technology.

Risk

Licensing technology does not always result in faster time to market. At the very least you have to invest time in learning the technology, integrating it into your solution, and verifying that it works correctly for your total solution. Building your own solution to meet your needs is sometimes faster. How do you know for sure? Conduct an economic analysis.

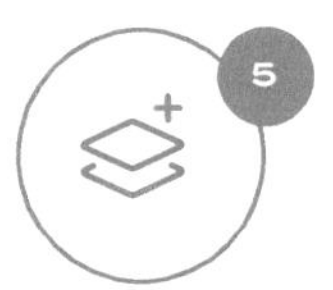

Increase quality

Vendor-created components may be higher quality than those you write on your own.

Risk

Many times this just isn't true—in-licensed technology is often lower in quality than what you might create. Accordingly, make sure that you do your research and factor quality into your selection criteria.

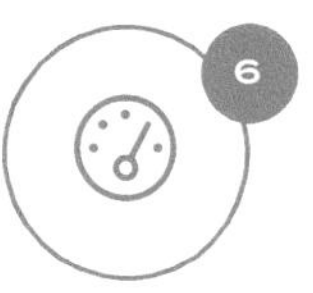

Increase Performance

While many product leaders live in the cloud where seemingly infinite storage and compute resources free them from worrying about pesky constraints such as memory consumption or storage, many of business leaders still have their feet firmly embedded on the ground or in embedded systems. This means they do have to worry about storage, compute, and other resources. This leads to another common motivation for technology in-licensing: performance. Vendors that have optimized performance can provide solutions that consume less memory, run on cheaper/lower-cost hardware, or use less disk space. All of these factors can create a positive economic impact on your solution.

Risk

In-licensed technology may be surprisingly heavy, consuming more resources or running more slowly than code you write on your own. Moreover, it is nearly impossible to substantially tune the performance of most in-licensed technologies. Unless you have the source code, which you probably don't, you can't recompile it to turn on multithreading or modify the code to perform I/O operations more efficiently. And if you could, you probably shouldn't, because this kind of change inhibits adopting future releases from the vendor. Accordingly, make sure that you include technical items in your roadmap and backlog to conduct feasibility assessments when considering in-licensing components for optimizing your work.

10 MOTIVATIONS - AND RISKS - OF IN-LICENSING

Maintaining currency with your Solution Context

Every software enabled solution has to stay current with its Solution Context - the 'container' that runs your solution. If you control the entire container - great. You get to control more of your destiny. Licensing a component relieves some of the burden associated with technology currency because the vendor will be continually improving the component.

Most of us, however, provide solutions that operate in someone else's 'container':

Smartphone apps run in the 'container' of the phone and its operating system

Cloud Solutions run in the cloud provider's context

Desktop apps run in the operating system of the vendor, typically Apple, Microsoft, or Linux

Staying current with that Solution Context can be tricky. Which leads to another common motivation for technology in-licensing: ***Currency.***

Risk

Vendors don't always update components as fast as needed. Sometimes they drop support for other components that you must still support, such as an OS. Accordingly, you may find that the technology you've licensed that originally accelerated your solution now puts a brake on innovation.

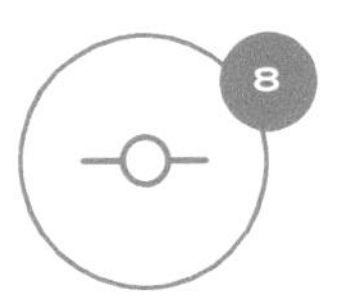

Gain access to state-of-the-art capabilities

Your developers originally built your solution on C, Perl, Ruby on Rails or Java. And it worked. While that boring old app was actually working, along comes...Scala, Python and Go. And suddenly the cool new technology choices magically convince your developers that your old application is tragically—no—horrifically broken.

Unless you upgrade, you'll fail. And if that doesn't convince you to change, you'll find that nearly overnight your app has become so overloaded with technical debt that you can no longer afford to make investment in new capabilities, let alone make the interest payments on the existing debt. The sweet lure of innovation, for developers, isn't just creating cool stuff for your customers. It also includes using cool stuff.

It isn't just developers who succumb to the siren's song. Plenty of business leaders find ways to justify something cool. They just *climb the ego-innovation mountain from the North face, instead of the East wall,* by showing how a critical customer need can only be solved by using a super cool technology that they secretly wished they had patented.

The desired benefit is that a technology provider's component (or language) is state of the art, and using it will future-enable your application and/or give your customers an amazing capability.

Risk

This sounds like resume driven design, in which developers and product managers seek to use a technology because it is cool. Use the razor of economic thinking to cut egos down to size.

If you can't justify the use of a given technology based on your real needs, drop it. Avoid any new technology that cannot be shown to generate more profit for your Profit Stream.

10 MOTIVATIONS—AND RISKS—OF IN-LICENSING

Reduce support, service, or operating costs

Licensing components will reduce service and support costs because the licensed technology has fewer bugs. Solutions licensed from hosted or SaaS providers will be cheaper to operate than solutions developed in-house.

Risk

Providing support for in-licensed technologies is one of the biggest challenges faced in creating a winning solution. While a mature component may have fewer bugs, in-licensing introduces new possibilities for errors.

Suppose you in-license three technologies: A database management system, a search engine, and a report writing tool. When your customer calls for support, you're going to have to determine the source of the problem and how it should be fixed.

There are several potential sources of the problem. It could be a previously undiscovered bug in your code or in any of the in-licensed components. It could be a bug in how you've integrated the component or in how the components interoperate with each other.

When the situation is tense, it can become quite easy for each vendor to blame the other. Your customer doesn't care about this infighting; they just want you to fix the problem. Make certain that you can properly support a component before choosing to in-license it.

The lack of control over operating costs means that changes outside of your control can significantly impair your profitability. Ethereum (ETH) is a decentralized, open-source blockchain with smart contract functionality. Financial applications built on top of ETH pay a "gas fee" for every transaction. When ETH was first released, these fees were cheap. Unfortunately, as ETH became more successful, the underlying blockchain technology that powered ETH (known as 'Proof of Work') made using ETH prohibitively expensive for most applications. Previously profitable solutions lost economic viability, causing significant disruptions to companies that relied on ETH. Fortunately, the ETH community changed the underlying technology in a manner that dramatically lowered gas fees, enabling ETH to once again become a financially viable technology for many applications.

Lower development costs

We saved the best for last. Done properly, licensing technology is cheaper than building it from scratch.

Risk

The claim that it is cheaper to license a technology instead of building what you need directly is usually based on estimating the cost of creating an ***equivalent replacement***.

Hold on! You may not need an equivalent replacement!

Instead of developing a full replacement, you may be able to limit scope by focusing on a much smaller set of functionality. This can substantially lower forecasted development costs, to the point where you are better served developing what you need instead of acquiring a license. License fees can enhance profitability by lowering your development costs. They can also hurt profitability when you acquire more functionality than is required.

Before deciding to in-license, do the necessary financial analysis to validate which approach is most financially attractive.

Contracts
Where the **action** is

The heart of any technology license is the contract that defines the terms and conditions associated with its use. Understanding how these terms enable or constrain your solution is essential to your Profit Stream. Before you can understand how the terms of in-licensing agreements and if the terms can affect your solution, you have to have an idea of what kinds of terms exist.

This section discusses terms commonly found in technology in-license agreements.

DEFINITIONS

A precise, legal description of all important items or terms referenced in the license agreement. Definitions of technology often go something like this:

Software means the object code software proprietary to {licensor} and listed on the pricing schedule.

OR

Software means the object code software proprietary to {licensor} and listed in Attachment A of this license agreement.

Pay attention to what is listed, because the definitions will often include specific version numbers, supported operating systems, hardware considerations, and so forth.

If you need support for something that isn't defined, you may be unable to obtain it.

If you're expecting upgrades and upgrades aren't covered in this term (or another term), you'll have to create another contract to pay your supplier to provide you with the needed or required technology.

USAGE OR GRANT

The manner in which the in-license technology can be used.

This section may be one of the longest in the agreement, as it often contains many of the other terms discussed here.

DURATION OR TERM

When the agreement begins and ends.

By working together, and by negotiating precise agreements about specific dates, business and technology can create a better overall result.

To illustrate, suppose that you agree to license a key technology for three years for an embedded system for an annual license fee. You estimate that it will take you:

Four months to integrate the technology

One month to perform final end-to-end field testing

Two months to distribute the solution through your channel

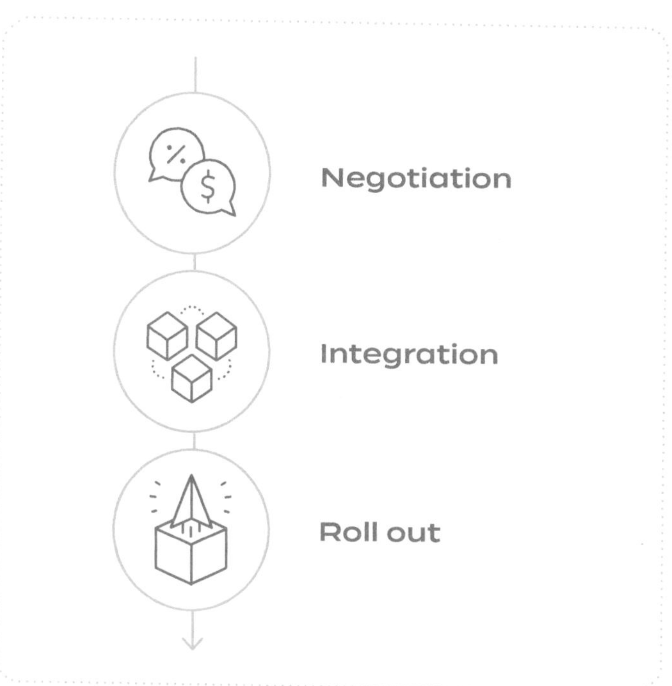

From your perspective, the best deal will allow development with the new technology to commence once the contract is signed but will delay payment of the initial annual license fee until the technology is actually delivered to customers, the reason being that until the technology is used by your customer it is merely a cost, with no positive economic value.

From the perspective of the technology provider, payments should begin when the contract is signed because they are not responsible for how long it takes you to integrate the technology and you're getting the benefits of it from the moment it is delivered. Who's right depends on your role in the negotiating process.

Most in-license agreements specify a variety of other important dates beyond the beginning and end of the agreement. If you don't understand these dates you can be headed for a lot of expensive trouble. Look for and keep track of the following dates:

Date	The date the agreement is executed.
Effective	Date the agreement is considered in effect.
Expiration	Date the agreement is ended. May be specified any number of ways, including an absolute date, or a calculated date, such as adding a fixed period of time to the effective date.
Payment	Dates when fees are due, usually listed along with payment terms (e.g., Net 30 or payments shall be made the fifteenth and the last day of each month).
Audit Periods	Period during which the licensor can audit how the technology is being used. Audit rights will be defined by other clauses, and audit rights can extend past the expiration date.
Termination Notice	Amount of time allowed to terminate the contract. It should be long enough to properly replace the terminated technology. Many agreements do not specify a long enough period of time, which puts the licensor (you) at a disadvantage when negotiating subsequent agreements.

Other

A wide variety of additional dates depending on license and contract requirements. The license might be required to report usage according to a well-defined schedule. OEM and partnership agreements may specify quarterly, biannual, or annual technology reviews. Timetables associated with new releases may be listed in the contract, along with penalties should these dates be missed.

A variant of the expiration date is the **"automatic renewal"** associated with many contracts. With an automatic renewal, once the contract has been signed it automatically renews unless you explicitly cancel it.

It is vitally important that you remain aware of these renewals. Circumstances change, and you may not want to re-up.

TERRITORY

The geographic territory where the in-licensed technology can be used. It is especially important to be careful of geographic restrictions because they can be very hard to honor in our internet-connected world.

EXCLUSIVITY

The degree to which the licensee agrees not to license the technology to anyone else. In general, exclusivity is hard to obtain, although there are ways to obtain it.

For example, suppose that you want to license a key technology but only intend to use it in Europe. It might be possible to obtain exclusivity for the European market. Exclusivity can sometimes be obtained for higher fees. In most circumstances you don't really need exclusivity, so it isn't something you should worry much about.

SPECIFIC USE

Specific use is a term that defines specific uses of the in-licensed technology. Examples:

A development license is used only for development purposes. A subsequent license will cover commercial use.

A quality assurance or verification license allows you to assess the potential technology before making a commitment.

A commercial use license gives you the green light to release your offering.

General terms are sometimes captured in one agreement while specific terms are captured in other, related agreements.

SUBLICENSE

The degree to which you (the licensee) can license the technology to a third party.

Sublicense rights are usually required for embedded technologies.

Suppose, for example, that you license a core technology for use in a hardware solution that will eventually be included in another hardware solution.

Chances are very good that you're going to license your solution to your customers, which requires a sublicense right from the technology's vendor.

TERMINATION

The many ways in which one party may terminate the contract are contained in the termination clause.

Here are some common termination clauses:

Breach

These clauses allow either party to withdraw from the agreement if there is a breach in performance. Performance breaches are usually specifically stated, such as failure to deliver by a specific date or failure of a system to meet defined processing requirements. Withdrawing from a contract because of breach is harder than it seems, because there is usually a process for recovery from the breach (the remedy). Enumerating potential breaches and their associated remedies is one of the more time-consuming aspects of contract negotiation.

For any reason—or no reason!

Many technology licensing contracts allow either party to withdraw from the agreement provided that they give the other party sufficient advance warning, ranging from as little as 30 days to as much as one year. Always try to negotiate the longest period of time possible.

Replacing an in-licensed technology with another one or with technology developed inhouse always takes longer than planned.

Financial performance or bankruptcy

The contract can be terminated if either party goes bankrupt or fails to meet defined financial criteria, if one party elects to drop support for the technology, or if there is a substantial change in control (such as when a competitor acquires a technology provider).

Although termination sections can get quite lengthy, it pays to read them carefully.

FEES / PAYMENT TERMS

The foundation of a valid contract is some form of consideration.

Remember:
Your technology provider is reading this book.

So you can expect they will develop a creative Profit Stream that will keep them in business - and you on your toes!

What is vitally important is that your technical architecture supports the payment terms required. If you are in-licensing a technology based on a transactional value exchange model, your technical architecture may also need to support transactions. And when the value exchange and/or business model required in the license is different from the one you use with your customers. Such differences can often be resolved only through careful negotiations, as explored later.

RENEWAL

Technology license agreements often contain one or more renewal clauses. These clauses may be automatic, which can actually cause you to pay more than you should, especially if your solution no longer needs the in-licensed technology. While convenient, proceed cautiously with automatic renewals.

DEPLOYMENT RESTRICTIONS

Some license agreements restrict one or more deployment options associated with the technology. For example, the vendor may require one agreement to use the technology for a customer deployment and a different agreement if the licensed technology is to be used in the cloud.

OTHER OR GENERAL RESTRICTIONS

In addition to the terms that define what you can do, license agreements also carefully define what you cannot do. As with the other terms, any of these restrictions can have an impact on your solution. One example is the very common restriction against any form of reverse engineering or modification of the licensed technology.

The practical effect of this kind of restriction can be fairly surprising. Suppose, for example, that one of your developers finds a bug in a licensed component. A restriction against reverse engineering may prevent them from analyzing the technology to identify the bug.

Let's say that this restriction doesn't exist, that you're facing a technology outage, and that you instruct your developers to research and fix the bug if possible. Assuming this is even possible, you may still be out of luck as a restriction against modifications means that you can't apply it. You may only be allowed to supply the fix to the vendor and wait for them to issue a patch or a new release. Since the best thing you can do is influence their development plans, you might be waiting a long time, unless they've hired Applied Frameworks to help them adopt Agile Software Development practices!

NONCOMPETE

Vendors may require that the solution you create does not compete with their own technology. In other words, you have to create a new offering. This may sound silly, but it prevents people from doing things like licensing a complete solution under the pretense of integrating the technology into a new product without really creating a new product. The net result would be a new solution that competes with the original vendor's solution.

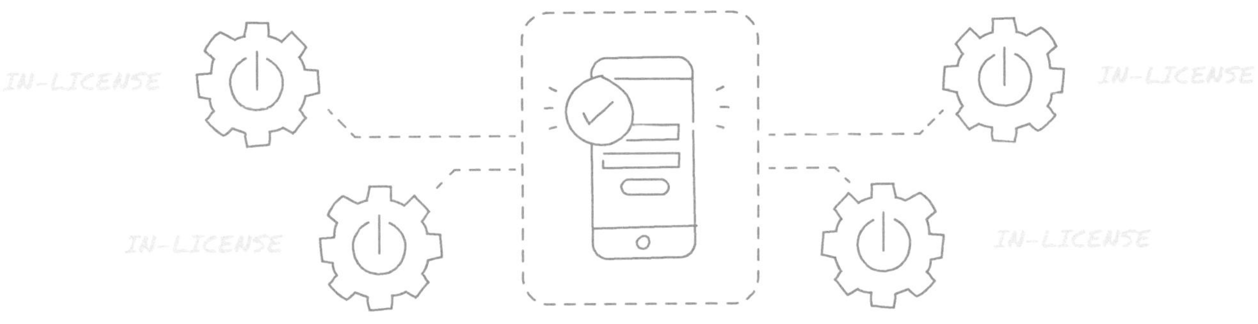

ACCESS TO SOURCE CODE

Technology agreements often specify that a copy of the source code be placed in escrow and given to the licensee should the licensor breach. In theory, this is great because it makes certain that you can get full and complete access to the technology you need.

In practice, however, it is often worthless. Suppose that the vendor does breach and you're given access to the source code. What then? Chances are good that you won't have the resources to absorb it.

MARKETING REQUIREMENTS

The agreement may obligate you to issue a press release or allow the licensee or the licensor (or both) the right to use the name or corporate logo of the other on their website.

Any number of other marketing-related requirements associated with the technology may be laid out, so read these sections carefully. Marketing and branding requirements can mean nasty surprises for your solution.

When business models collide, negotiations ensue.

Before you actually license any technology, you have to make certain that your business model is **compatible** with your provider's business model.

If the two are not compatible, you're going to have to **negotiate** an acceptable agreement. These choices can have a significant impact on your underlying technical architecture.

Suppose, for example, that you're building an enterprise application and you want to base your business model on concurrent users.

You want to integrate a search engine, for which your preferred vendor will charge an annual fee. While the business models are different, this situation can be fairly easily resolved. If the annual fee is low enough, you can just pay it. If it is too high, you might be able to negotiate something more acceptable and, again, pay it.

A more complex strategy is to negotiate a license fee based on the projected revenue from your concurrent users, with a floor (a guaranteed minimum amount you'll pay) and a ceiling (the maximum amount you'll pay).

You can pay the floor to gain access to the technology and, at the end of the license term (one year), provide the licensor with a statement that details your actual revenue and the amount of money you owe.

This isn't an easy choice because it requires you to disclose potentially sensitive information to your provider (such as the number of concurrent users and your annual revenue). Along the way, your technical architecture or, more likely, your back-office systems will need to be checked to ensure that you can **meet your license payments.**

Let's invert the above example and see what happens. In this case, your business model is based on an annual license and your technology provider's business model is based on concurrent users. You can resolve these incompatibilities by creating a mutually agreeable estimate for the number of concurrent users accessing your system for a given annual license, by negotiating with your technology provider to accept an annual license instead of charging by concurrent user, or by offering your provider's technology as an "optional" module and licensing it as a concurrent user option. If you really need this technology and you can see no realistic way to make it an optional module, and if the provider is adamant about maintaining its business model, you may have no other choice but to convert to a concurrent user business model.

The point is that you must understand the business models of all your technology suppliers and how they relate to your own.

A special case of business model negotiation is required when you change technology vendors.

Let's say that you've created an enterprise application and have licensed a search engine from technology vendor A. Sometime later, for whatever reason, you decide to change to technology vendor B. Along with the fees associated with new systems sold using vendor B's technology, you're going to have to calculate the fees associated with upgrading from vendor A's technology to vendor B's technology. Depending on your licensing agreements, you may or may not be able to charge your customers for the upgrade and/or change.

Business leaders must model the complete costs associated with changing technology vendors, including the cost of converting the installed base.

Honoring **license agreements.**

Just about anything you can think of has, or will be, specified in a license agreement. Examples of issues that are commonly covered in license agreements that are likely to affect your solution include the following:

DEFINITION OF TECHNICAL TERMS

This is probably the biggest area of license compliance and one that architects should be familiar with.

- *Do all the definitions reflect the actual solution under development?*
- *Are the version numbers in the contract correct?*
- *What about the defined operating systems and operating environments?*
- *Do you have the rights to use the solution in the manner envisioned by your business plan? More specifically, can you operate the in-licensed technology in a way that supports all your deployment architectures?*
- *Can you fully embed the technology in your solution?*
- *What is the degree or nature of the embedding?*
- *Are there any geographic or export restrictions?*

SUPPORT

Who fields what support questions? What kind of information must you capture and forward to the third party? License agreements can get very precise about the support information required, affecting both your architecture and other corporate processes.

APIs

Can you simply expose any third-party APIs provided in the license agreement? Chances are you can't, and trivially wrapping third-party APIs with your own API won't cut it. Most license agreements require you to substantially enhance the functionality of an API before it can be exposed (whatever that means).

BRANDING

Do you have to include visible or direct attribution of the third-party component? Consider the ubiquity of the "Intel Inside" marketing campaign to get a sense of just how important third-party technology suppliers consider such attributions.

Managing **in-licensed** technology.

A proven technique for managing in-licensed technology is to create a "**wrapper**" or "**adapter**" for it. Instead of programming to the API provided by the vendor, you create an abstraction that you can replace if needed.

Wrappers may make it easier to replace one vendor's technology with another's, but they aren't without their drawbacks.

Wrapping frequently introduces a least-common-denominator approach, in which the development team cannot use superior but proprietary technologies.

WRAPPING TAKES TIME AND MUST BE TESTED.

If the in-licensed technology is never replaced, or replacement is extremely unlikely, then the additional expense associated with wrapping may not be justified.

The decision to insulate or protect your solution from direct access to an in-licensed component must be made with the support and involvement of business and technical leaders.

Open Source Licensing

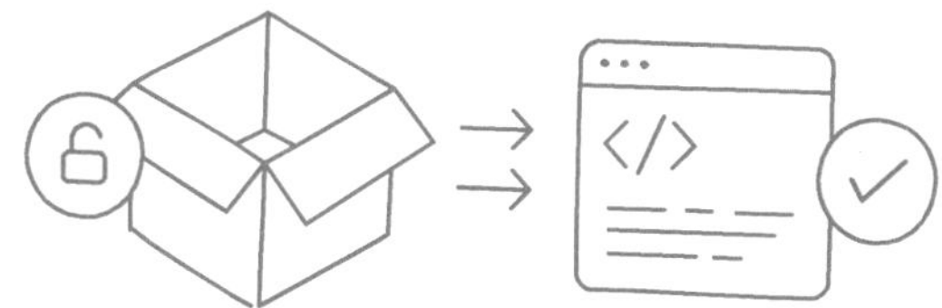

Open Source software presents a wide variety of options.

Using key open source technologies within your solutions can provide substantial benefits to you and your customers.

This section assumes that you've evaluated a given Open Source technology against your technical requirements. It is neither a blanket endorsement nor an indictment of the quality or appropriateness of a given technology but merely accepts that, for whatever reason, you want to use an Open Source technology as part of your overall solution.

The first step is to read the specific license that governs your technology, as all open-source licenses are not equal. It may seem that the differences are minor, but they are the stuff that lawyers love to charge for!

When you're finished reading the license, look for the sections that govern how the licensed technology can be incorporated into other technologies—this is likely to be your most important area of concern.

Your fears are likely to be unfounded as it is entirely permissible to incorporate a portion of an Open Source technology into your solution (see also the GNU Lesser General Public License), provided that you maintain the same rights for the incorporated technology and that you meet the other terms of the specific license.

It is beyond the scope of this book to provide detailed legal advice (we're not lawyers), but practically this means that you can use a variety of Open Source technologies to create a new, for-profit work. This is an advantage, and Open Source strategies should be considered as a valid option for your Profit Stream.

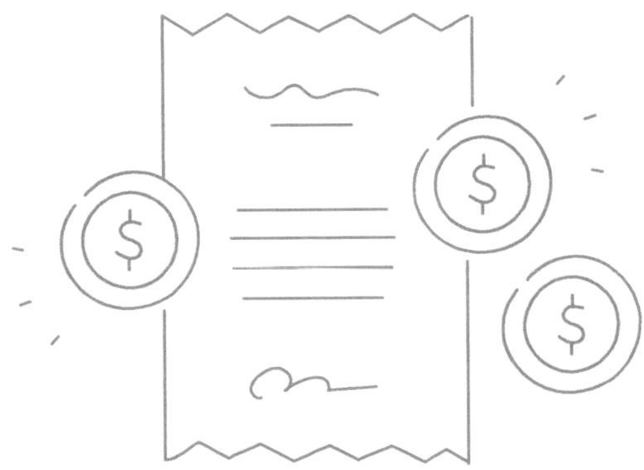

License **Fees**

Third-party technologies come with a variety of license fees. A good way to think about these fees is that **anything you license represents the business model of some technology provider.**

As a result, you may have to deal with any of the previously described business models or, for that matter, any business model the vendor has identified as being useful. Fortunately, technology providers tend to limit the business models they use to a manageable number of options.

The most common approaches, and their likely impact on your solution, are described next.

PREPAID FEES

In this arrangement you pay an agreed-upon fee for the time-based access or usage of the technology, whether or not you actually use it. Such an arrangement usually results in minimum impact on your solution, as you are given maximum flexibility in integrating the technology into your system. The fee must be included in the solution cost estimates provided to justify initial development and in the ongoing costs associated with maintaining the system.

USAGE-BASED FEES

In this arrangement you pay an amount based on some measured usage of the in-licensed technology, often with a minimum payment required to access it (metering). Such an arrangement always has an impact on your solution because you must ensure your compliance with the license agreement. Specifically, you must make certain that your solution can capture the metering data. Clearly, it is advantageous to negotiate a usage model that is conveniently implemented.

As described earlier, when the fees are variable the in-license technology vendor will often require a minimum payment, referred to as a floor. You'll want a ceiling, or the maximum amount you'll have to pay—which the vendor will resist.

The strength of the technology supplier, the kind of technology being provided, the quality of the relationship, and the overall volume of the expected deal are all factors that play a part in negotiating usage-based fees.

TRAINING/DEVELOPMENT COSTS

You may be able to obtain free or discounted training or educational materials, preferential access to support or development organizations, or special review meetings in which you can meet with key representatives of the technology provider to make certain your needs are being met.

Whatever the licensing arrangement offered by your provider, actual costs must be used for proper financial modeling.

Simply put, too many license agreements, or even just one with onerous terms, can seriously erode any profit margins you expect for a solution. In extreme cases the wrong fee structure can actually kill a project.

PERFORMANCE

In this arrangement there are no up-front fees to license the technology; instead, you pay the provider a percentage of the gross or net revenue gained from its use. Get ready to spend time clearly defining the meaning of performance, as this fee structure must be precisely defined. Keep in mind the following as you negotiate. You'll want:

Milestone Payments

Be wary of the following costly mistake: licensing a key technology from a vendor, paying a very large up-front fee, and subsequently failing to deliver their technology to the market. A better approach is to base fees on key milestones that represent revenue you're going to receive from the use of the technology. Say that you've decided to license a core technology based on an annual fee (the usage fee). During initial development, when the technology is being incorporated into your solution and you're not making any money, the most you should pay is a small access or development fee. The next payment, and typically the largest, should be upon release or launch of your solution. The final payment may be due after the solution has been in the market for some months.

Protection from Product Obsolescence

Business leaders need to know that technology providers are going to be able to support their needs for as long as necessary. Choosing providers who are sustainably profitable is a good start, and aligning roadmaps with strategic providers is a best practice.

Protected Pricing

Whatever fee structure is chosen, business leaders should try to negotiate such provisions as capped price increases, favored pricing plans (in which no other licensor will be given better terms than the licensee; should such better terms be offered, they will also be automatically applied to the licensee), and volume or usage discounts.

* *The majority of this content is derived from Beyond Software Architecture, with a smile from the author.*

COMPLIANCE BLOCK

RELATIONSHIP SUSTAINABILITY

COMPLIANCE FOCUS

Compliance

Compliance is the process by which a company adheres to imposed or chosen **laws, regulation, standards, and agreements.**
We'll cover:

- → *The risks and rewards of compliance*
- → *Systems thinking and compliance*
- → *Techniques to integrate compliance into a Profit Stream*

Compliance is the process by which a company adheres to imposed or chosen laws, regulation, standards, and agreements.

The severity of non-compliance varies based on the industry, the nature of the solution, and the social or economic costs of failure.

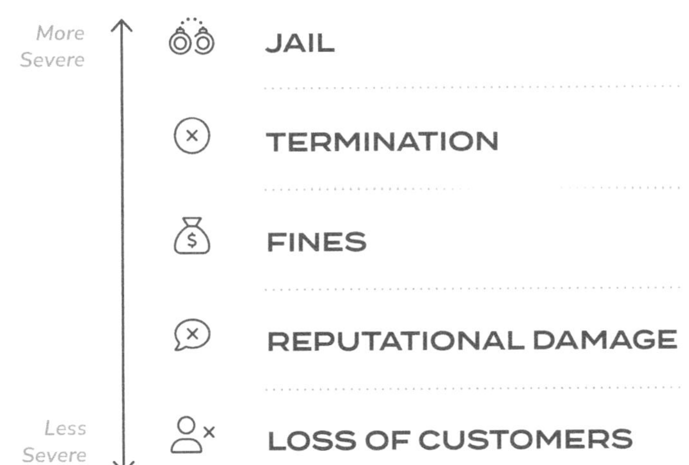

Effective compliance strategies provide a number of benefits.

Operating necessity

Solutions designed for healthcare, educational, financial, and safety related markets must be compliant with applicable laws and regulations within a jurisdiction.

While not a law, some industry standards are considered so important as to govern behavior as a law.

PCI-OSS and SOC standards are examples of such standards.

Continue with Regulations ⟶

Regulations:

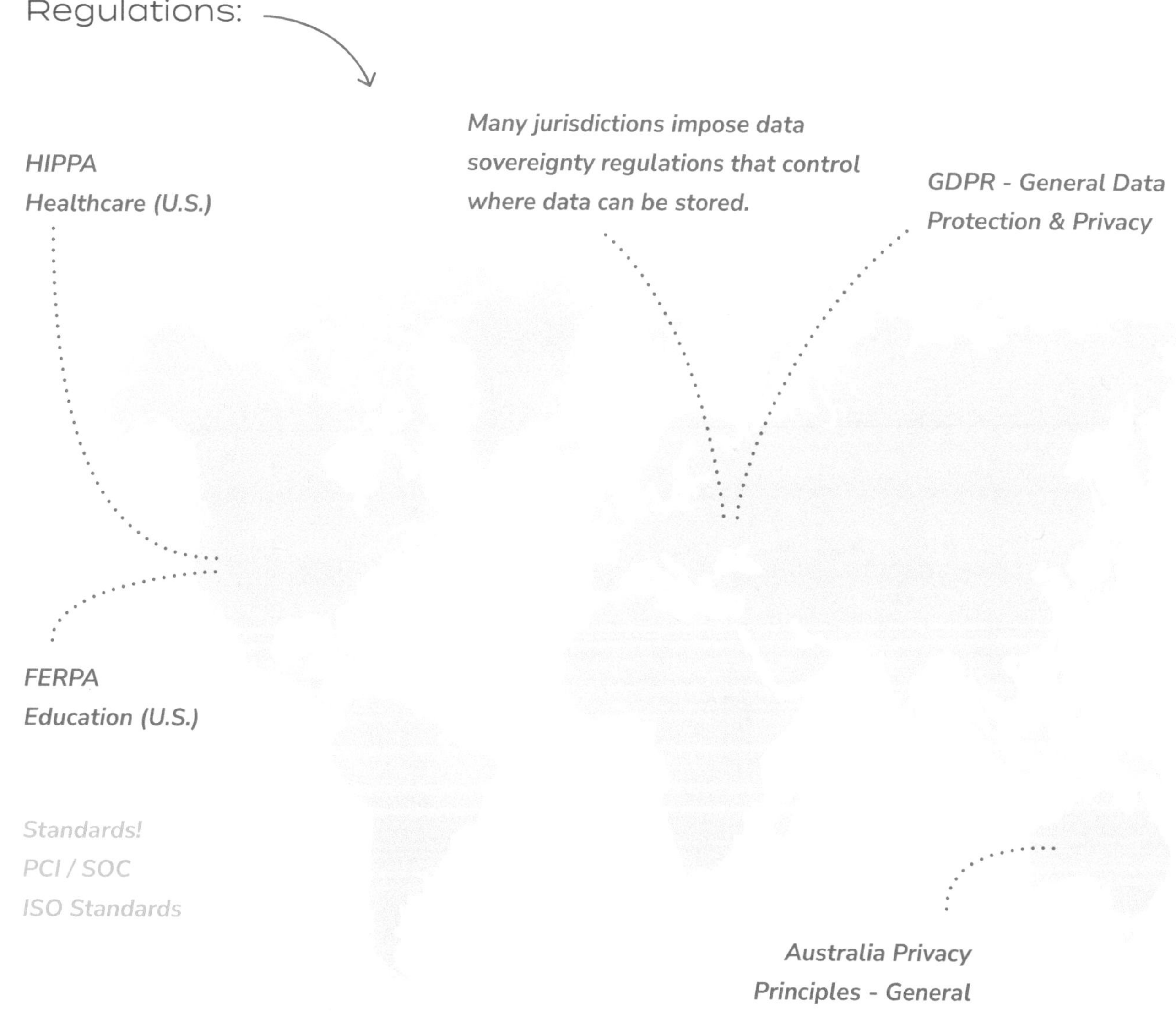

These are just a few examples. Business leaders must do the work required to determine **which laws and regulations apply to their solutions.**

Access to new markets

Voluntary compliance with regulations and standards can give solution providers access to new markets.

- We can target children if we're COPPA compliant.

AutoDesk created TinkerCad, a free version of Autocad that complies with the U.S. COPPA regulation. TinkerCad enables AutoDesk to help children learn design skills and creates future customers for AutoDesk!

- We can target EU customers if we're GDPR compliant.

Conteneo retained and expanded within the EU through GDPR compliance.

+ ***ACCESSIBILITY.*** *We can target older voters by following W3C Accessibility guidelines.*

Competitive advantage

Providers who develop solutions that comply with multiple standards can gain a significant competitive advantage over competitors.

Our flexible rules engine enables us to create a driver compliance solution that spans the Americas.

In order to determine which segments value compliance, model each aspect of compliance as part of your customer benefit analysis and Solution Benefit Map.

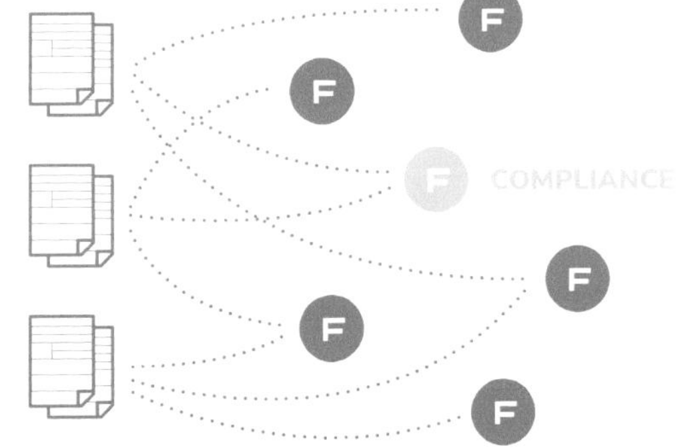

Improvements to intangible attributes

Compliance enhances such intangible attributes as trust in your brand because compliance signifies that the solution, and the manner in which it was built, and/or the results it creates, meet specific external criteria. In some cases, compliance is verified through a third party, further increasing our trust.

Use your Whole Product Model to help determine the degree of competitive advantage.

Change this: GDPR compliance is an expected part of a solution for European customers.

Compliance features that are unique to your offering or otherwise differentiated, create opportunities for competitive advantage.

Customers have learned to trust solutions certified by Underwriters Laboratories.

Parents trust websites and solutions certified by KidSAFE or iKeepSafe as being COPPA compliant.

SaaS vendors that comply with Cisco's Cloud/Application Service Provider Remetiation (CASPR) have passed an extensive security audit that increases trust with corporate IT shops.

Risk reduction

Business leaders can reduce risks through the selection and implementation of applicable laws and regulations.

Providers of mission or safety critical solutions can minimize damages through the definition of, and adherence to development process compliant with applicable standards.

Improved technical choices

While many compliance choices require an initial investment, the technical choices required to implement compliance can create unexpected future benefits.

Developing and following modern, agile-centric processes for solution development can increase solution delivery and quality.

Lower operating costs

It is typically cheaper to implement compliance policies than to fight them.

OWASP.IO defines a set of security standards for SaaS solutions. It is cheaper to implement compliance with OWASP.IO than pay to clean up a data or security breach that OWASP.IO compliance could have prevented.

Compliance & Systems Thinking

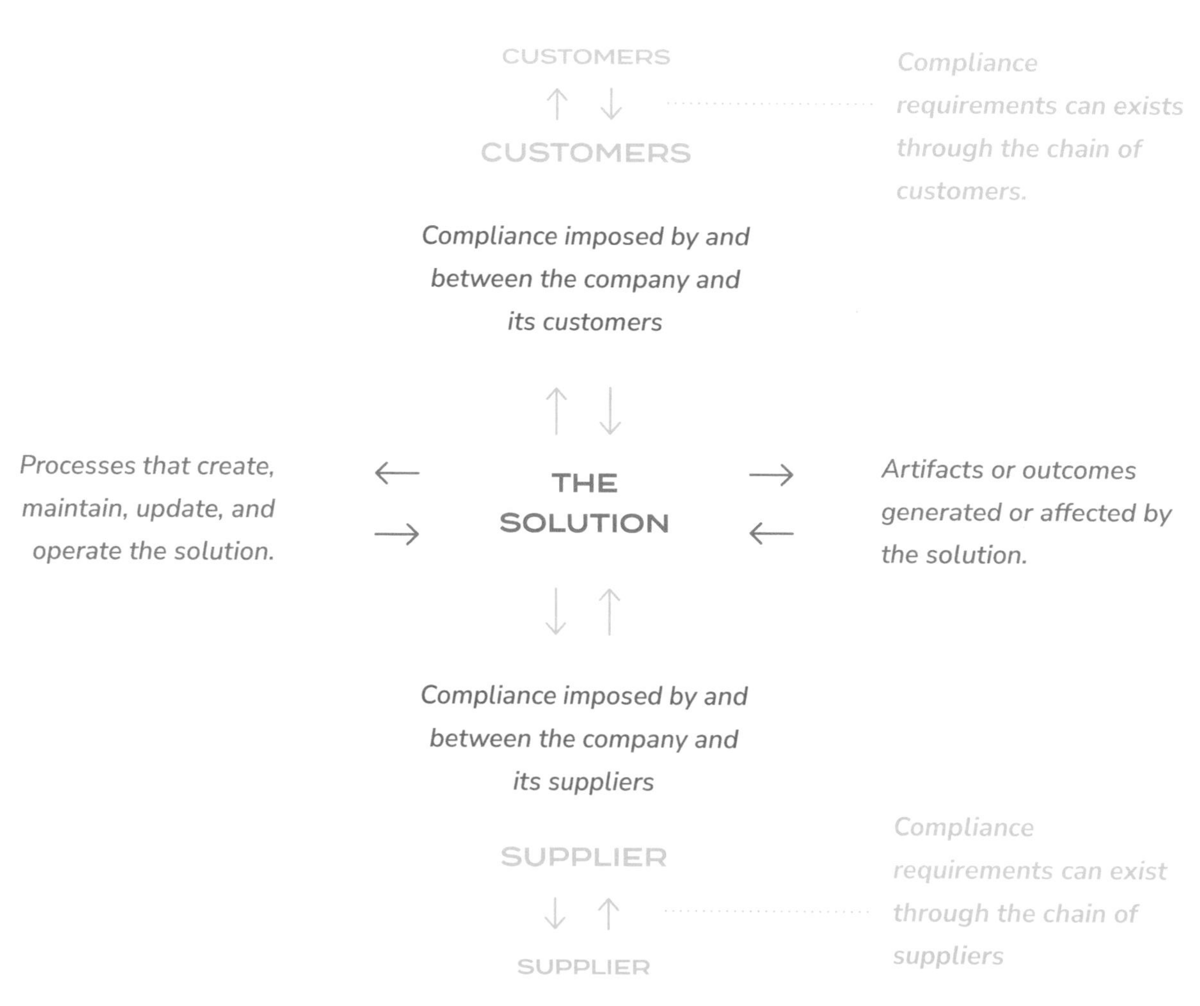
CUSTOMERS
CUSTOMERS
Compliance requirements can exists through the chain of customers.
Compliance imposed by and between the company and its customers
Processes that create, maintain, update, and operate the solution.
THE SOLUTION
Artifacts or outcomes generated or affected by the solution.
Compliance imposed by and between the company and its suppliers
SUPPLIER
SUPPLIER
Compliance requirements can exist through the chain of suppliers

Any or all of these entities may be subject to compliance requirements.

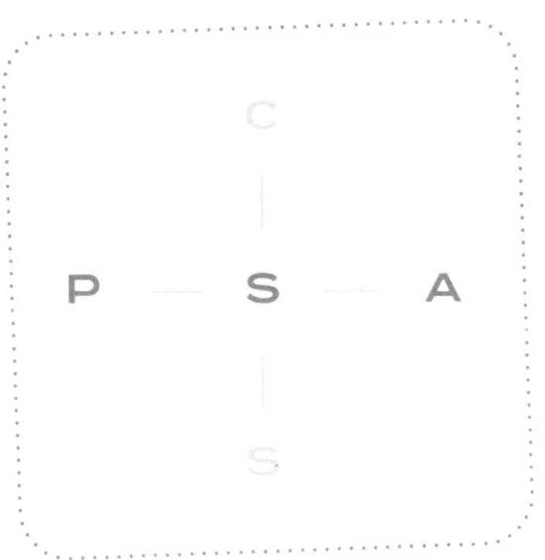

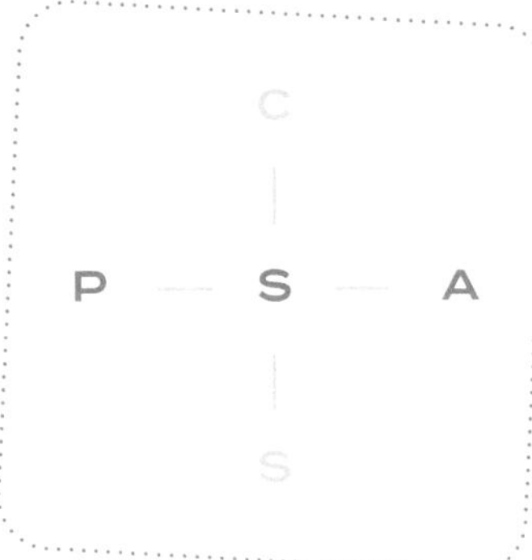

All entities may be subject to industry-wide laws or standards such as HIPAA, GDPR, PCI.

You may wish to impose certain regulations on your customers.

Certain market segments may require compliance with such standards as the Web3 Accessibility guidelines.

Certain industries, such as medical devices, may have unique process standards like ISO13485.

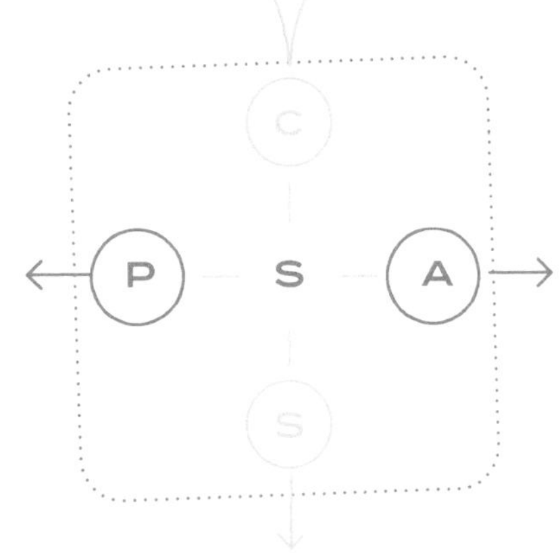

Specific artifacts may be required to comply with standards related to data output, like the SCORM specification for sharing data in learning management systems (LMS).

Suppliers want the provider to comply with their agreements.

Integrating **Compliance** into the **Profit Stream**

The following process enables business leaders to integrate compliance into their Profit Stream.

The compliance ecosystem is dynamic. Your solution will be impacted by updated or new laws, regulations, standards, and agreements over the course of its existence!

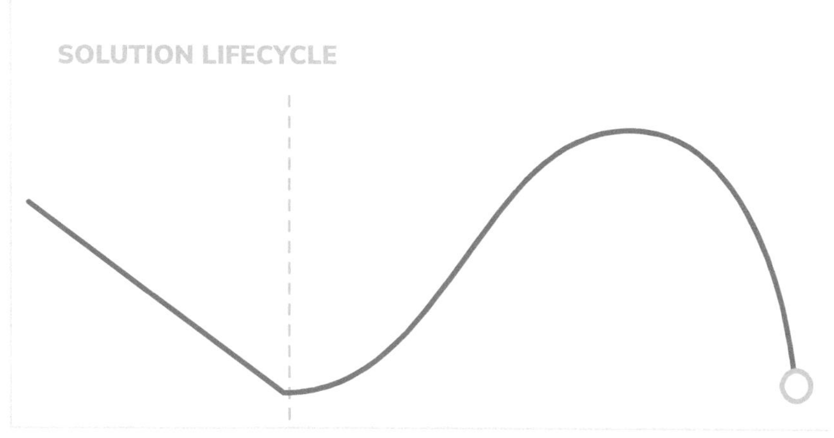

Compliance is part of every stage in the Solution Lifecycle, including the end.

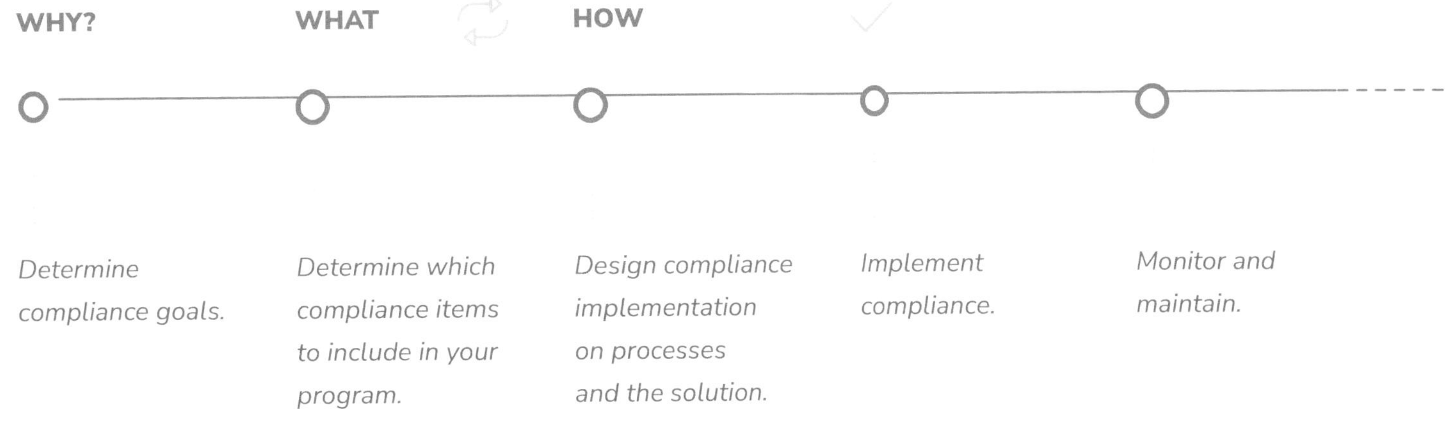
WHY?
WHAT
HOW
Determine compliance goals.
Determine which compliance items to include in your program.
Design compliance implementation on processes and the solution.
Implement compliance.
Monitor and maintain.

Avoid complicating compliance

Simple statements and straight forward responses are typically the best choices!

EXAMPLE.

We are building a game for kids, so let's make sure we are COPPA and GDPR compliant.

WHY?

Determine compliance goals

Using the motivations described early, determine your compliance goals. Develop the underlying economic rational, and include any adjustments to your customer and Solution ROI models.

If needed, include the economic risks associated with non-compliance.

Compliance can be part of your Profit Engine.

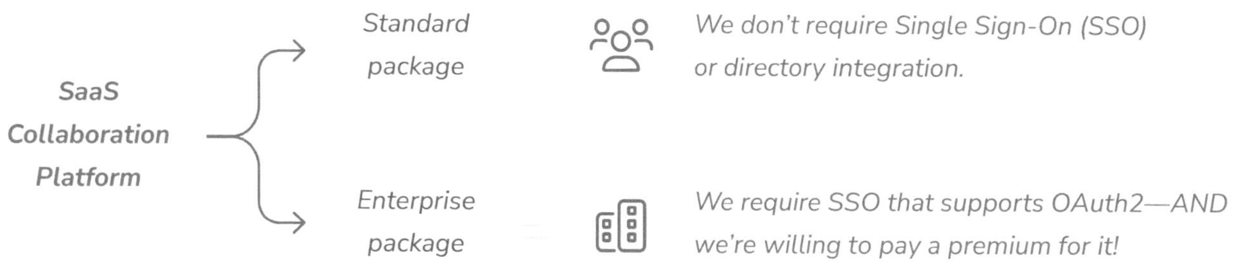

SaaS Collaboration Platform
Standard package
We don't require Single Sign-On (SSO) or directory integration.
Enterprise package
We require SSO that supports OAuth2—AND we're willing to pay a premium for it!

Because many segments care about compliance, make certain your compliance programs are included in marketing campaigns and sales processes.

WHAT?

Determine what is included

Determine which laws, regulations, standards, and agreements that will be included in your compliance program.

There is no substitute for domain knowledge and experience, so be certain to survey your customers and your target market.

Engage your target market to understand compliance requirements.

B2C *Markets may not know or understand their compliance needs.*

B2P / B2B *Markets will often provide detailed lists of compliance requirements upon request.*

WHY? **WHAT?**

Values *Purpose* *Mission*

*The **WHY** and the **WHAT** of compliance programs are part of the DNA of your company.*

The most notable examples of compliance are the sad examples of non-compliance:

- *Banks that violate privacy laws*
- *Social media companies that ignore regulations, designed to protect children*
- *Gig economy companies that ignore labor laws*

Design **compliance** implementation

The specific implementation of compliance is a design choice that strives to meet the goals and needs of all stakeholders.

How do we want to implement the GDPR right to erase ('right to be forgotten')?

How will we evolve our solution to remain in compliance with PCI-DSS?

What changes do we need to make in our technical architecture to fulfill the reporting requirements of our new partner agreement?

Consider...

Process changes

Training for staff, customers, suppliers, and partners

IMPLEMENTATION

Timelines and adjustments needed for customers, to integrate your solution into their compliance programs

Reporting and remittance requirements

Implement **compliance**

Implementation of compliance includes necessary validation and verification activities, not just once, but continuously, across every release.

WHO VERIFIES?

Verification can be performed by you, your customers, or third parties.

Who do you trust?

Who do your customers trust?

Who do regulators trust?

Who might a court trust?

Verification is another example where intangible attributes such as brand can dominate our decision-making.

A 'low cost' verification service might 'cut corners' and put a provider at financial risk.

MONITOR AND MAINTAIN

Business leaders must implement policies and practices to monitor and maintain compliance.

Ensure your roadmaps include planned updates to maintain or enhance your compliance.

Have you integrated compliance activities into your processes? How do you know? How would your customers or auditors verify this?

SECTION 03

Applications

ations

There are two main applications of the **Profit Stream Canvas**

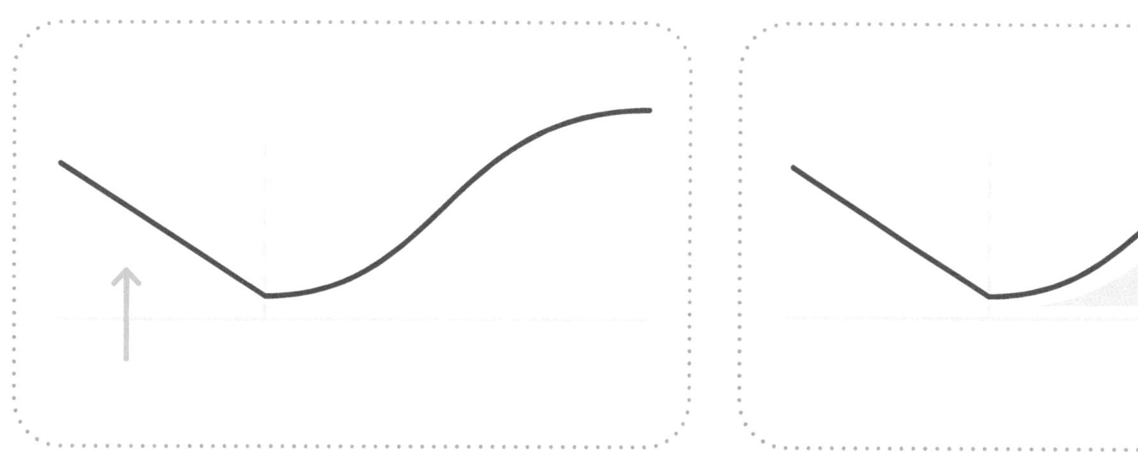

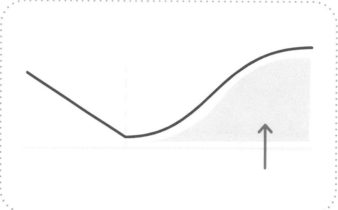

New Solution Development

Common examples:

- Startups creating their first solution
- Established companies creating a new solution within a portfolio
- Established companies replacing old solutions with a software-enabled solution
- Spinouts / Carve-outs—Existing companies offering an internally developed solution to external customers

Solution Lifecycle Management

Common examples:

- Adjusting prices
- Adjusting packages
- Fine-tuning profit engines
- Responding to competitive threats

In both applications, the use of the canvas follows a **similar pattern**:

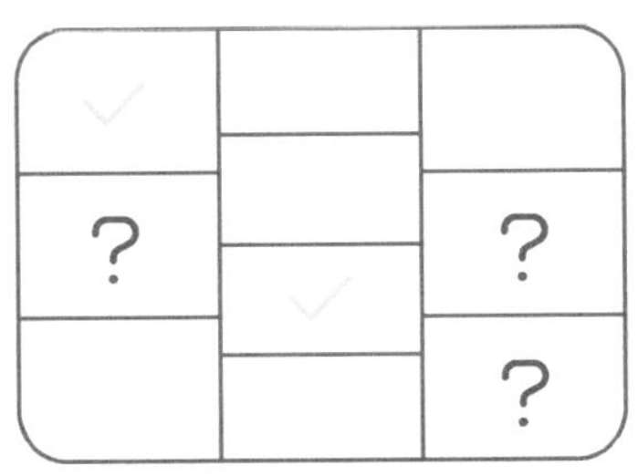

Identify what aspect of the canvas needs to be added or modified.

Some choices constrain future choices. Some choices are dependent and others are interdependent.

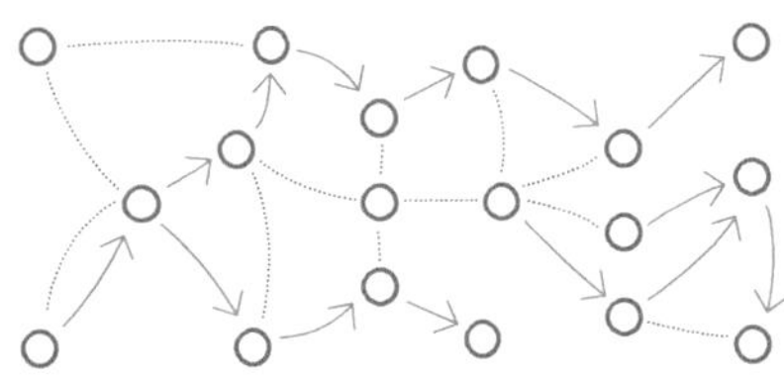

Develop choices, exploring their impact and effects on other parts of the framework, continuing the process until...

...all elements of the system are working together to enhance your Profit Stream.

This process is informed by data, experiments, and the wisdom of the participating business leaders.

Using the Profit Stream Canvas helps ensure you've made a complete set of choices.

"Where should I start?...
?
!
...If I change this, these other things must change"

Making choices in a causal system can feel overwhelming. Here are four strategies for managing this complexity.

1 Pick a block and explore its impact on other blocks.

A supplier has announced that they will no longer support a key component of your solution.

Start with the Solution Licenses and explore how this change affects the other blocks.

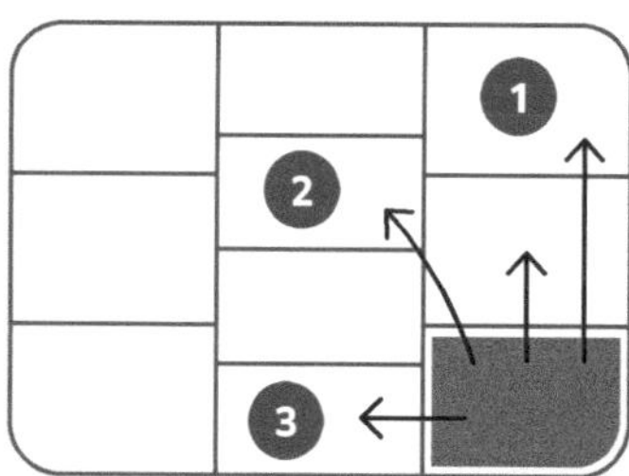

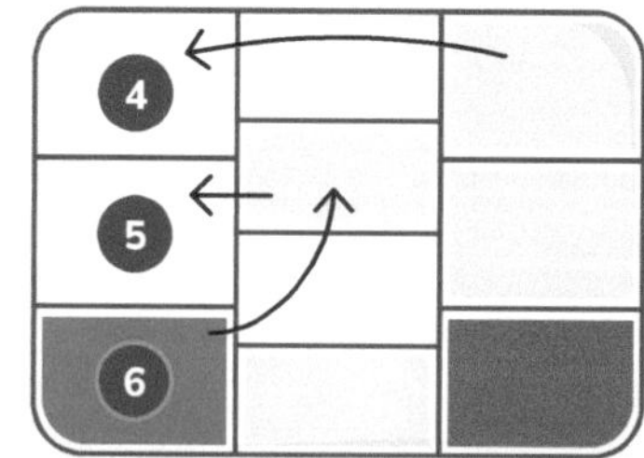

Your specific context or scenario will dictate where you start. Later in the book we will share patterns that help you navigate the system.

1. Your solution will change, Solution ROI may change
2. Your pricing specifics may change
3. Your compliance choices may change
4. Changing your solution may impact target customers or packaging choices
5. Changing pricing may cause updates to your Customer ROI models
6. Customer license agreements may constrain price or packaging choices

Explore the system by exploring the impact of provisional choices

No choice

No choice for a given block means that other blocks will be the primary determinant of this block or that it is largely independent from other blocks.

Preliminary choice

Preliminary choices enable business leaders to explore the Profit Stream as a system.

Working draft

A working draft provides a final opportunity to explore the choices.

Release

A release of a solution means that all elements of the Profit Stream Canvas were defined. The first release represents a baseline of choices that will evolve with the solution across the Solution Lifecycle.

Example:

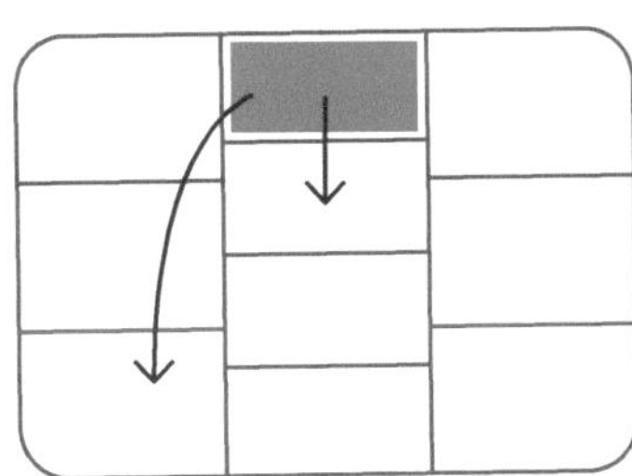

The Value Exchange Model strongly influences the price structure and the Customer License.

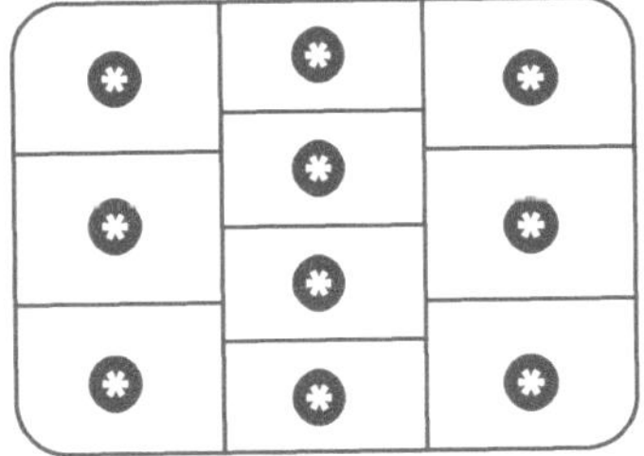

Preliminary choices enable different functional areas to explore, understand, and design the choices as a system.

You're welcome to change this scale. Just keep it as simple as possible.

Reverse the direction of a relationship to create new possibilities.

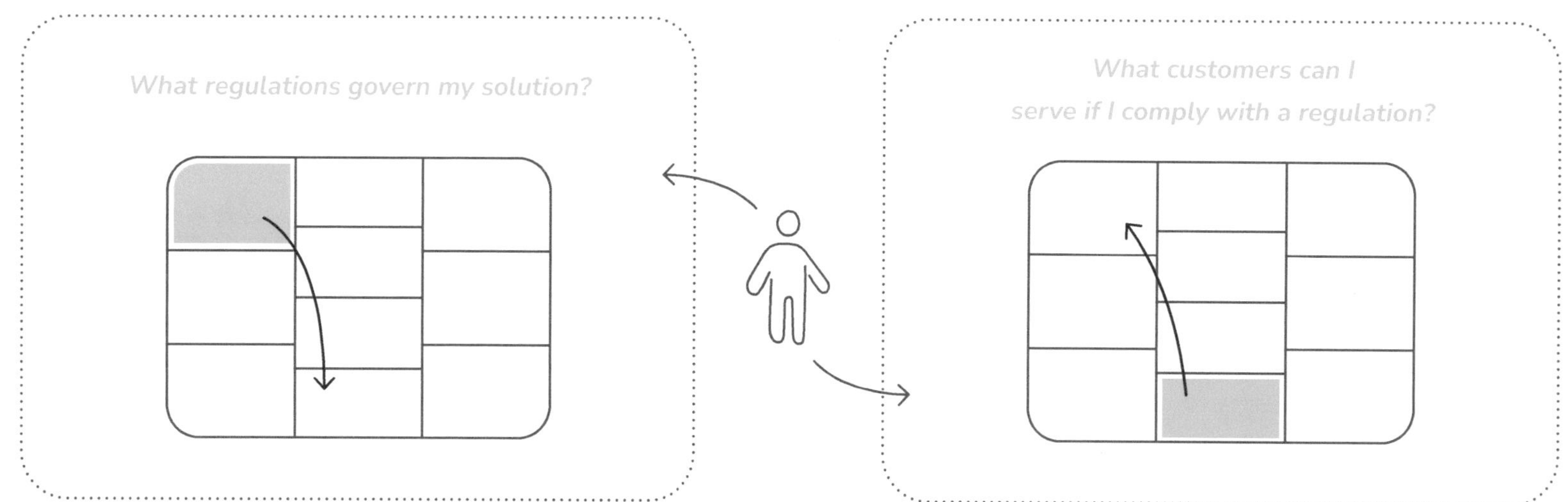

What regulations govern my solution?
What customers can I serve if I comply with a regulation?

All perspectives are helpful

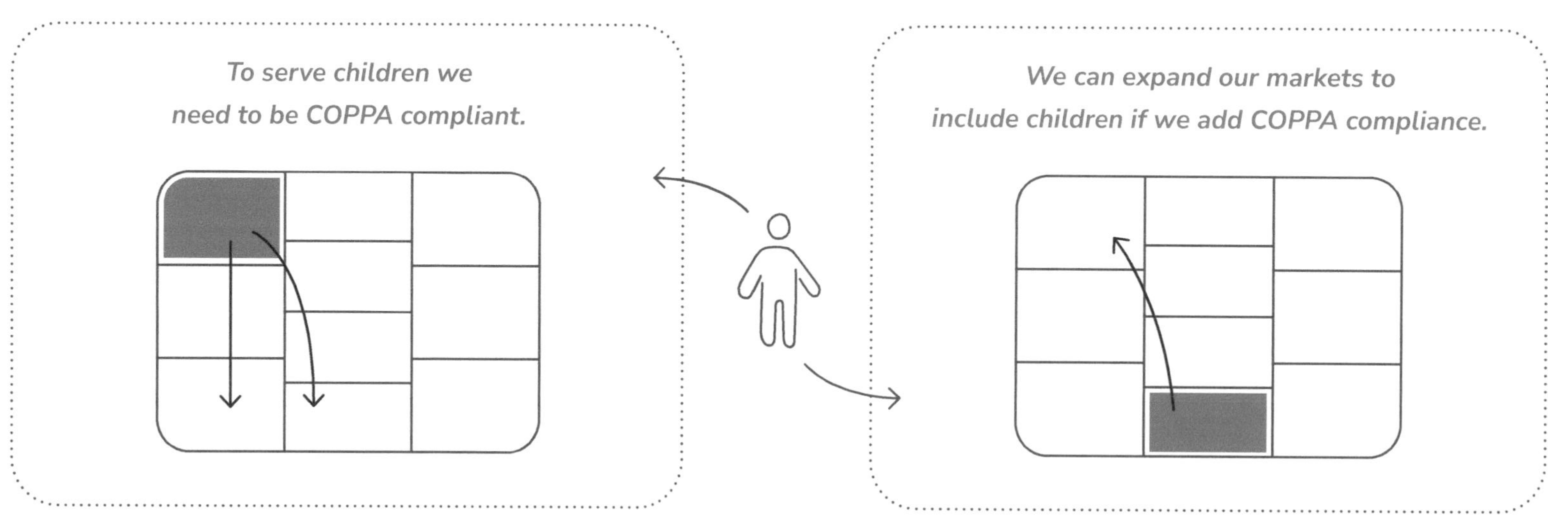

To serve children we need to be COPPA compliant.
We can expand our markets to include children if we add COPPA compliance.

Use multiple canvases to explore systemic change.

A solution that must address a performance gap, such as a forecasted revenue shortfall, should isolate and explore several options.

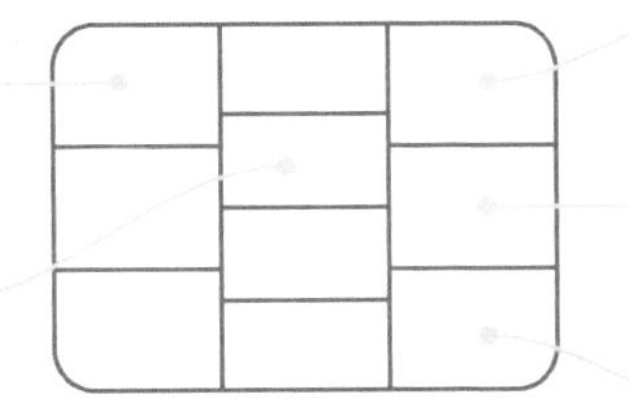

Have we missed aspects of value?
Can we change pricing?
Can we increase value by adding features?
Can we lower internal costs?
Can we lower supplier costs?

Capturing the answers to these questions in separate canvases enables business leaders to explore options before finalizing their choices.

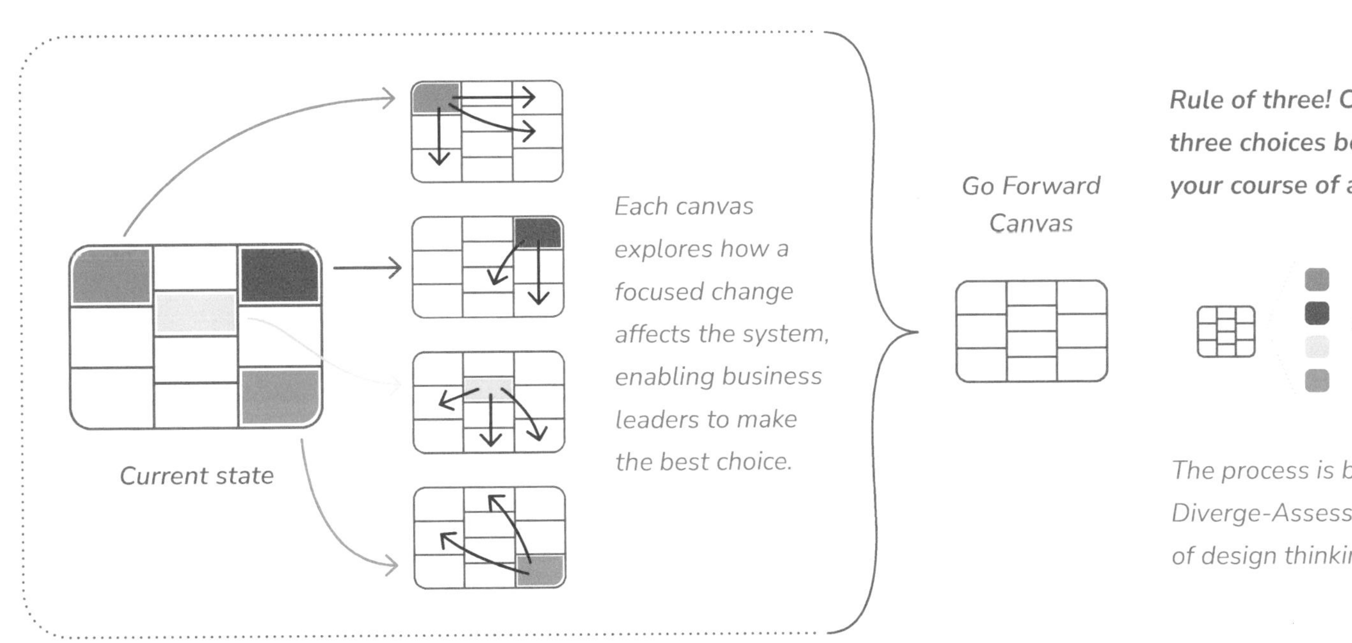

Current state
Each canvas explores how a focused change affects the system, enabling business leaders to make the best choice.
Go Forward Canvas

Rule of three! Create at least three choices before finalizing your course of action.

The process is based on the Diverge-Assess-Converge model of design thinking.

Checking the System

As you develop your canvas, it is helpful to periodically check your work to ensure the system is operating as a system. Adopting a different perspective can help.

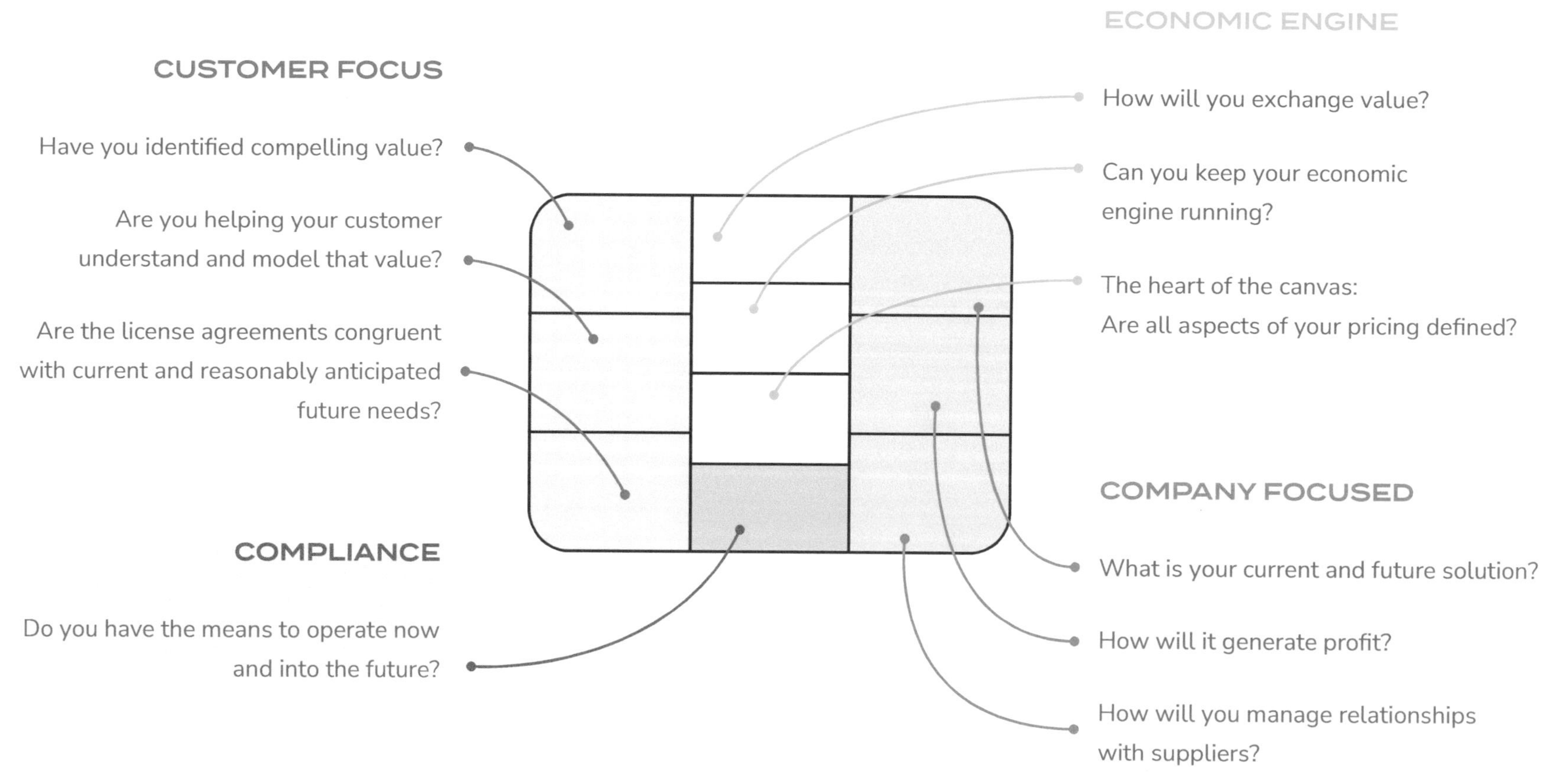

CUSTOMER FOCUS
Have you identified compelling value?
Are you helping your customer understand and model that value?
Are the license agreements congruent with current and reasonably anticipated future needs?
COMPLIANCE
Do you have the means to operate now and into the future?
ECONOMIC ENGINE
How will you exchange value?
Can you keep your economic engine running?
The heart of the canvas:
Are all aspects of your pricing defined?
COMPANY FOCUSED
What is your current and future solution?
How will it generate profit?
How will you manage relationships with suppliers?

PRACTICE, PRACTICE, PRACTICE!

There is an old joke about Carnegie Hall, the famous music venue in New York City. The joke goes something like this:

A tourist visiting NYC was standing on the corner looking at a map. A native New Yorker walks up and the tourist asks "How do you get to Carnegie Hall?" Without missing a step, the New Yorker replies, "Practice, practice, practice".

Learning how to design **Profit Streams** is a skill that gets better with practice.

Practice on competitors

Reverse-engineer how your competitors have designed their Profit Streams. What can you do better?

Practice on other businesses

Reverse-engineering the Profit Streams of other companies can spur your creativity, help you identify investment opportunities, and enable you to expand your career.

Practice together

Designing a Profit Stream is a team sport - so practice as a team. What are you learning about your colleages? How can you better leverage their unique strengths? How can they better leverage your abilities?

PROFIT STREAMS FOR STARTUPS

Designing a Profit Stream for a Startup starts by capturing the vision of the founder(s).

Solo entrepreneur

"I want to create a low-cost SaaS solution to help low-income students secure jobs in their own country, or sponsored internships in wealthier countries".

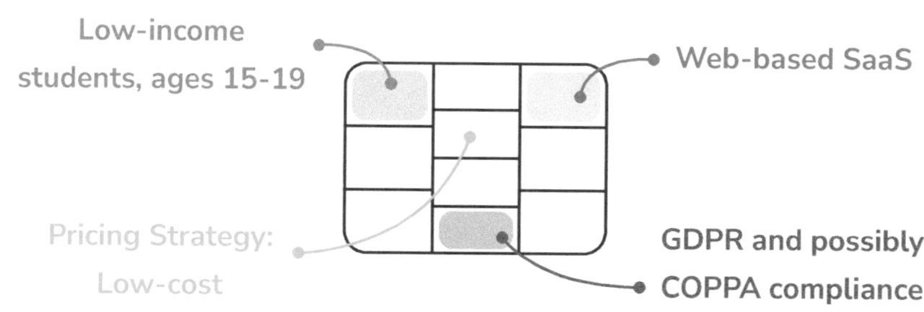

A founder's vision can emerge in a moment of inspiration or through years of hard work.

Research team in a University starting a new company

"We have developed a new software controlled hardware device to remove microplastics from oceans and lakes".

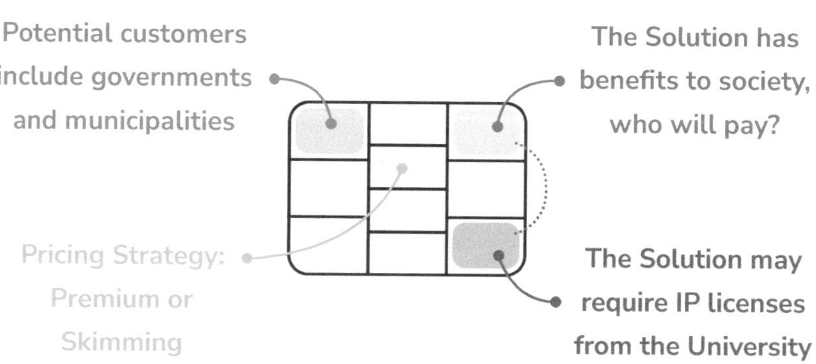

It is rare that the vision will encompass all aspects of the canvas, and that's OK!
Your job is to use the canvas to help you launch a sustainable business.

Three patterns capture the origin story of startups creating software-enabled solutions.

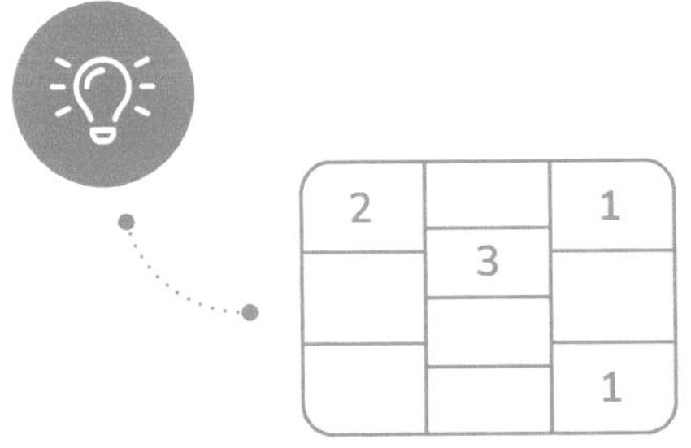

TECHNOLOGY-CENTRIC

A novel technology, often created through basic research, or a set of substantially improved technologies, enable founding teams to envision new solutions to old problems.

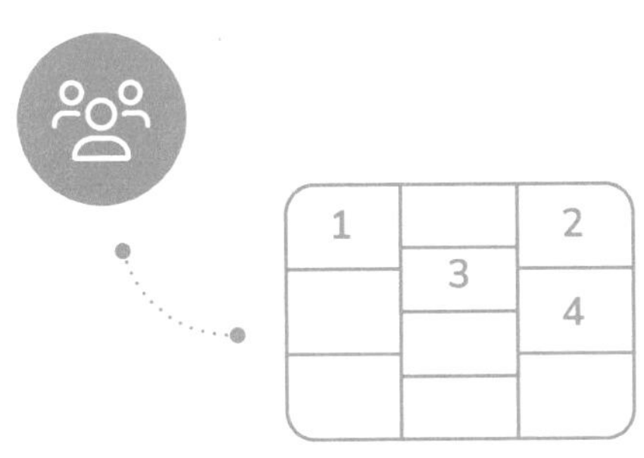

CUSTOMER-CENTRIC

A customer segment is identified and the founding team engages in detailed market research to identify and validate problems that, if solved, would create a Profit Stream.

It is common for teams using this pattern to have prior knowledge of the Customers.

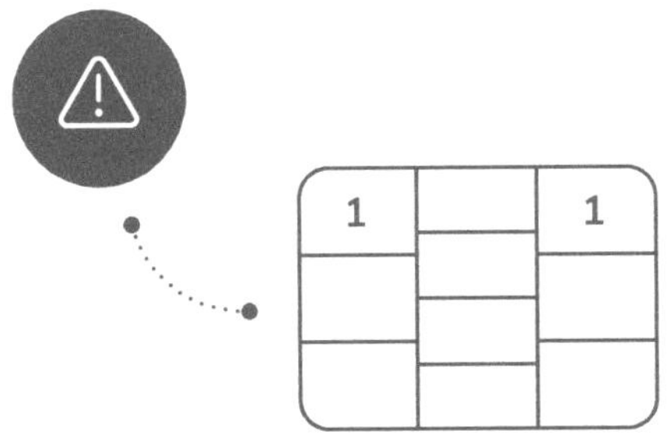

PROBLEM-CENTRIC

A specific problem is identified by a single customer or the founding team. Solving this problem entails the development of the solution.

Companies often develop custom solutions that can form the foundation of a new company's Profit Stream.

Because these patterns are closely related, it is most useful to consider them as **starting points** towards completing a **Profit Stream Canvas.**

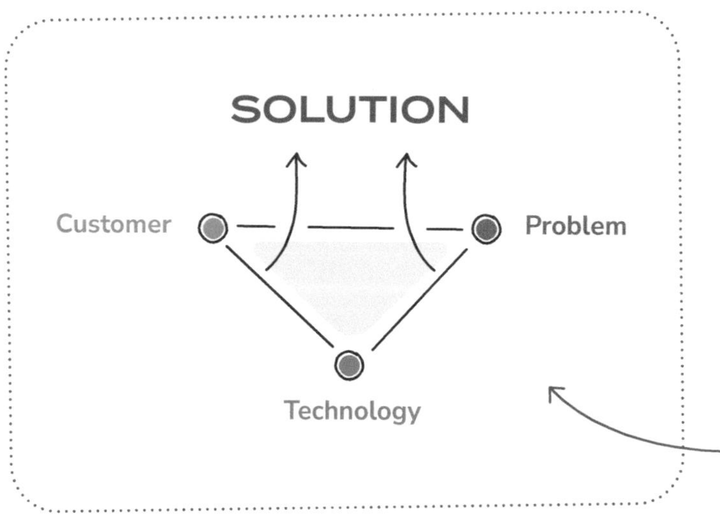

Once the vision has been captured, it is helpful to complete the rest of the canvas through a structured process that promotes systems thinking and the exploration of ideas.

ANY AND ALL OF THESE INSPIRE SOLUTIONS!

Next, we present a typical flow through the canvas...

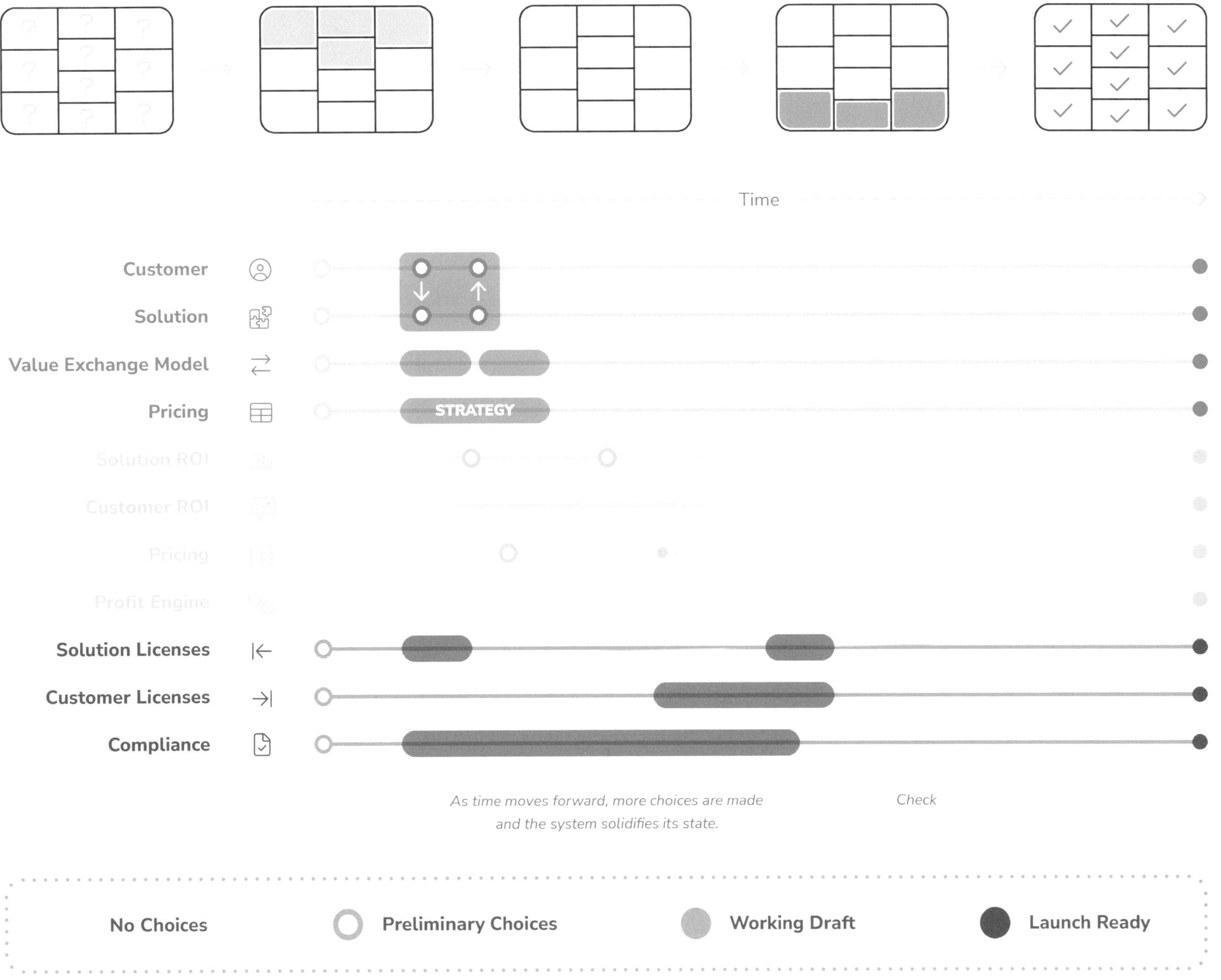
Time
Customer
Solution
Value Exchange Model
Pricing
STRATEGY
Solution ROI
Customer ROI
Pricing
Profit Engine
Solution Licenses
Customer Licenses
Compliance
As time moves forward, more choices are made
and the system solidifies its state.
Check
No Choices
Preliminary Choices
Working Draft
Launch Ready

10 tips that make developing Profit Streams in Startups less turbulent.

Build as much of your solution and business practices on your in-licenses as possible.

Consider a SaaS solution based on a monthly subscription fee. Don't build the subscription solution, just use one provided by Stripe or Paypal.

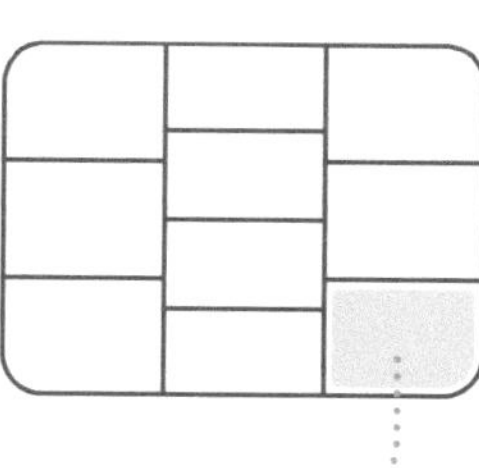

Understand reference pricing.

Even if your solution is new, you're going to be compared to a reference price.

Price high, not low.

A common challenge in Startups is that they price their initial solution too low. This doesn't mean that every Startup should pursue a premium pricing strategy. It does mean that your price should always start as high as possible.

Remember that it is easier to lower prices than to raise them!

Keep your pricing policies simple.

Avoid too many discounts.

Identify when a Customer ROI is needed, and build it.

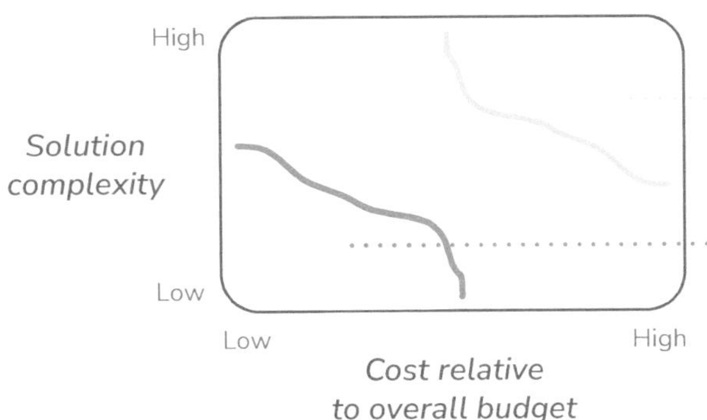
High
Solution complexity
Low
Low
High
Cost relative to overall budget
ROI tools are highly beneficial for high cost, high complexity solutions.
ROI tools are not needed for low cost, low complexity solutions.

Pick no more than five benefits.

Startups don't need dozens of benefits. Indeed, a Startup often only needs one or two benefits to motivate customers to purchase their solution. Focus on the benefits that create the highest impact.

Establish price metrics that align with your Value Exchange Model

Failling to align price metrics with Value Exchange Models is a common mistake that costs time and money to fix.

10 tips that make developing Profit Streams in Startups less turbulent.

Ensure that your roadmap includes how your Profit Engine fuels sustainability.

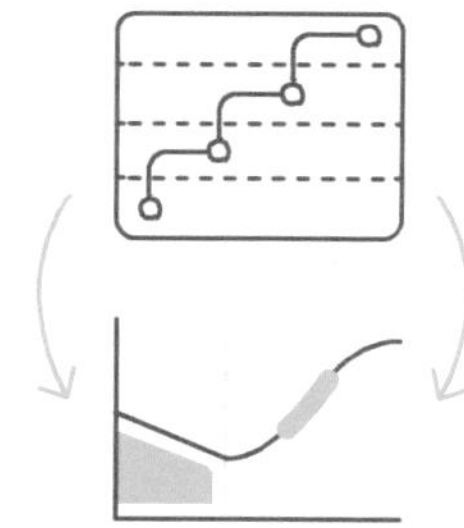

Roadmaps that guide development before launch...

...should guide sustainable, profitable growth after launch.

Select competitors with similar pricing strategies.

When establishing price ranges for competitive offerings, take care to use competitors employing the same price strategy. For example, it doesn't make sense to compare your prices motivated by your "low cost" strategy with prices from a "premium competitor" because you're targeting different customers. Instead, compare your "low cost" prices with other "low cost" providers.

Avoid the GOOD-BETTER-BEST Profit Engine at launch.

Even if creating GBB packaging is part of your solution roadmap, creating one complete offering at launch and then developing segments based on actual use gives you more data on how to create the packages.

Creating new solutions within an existing portfolio.

Developing a new solution in the context of existing solutions starts with an understanding of how the new solution is differentiated from existing solutions, along with the intended relationship that will be created between the new solution and existing solutions.

Starting with the intended relationship between the new solution and prior solution(s), there are three main relationships.

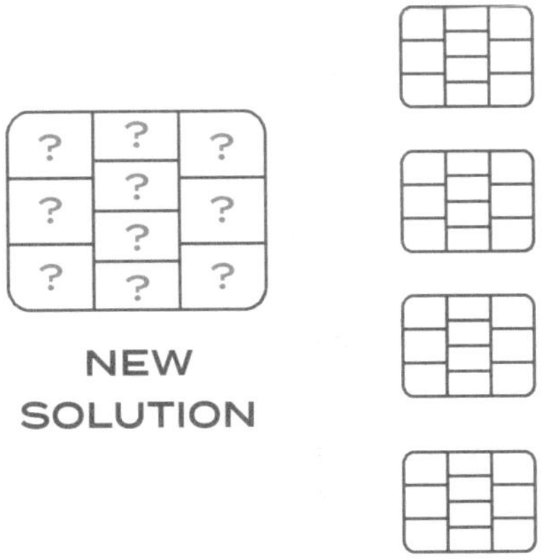

NEW SOLUTION

Will the new solution target the same customers?

Will the new solution leverage technology or components of existing solutions?

Will the new solution be based on the same Value Exchange Model and Pricing Strategy?

How does the pricing of the existing solution impact the new solution? Should the old solution's price be adjusted?

01

NEW REPLACES OLD

The new solution is designed to replace the old solution, typically preserving the target market and possibly expanding it.

02

NEW TARGETS OLD

The new solution expands customer relationships, benefiting from lower sales and marketing costs, and creating opportunities for promotions and packaging, such as solution bundles.

03

NEW TARGETS NEW

The new solution expands the scope of the portfolio, often leveraging core assets and knowledge acquired from the existing solution.

Creating new solutions within an existing portfolio

NEW CO-EXISTS WITH OLD...

01

NEW REPLACES OLD

Examples:

On-premise software providers have replaced these solutions with new SaaS based cloud alternatives.

While often marketed as an upgrade, under the covers these are often entirely new solutions, just like Adobe Creative Cloud replaced Adobe Creative Suite.

02

NEW TARGETS OLD

A classic example are video game franchises, in which new editions of the game co-exist with prior versions.

Note that each game can continue to evolve and grow, with updates for many years.

03

NEW TARGETS NEW

Apex Group provides a number of financial compliance solutions that serve related, but distinct markets.

The evolution of the solution, such as upgrading a B2B platform from Release 2.4 to Release 3.0, or the frequent upgrades to SaaS solutions are covered in the next section, on the evolution of solutions in the Market Lifecycle.

Efficiently serving distinct customer segments with common technical platforms is a sophisticated form of architectural engineering. The investments—and returns—can be quite substantial.

After you have established the relationship between the proposed solution and existing solutions, you can leverage the canvas **to guide and accelerate decisionmaking.** New solutions motivate a review of every block in the canvas. This table will guide you through your choices.

		NEW REPLACES OLD *Targets same customers*	**NEW CO-EXISTS WITH OLD** *Targets same customers*	**NEW TARGETS NEW** *Targets new customers*
	Customer	*Update CBA. Determine if any segments will be dropped.*	*Update CBA.*	*Develop new CBA.*
	Solution	*Determine which features are included, which are deprecated, and what new features will be delivered.*	*Differentiate solutions to minimize confusion among customers.*	*Develop new Solution Benefit Map.*
SOLUTION	**Roadmaps**	*The old solution roadmaps clearly show End of Life and how customers will be transitioned.*	*Each solution has a separate roadmap that reflects their unique evolution. Roadmaps and underlying technical architectures are exploited for synergies.*	
	Strategy	*You will typically use the same pricing strategy.*		*You may use the same or you may use a different pricing strategy for the new customers you're targeting.*
	Structure	*The structure is usually the same.*	*Structure changes to reflect the new solution and/or the new customers.*	
PRICING	**Specifics**	*Prices are typically the same or increased to reflect additional value.*	*Prices are set for the new solution with awareness of the TCO for customers who seek to purchase multiple solutions.*	*Prices are set uniquely for the new market.*
	Policies	*Discounts or other limited policies may be offered to motivate customers to move to the new solution.*	*Policies are set in a way that is consistent with previously established choices.*	*Policies are set uniquely for the new market.*

<table>
<tr><th></th><th>NEW REPLACES OLD
Targets same customers</th><th>NEW CO-EXISTS WITH OLD
Targets same customers</th><th>NEW TARGETS NEW
Targets new customers</th></tr>
<tr><td rowspan="2">Solution ROI & Customer ROI</td><td rowspan="2">Update both the Solution and Customer ROI to reflect the new solution. Consider any additional costs associated with deprecating the old solution or one-time costs required to transition to the new solution.</td><td colspan="2">Develop new Solution & Customer ROI models to reflect the new solution.</td></tr>
<tr><td>Consider extending all related ROI tools to promote cross-selling.</td><td>Tailor your customer ROI model to the new segments.</td></tr>
<tr><td rowspan="2">Profit Engine</td><td rowspan="2">Your new solution will likely use the same Profit Engine. Prepare carefully for any Profit Engine changes, as these can be more substantial than you might expect.</td><td>Consider using the same Profit Engine as this will be familiar to your customers and internal operations.</td><td>Explore the Profit Engines that best align with this new segment. Consider your underlying technical architecture as you make these choices.</td></tr>
<tr><td colspan="2">The synergy between Google's acquisition of YouTube is obvious when considered from the perspective of Value Exchange Model and Profit Engines: both use the same Value Exchange Model and similar Profit Engines.</td></tr>
<tr><td>Solution Licenses</td><td>Review your Solution Licenses to confirm your replacement Solution is supported.</td><td colspan="2">Audit all new In-Licensed technologies to ensure your new solution is supported. Explore ways to negotiate better terms with suppliers if your new solution enhances your relationship.</td></tr>
<tr><td>Customer Licenses</td><td>Carefully review so that you can maximize your operating freedom and pricing choices.</td><td colspan="2">Develop new license agreements, or extend existing license agreements to integrate the new solution or support the new customers. Ensure your backend systems are prepared for multiple license agreements.</td></tr>
<tr><td>Compliance</td><td>Review your requirements and commitments to confirm your replacement solution is supported.</td><td>Chances are good that your new solution will fall under the same set of compliance choices as your present solutions. That said...don't guess; check to be sure!</td><td>Serving a new market requires a compliance audit to make certain you are not making any assumptions that could harm your company.</td></tr>
</table>

Are we done yet?

Even if your new solution can leverage aspects of existing solutions, keep going until all blocks of the canvas have been completed.

A completed canvas helps every part of the organization succeed.

- Sales
- Marketing
- Legal
- Compliance
- Product Development
- Engineering
- ...

When software eats hardware.

New solutions created by software!

Technological advances and lower costs for CPUs, memory chips, and ubiquitous network infrastructure provide extraordinary opportunities for traditional companies to create Software Profit Streams by integrating software into old solutions.

The result?
New solutions that drive innovation and growth.

Traditional companies that base their pricing and licensing practices on hardware models face significant challenges because software is not like hardware. Understanding why software is special is particularly important to companies creating their first Software-Enabled Solutions.

Here are twelve ways in which software is different than hardware, each of which can fuel a new Software Profit Stream. Review this list, and then follow the guidance for creating a new solution in a Startup.

12 reasons why software is special

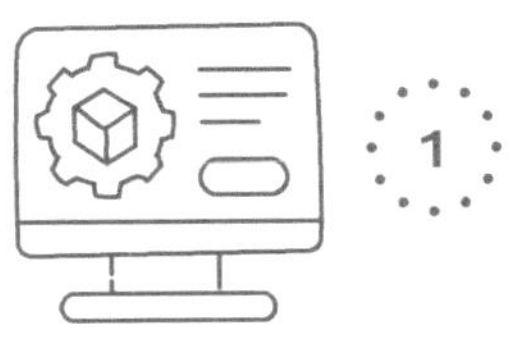

Software is not a physical thing, it is intellectual property.

Unlike a physical good where the customer can transfer ownership rights, a software license restricts customers on what ownership rights may be transferred, if at all!

When you purchase a pen at the store, you own it, and can give it someone else. When you license a software solution, you do not own it, and what you can or cannot do with the software is determined by the license agreement.

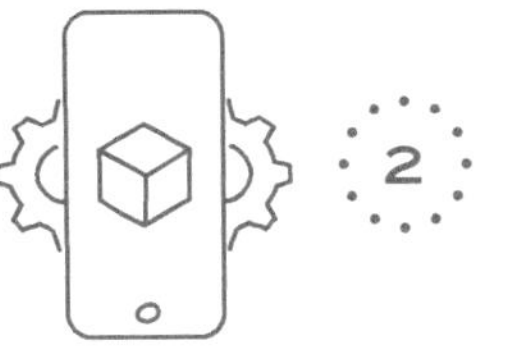

Software requires a physical environment, hardware, to run.

Sometimes the customer will provide all of the hardware, such as when you download an app onto your phone. Sometimes multiple entities provide hardware, such as when you access a Software-as-a-Service (SaaS) solution like Netflix or LinkedIn via your personal computer: you provide the personal computer / browser that accesses the software running on the hardware provided or managed by the SaaS provider.

There is a always a solution context for any solution - a hammer needs a nail. The specific hardware for software is unique and must be defined.

12 reasons why software is special

3

Unless the software is specifically designed to be extended, the average customer cannot modify it.

This stands in stark contrast to most hardware. In fact, in the United States Uniform Commercial Code (UCC), the Implied Warranty of Merchantability burdens manufacturers with the responsibility of providing customers with spare parts, which means the customers can generally repair, modify, and even extend what they've purchased. Before cars became software-enabled, it was easy to hot rod your car by replacing the original parts with aftermarket parts designed to increase acceleration, speed, and power.

Most software license agreements explicitly reject the types of warranties found in the UCC, which means you'll only be hot rodding your car if you're willing to violate the terms of the license agreement. And if you think this is about having fun driving down a highway, you're missing the point: the 'right to repair' equipment has emerged as one of the most contentious issues in the licensing of software-enabled solutions.

Business leaders must remain aware of the specific regulations that govern the 'right to repair' or the 'right to modify', as these laws vary around the world.

While there is effectively zero-cost to replicate and distribute software, the costs to maintain, extend and decommission software can be expansive - and expensive.

Solution costs can be organized into five main categories: creating the release or unit, creating subsequent releases or units, operating the solution, maintaining the solution, and decommissioning the solution. While there are many similarities in the design and initial production costs for the first release or first unit of software and physical solutions, the ongoing creation of the next unit of a physical good incurs costs based primarily on raw materials, manufacturing/production, sales, and distribution. In contrast, it costs virtually nothing to replicate or distribute additional versions of software, although there are other expenses associated with software that affect both customers and producers, notably operations, maintenance, and decommissioning.

For enterprise or business software, these costs can be extensive, with the total lifetime cost of the software maintenance far exceeding the initial purchase cost. We explore costing models extensively in our treatment of Economic Sustainability.

Software can be pretty easy to steal.

Every business has to deal with theft. Physical goods that are cheap, like pens, aren't typically worth stealing. Expensive physical goods, like cars, are protected in such a way as to make them harder to steal. The level of protection and/or security increases based on the value of the goods and can reach quite significant levels for extraordinary or priceless items such as art or fine jewelry. Similarly, software-enabled solutions exhibit quite a range of vulnerabilities to theft. Some software, like games or personal computer software, is relatively easy to steal. Software that is contained within hardware is stolen when the hardware is stolen. And while we may not be stealing SaaS software, sharing accounts on a movie streaming service is a different form of theft. Accordingly, business leaders of software-enabled solutions must understand how their offering is susceptible to theft and implement appropriate mechanisms to deter it.

While software doesn't wear out, it will become outdated, irrelevant, and lose value over time.

Many physical goods are consumed (bananas or diesel), wear out (running shoes or brake pads), or break (windows or coffee mugs). Software does not share any of these properties we find with physical goods. From this perspective, software doesn't wear out. Software does, however, embody the methodologies and constraints of the time it was delivered. For example, accounting software written on the earliest mainframe computers is functionally useless, a relic for hobbyists or museums. The implication is that software must be continually updated to provide value, a key mindset in the design of Profit Streams.

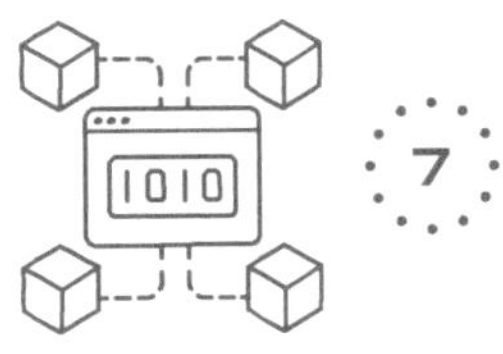

Software-enabled solutions are composed of multiple software components in complex value chains.

While these components provide value to the company creating the solution, business leaders must review the license agreements and business models of the in-licensed components to ensure they support the sustainability goals of the company. This is in contrast to physical goods which may—*or may not*—have in-licensed components.

12 reasons why software is special

Software is extended, updated, and improved while in the hands of the customer.

This promotes an organic mindset to growth that is considerably different from the relatively inorganic mindset associated with physical goods.

For example, we do not consider "upgrading" our couch, a shirt, or lawnmower. We use them until they are worn out, unfashionable, dull, or outdated. Then we buy the next model - which in most cases is better. However, our mindset changes once any of these physical goods become software enabled. When that happens, we tend to think of upgrading our car or improving the diagnostics in our lawnmower.

This organic mindset motivates an organic economic model, with benefits to all stakeholders: customers may not have to buy a new product to obtain an improvement and manufacturers may be able to avoid costly recalls.

More than 30% of Tesla's 'recalls' are handled via software updates!

Upgrading one software component can destabilize the solution.

One undesirable side effect of component-based solutions is that the improvement of any one component can destabilize one or more solutions that depend on it, or on which it depends. Upgrading your personal computers operating system to remove a security vulnerability may require you to also upgrade several applications. These upgrades may cost additional money. Purchasing the latest version of your favorite game may force you to purchase a new version of your smart phone or game console to run it.

With a small amount of architectural support, additional value can be easily added to a software product after its initial purchase or release.

At the same time, this is not usually the case for a physical good. This specialness of software opens up new opportunities to capture revenue for the business.

Software solutions generate data through their use.

Every software solution has the potential to generate usage data that creates value in a manner that traditional physical goods cannot. A traditional torque wrench provides feedback to a mechanic that helps them tighten a bolt to the correct tolerance. A software-enabled torque wrench provides the same feedback and can capture that feedback as data that can be used for longitudinal analysis to improve maintenance practices.

While a traditional board game is fun to play, a software version of that game can analyze your moves and help you become a better player. These data enhance existing Profit Streams and can serve as inspiration for new Profit Streams.

Software solutions can generate metadata that improves the solution.

Every software solution has the potential to generate metadata about how it is used in a manner that improves the system.

Cloud based software solutions track customer usage, enabling product leaders to identify features that can be added, improved, or even removed.

Hardware solutions with embedded software can be used to create 'digital twins' to develop individualized predictive maintenance schedules, lowering costs and extending the service life of the hardware.

Metadata can also help customers monitor their use of the solution, enabling them to change their behavior to better align to their goals. Health monitoring software on our phones helps remind us to take a break from our social media and go for a walk.

Spinouts

A Spinout is the process of taking a private, limited, and often internal solution and commercializing it into a Profit Stream.

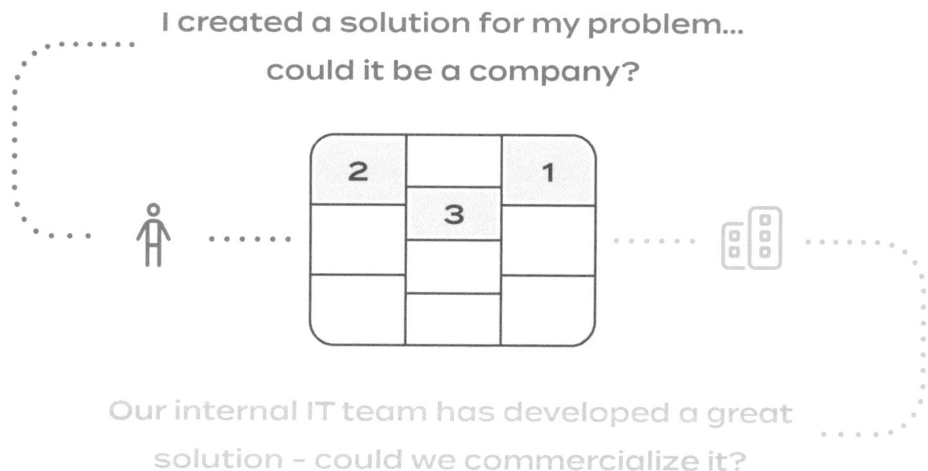

I created a solution for my problem...
could it be a company?
2
1
3
Our internal IT team has developed a great
solution - could we commercialize it?

Haier initially created CosmoPlat as an internal solution to manage procurement. Sensing a broader opportunity, Haier opened the platform to external companies, who use CosmoPlat to solve a host of supply chain challenges.

CosmoPlat has been celebrated for creating hundreds of millions of dollars in economic value for a diverse set of companies.

The online browser extension Honey, which saves consumers money by automatically finding coupons, was started by Ryan Hudson, a dad who wished he had a coupon when he was ordering pizza for his kids online. The solution resonated with others and Honey was acquired by PayPal in 2020.

Could Amazon Web Services (AWS) be the most famous—and profitable—Spinout of all time? We'll find out...

It is helpful for the Spinout team to **follow the sequence of steps for a customer-focused Startup** in which the first customer is the entity that created the solution.

Staffing the Spinout properly is key for success, structuring a Spinout as a new division or even as a new company is a best practice.

Additional questions and guidance are as follows:

You will have to design all aspects of your Profit Engine

Who are the customers? Will they obtain the same benefits?

Your solution was created on a forecast of economic benefits. How can this be leveraged to create a Customer ROI model?

Solution licenses must be designed for the new solution.

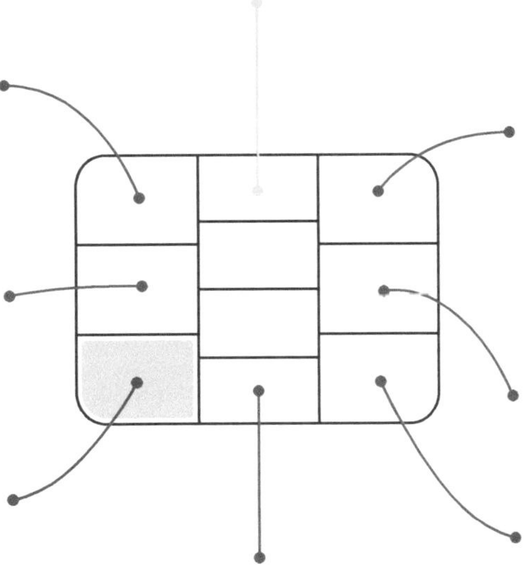

What new compliance factors must be supported?

What is the solution? Clear boundaries must be established to 'spin out' the solution. Once 'spun out', the solution will need to be reintegrated into the company. For example, APIs might need to be created to spin out a solution and then these APIs need to be used to reintegrate the solution.

What additional costs will be incurred to commercialize the solution?

Do any license agreements need to be adjusted to support the Spinout?

Solution Lifecycle Management

The evolution of the Profit Stream

The smooth curve of the Solution Lifecycle hides the stair-step nature of discrete releases of a solution. Each release is motivated by one or more discrete events.

Important or materially significant events serve as **triggers** that create opportunities for business leaders to adjust pricing, fine-tune Profit Engines and otherwise ensure the sustainability of the business.

The Profit Stream Canvas is the tool you will use to take advantage of triggers.

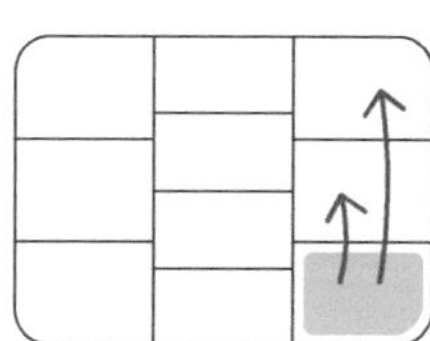

Switching to a low-cost supplier can create greater margins, may improve the solution, and contribute to sustainability.

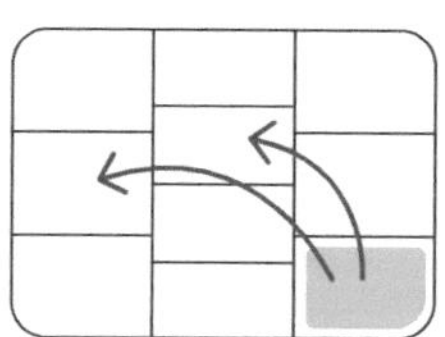

Or it may lower costs, improving Customer ROI.

Using the canvas promotes the systems thinking that creates greatest impact.

There are three primary **triggers**

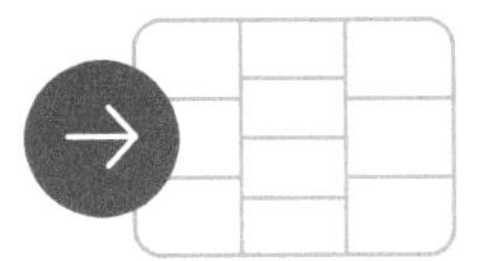

External Triggers

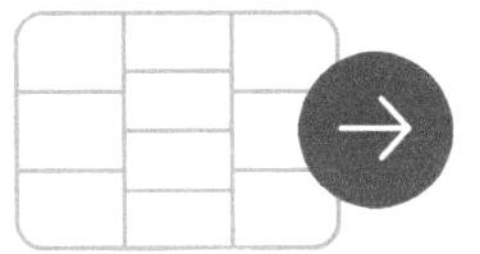

Internal Triggers

That create four primary opportunities:

Adjusting Pricing

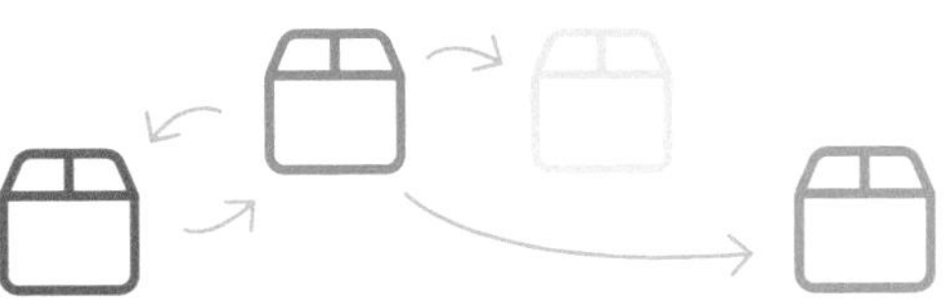

Adjusting Packaging

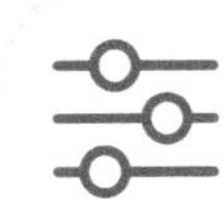

Fine-Tuning Profit Engines

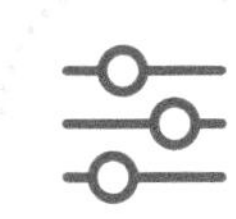

Adjusting Compliance

Time

The passage of time serves as a guardrail to ensure business leaders are evaluating their solution on a regular basis. The most common outcome is adjusted pricing.

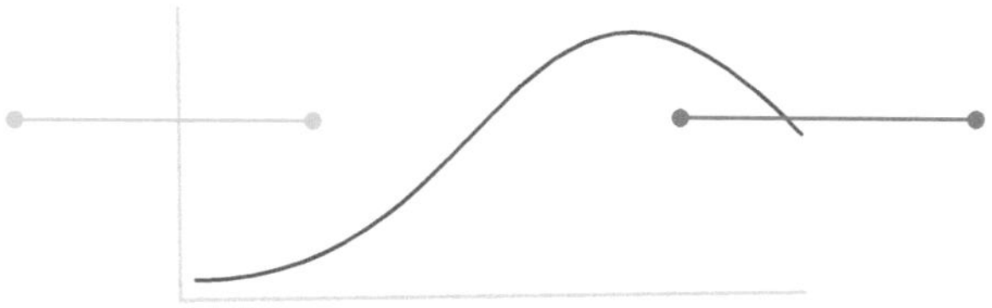

Solutions (and Startups) in the growth stages should evaluate pricing every 3-6 months

Mature solutions should evaluate pricing every 6-12 months

Salesforce establishes the right to raise prices by 5% or more annually in multi-term contracts.

Why establish a cadence for pricing evaluations?

Adjusting prices too infrequently creates unusually large price increases. For inexpensive solutions, this may be acceptable. For expensive solutions, this causes problems as customers may not be able to adjust budgets to absorb the new pricing, increasing the likelihood of expensive, protacted negotiations or customer defections.

Regularly exploring prices helps ensure you are capturing all of the value of your offering. Even if you don't increase your pricing, these reviews may uncover improved ways to capture and present your Customer ROI.

Review your Customer ROI model every significant release to find opportunities to promote the increased economic value of new features and related solution enhancements.

Market Rhythms & Pricing

The cyclical nature of Market Rhythms enables business leaders to plan discounts and promotions. Customers are prepared to spend money and the right discounts can accelerate sales in a way that does not harm overall margins.

When demand is low, targeted discounts and promotions can motivate purchases

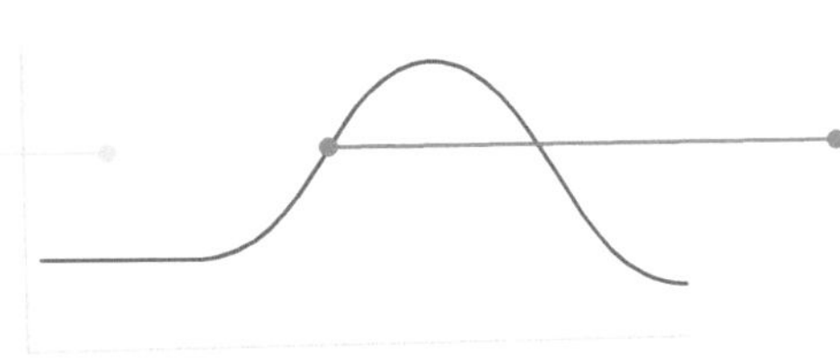

When demand can be forecasted, it creates an optimal release window for new solutions. Discounts and promotions should be avoided — customers don't need them to motivate the purchase.

Business leaders must be careful about the over-use of discounts to motivate demand. The frequent use of discounts can create an unintended event, shifting customers from their normal buying patterns as they seek lower prices.

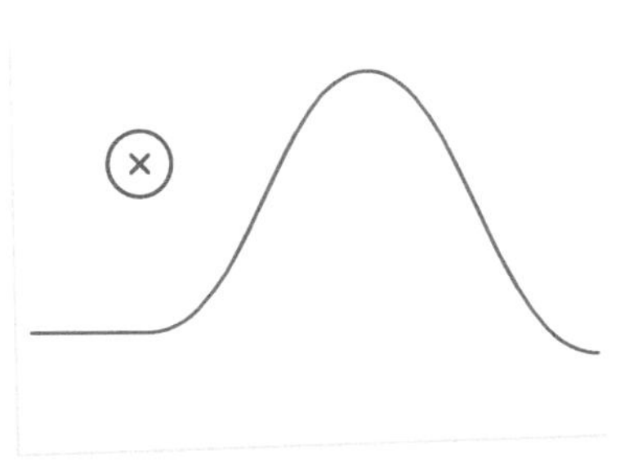

Consistently offering a discount at the same time...

...can create a new market rhythm that serves to lower overall revenue and profitability.

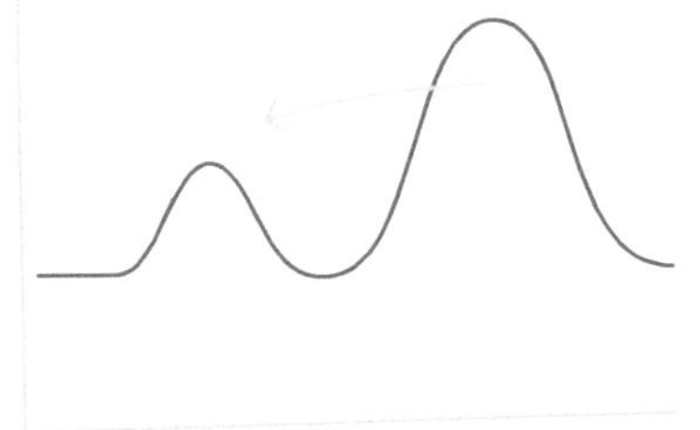

External Triggers

Businesses are impacted by external forces and events outside their control.

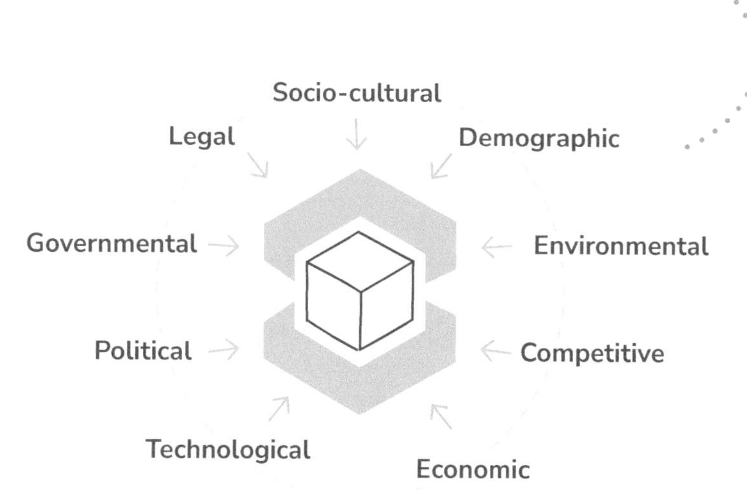

The scope, timing, rate of change, and impact of these external triggers vary:

Example: Legal, Competitive, Technological...

Changes flow through our systems...

RESIDUAL
Old-fashioned, on the way out, out-dated.

NOW
Dominant behaviors, uses of technology.

FUTURE
Emerging behaviors, laws, norms, trends, etc.

At different speeds, and with different impacts.

COVID
Rapidly developing, global in scope, significant impact to all industries.

AGING POPULATION
Slowly developing, global in scope, varying degree of impact.

Sustainable businesses capture these forces and events in their roadmaps and product trees, using them as triggers to promote sustainability. **The specific implications of these triggers can be assessed through the application of the Profit Stream Canvas.**

1 TECHNOLOGICAL TRIGGERS

Companies can evolve their solutions to benefit from advances in technology or face challenges in competing with them.

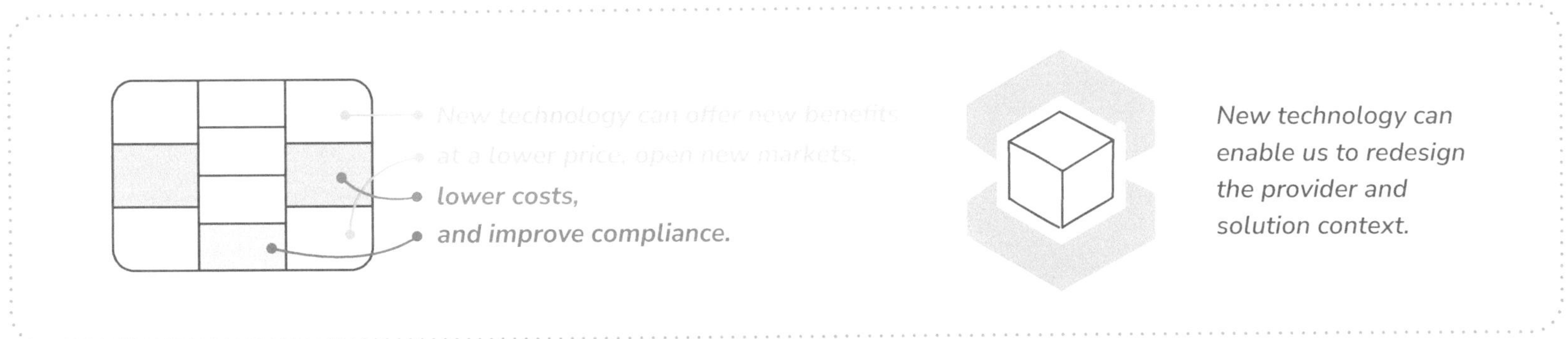
New technology can offer new benefits
at a lower price, open new markets,
lower costs,
and improve compliance.
New technology can enable us to redesign the provider and solution context.

2 ECONOMIC TRIGGERS

Economic triggers such as inflation, access to capital, rising or lowering costs, taxes, disposable income, access to resources, and a myriad of other factors impacts the solution.

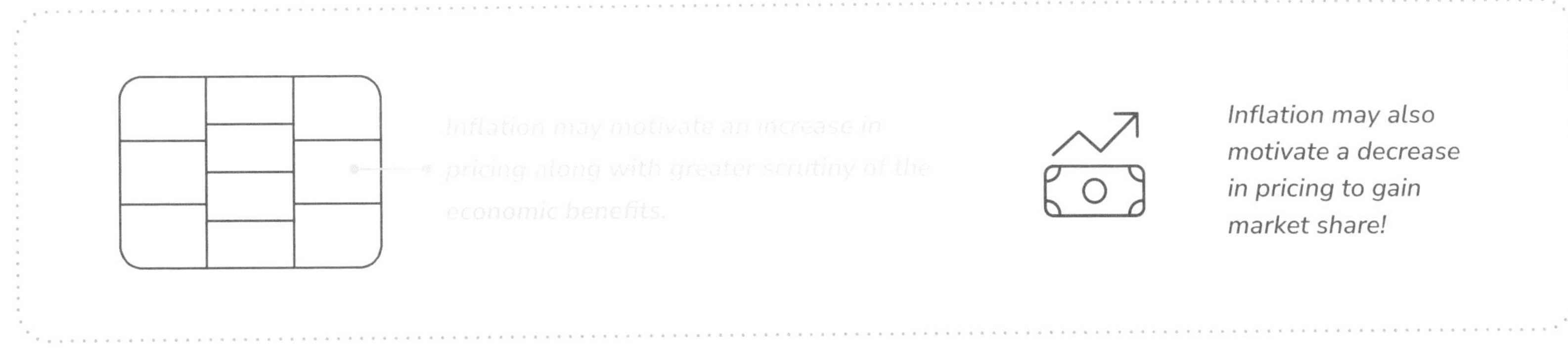
Inflation may motivate an increase in pricing along with greater scrutiny of the economic benefits.
Inflation may also motivate a decrease in pricing to gain market share!

EXTERNAL TRIGGERS

3 DEMOGRAPHIC TRIGGERS

Demographic triggers such as age, gender, race, nationality, marital status, occupation, education, income level, and more have the greatest impact in companies serving B2C and B2P markets.

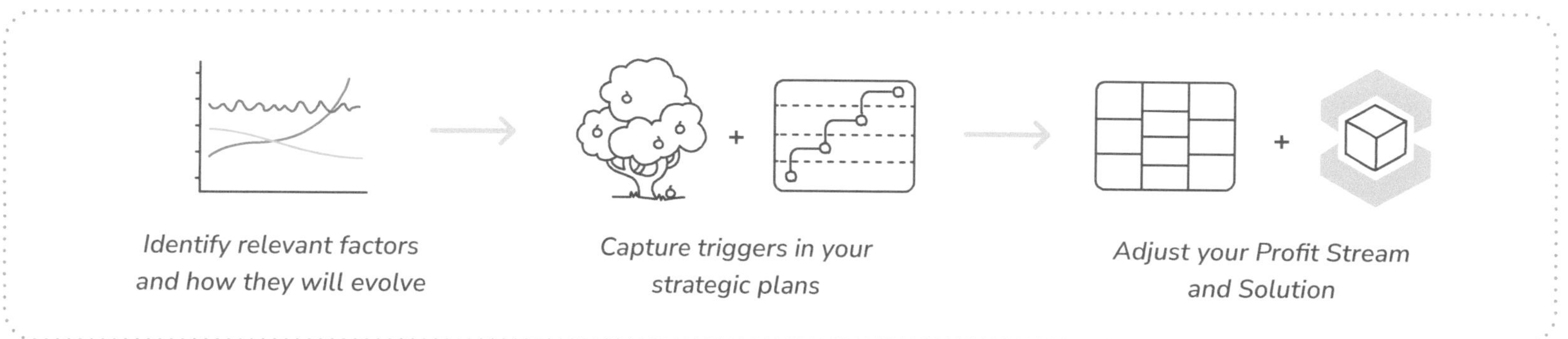

Identify relevant factors and how they will evolve
Capture triggers in your strategic plans

4 SOCIO-CULTURAL TRIGGERS

Socio-cultural triggers relate to values, beliefs, and attitudes that influence and motivate individual and collective decision making. These can change the mix or magnitude of desired benefits, including constraints of acceptable solution design.

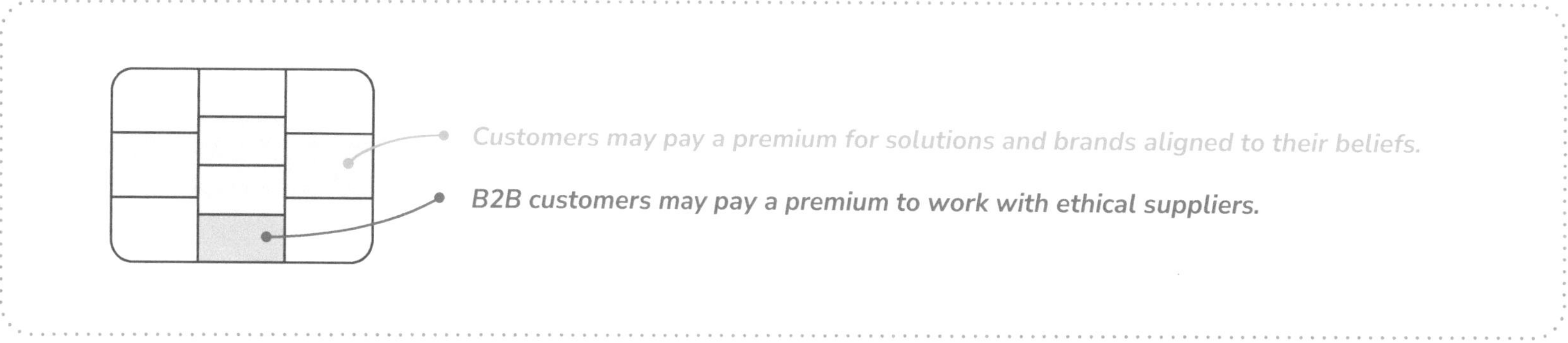

Customers may pay a premium for solutions and brands aligned to their beliefs.
B2B customers may pay a premium to work with ethical suppliers.

5 ENVIRONMENTAL TRIGGERS

Environmental triggers encompass changes in our physical world, such as weather, climate change, pollution, industrialization, waste. Software-Enabled Solutions can contribute to both positive and negative outcomes in these areas: Software can improve efficiency and reduce waste and it can contribute to e-waste as older hardware is discarded.

Our hope is that your definition of a sustainable business will include consideration of how you contribute to a healthy environment.

6 POLITICAL TRIGGERS

Changes in political parties and political structures directly impact businesses and their solutions through such things as tax policies, employment laws, tariffs, regulations, Intellectual Property rights, along with the political attitudes and structures of how these changes were made.

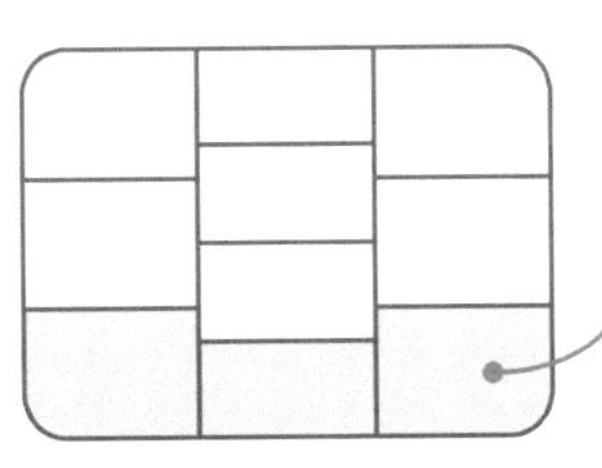

Political and legal forces tend to concentrate their impact in the relationship sustainability portion of the Profit Stream Canvas.

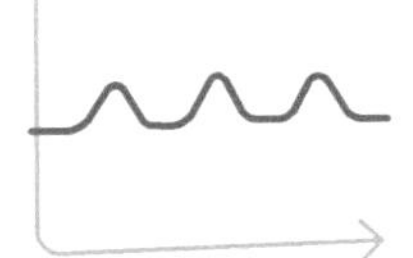

Longterm roadmaps can capture political rhythms, such as the timing for national elections.

EXTERNAL TRIGGERS

LEGAL TRIGGERS

Legal triggers primarily impact compliance, such as changes to export restrictions, data privacy, and data sovereignty. These changes tend to be made slowly and should be captured as Market Events in your solution Roadmap.

COMPETITIVE TRIGGERS

Competitive triggers capture the natural evolution of competitors within the Industry Lifecycle.

We advocate a relatively light approach to the identification and management of competitors and their actions. True sustainability comes from meeting customer needs, not responding to competitors.

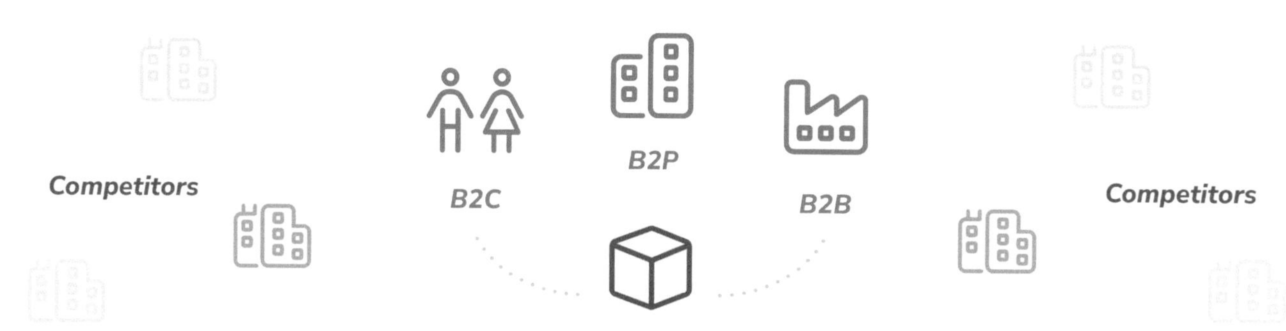

FOCUS ON YOUR CUSTOMERS...
NOT YOUR COMPETITORS.

Internal Triggers

Internal triggers are created by the actions of the company.

Common internal triggers include:

Use the canvas as a guide to help you identify and capture internal triggers so that you can act on them.

Releasing a new *-and improved-* solution.

This can motivate a new price increase. Remember that simply releasing your solution more frequently creates more potential for triggers that increase profit.

Exploring a performance gap, such as when sales are lower than expected or customers fail to renew/churn is higher than expected.

This can motivate a whole host of responses, including...

- *Adjusting the solution to create a better solution-market fit*
- *Lowering prices*
- *Changing the Value Exchange Model*

Be careful about changing the Value Exchange Model. It will almost certainly take longer and be more expensive than you expect!

Choosing to target a new market segment.

Extend your current solution or motivate the development of new solutions.

Choosing to target a new market event.

New market events create opportunities to do such things as adjusting pricing or serving new market segments.

Changing suppliers.

A new supplier can motivate a price increase to cover increased costs or a price decrease when the new supplier costs less.

Prioritizing for Profit

Business leaders are responsible for making an ongoing series of decisions that evolve the solution over the course of the solution lifecycle. This encompasses the identification, selection, and prioritization of new features, the removal of features that are no longer valuable, and related changes that create a more valuable solution, such as improving customer support.

The capital required to fund these investments comes from a variety of sources. In fast-growing startups, growth capital typically comes from investors. In mature solutions, the Profit Stream itself funds its own evolution. In organizations with a portfolio of Profit Streams, mature solutions provide growth capital for emerging solutions.

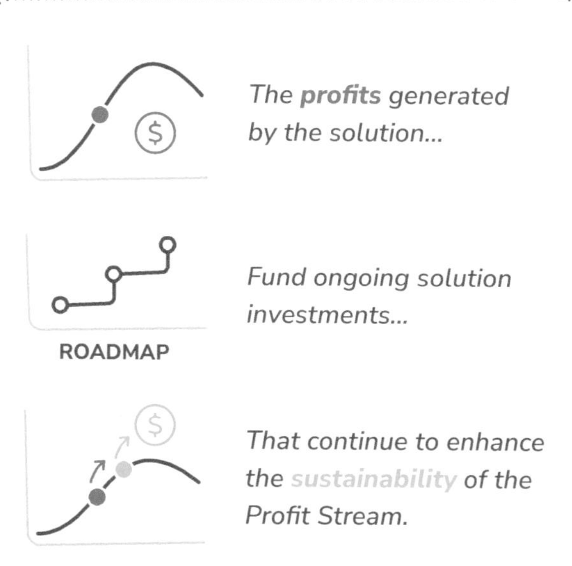

The **profits** generated by the solution...
ROADMAP
Fund ongoing solution investments...
That continue to enhance the sustainability of the Profit Stream.

Each change to the solution can be captured in the Customer Benefit Analysis, which serves to guide subsequent choices that promote sustainability. For example, adding a substantial new feature may motivate raising prices. The changes to the Customer Benefit Analysis include introducing a new benefit, changing the magnitude of an existing benefit, and/or adjusting the relationship between benefits.

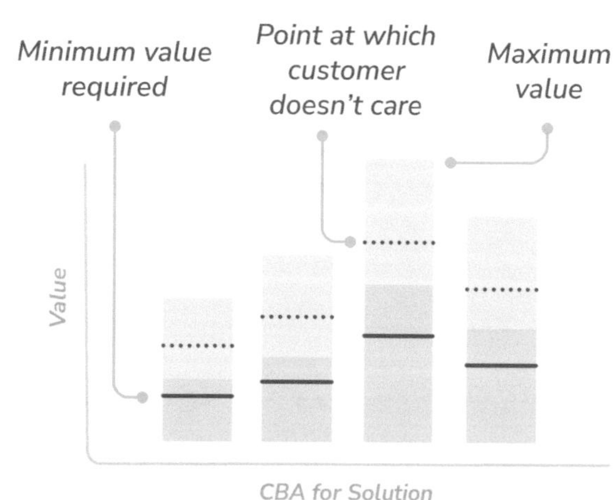

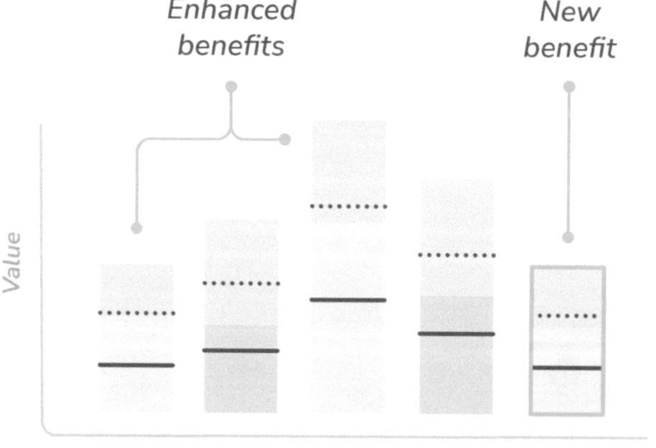

Growth capital required to advance the solution can come from many sources.

Visit www.profit-streams.com/growth-capital to explore additional sources of growth capital.

Customer perceptions of value change over time.

Value

Time

The introduction of new technology...

That increases performance can...

Raise the minimum acceptable level of performance.

CUSTOMERS EXPECT MORE OVER TIME.

A solution that provides compelling benefits...

Must maintain or improve these benefits over time to retain and/or increase customers.

Better TVs

Tech-infused clothing

Faster, cheaper phones

Better, healthier lives

Improved worker productivity

Lower costs for data storage

Greater price / performance

To understand how each feature or planned investment is intended to promote sustainability, classify them in one of three categories.

New Customers	Profit Engine	Operations
Investments designed to attract new customers	*Investments designed to leverage profit engines (existing customers)*	*Investments designed to lower costs and improve operational efficiency*

Each of these buckets will be emptied as the solution evolves and continually replenished with content from your roadmap, customer feedback, and many sources of innovation.

While it is OK to create additional categories, avoid creating more than 5. Too many categories introduces unnecessary complexity.

The **Solution Lifecycle** provides guidance on how investments should be allocated across these categories.

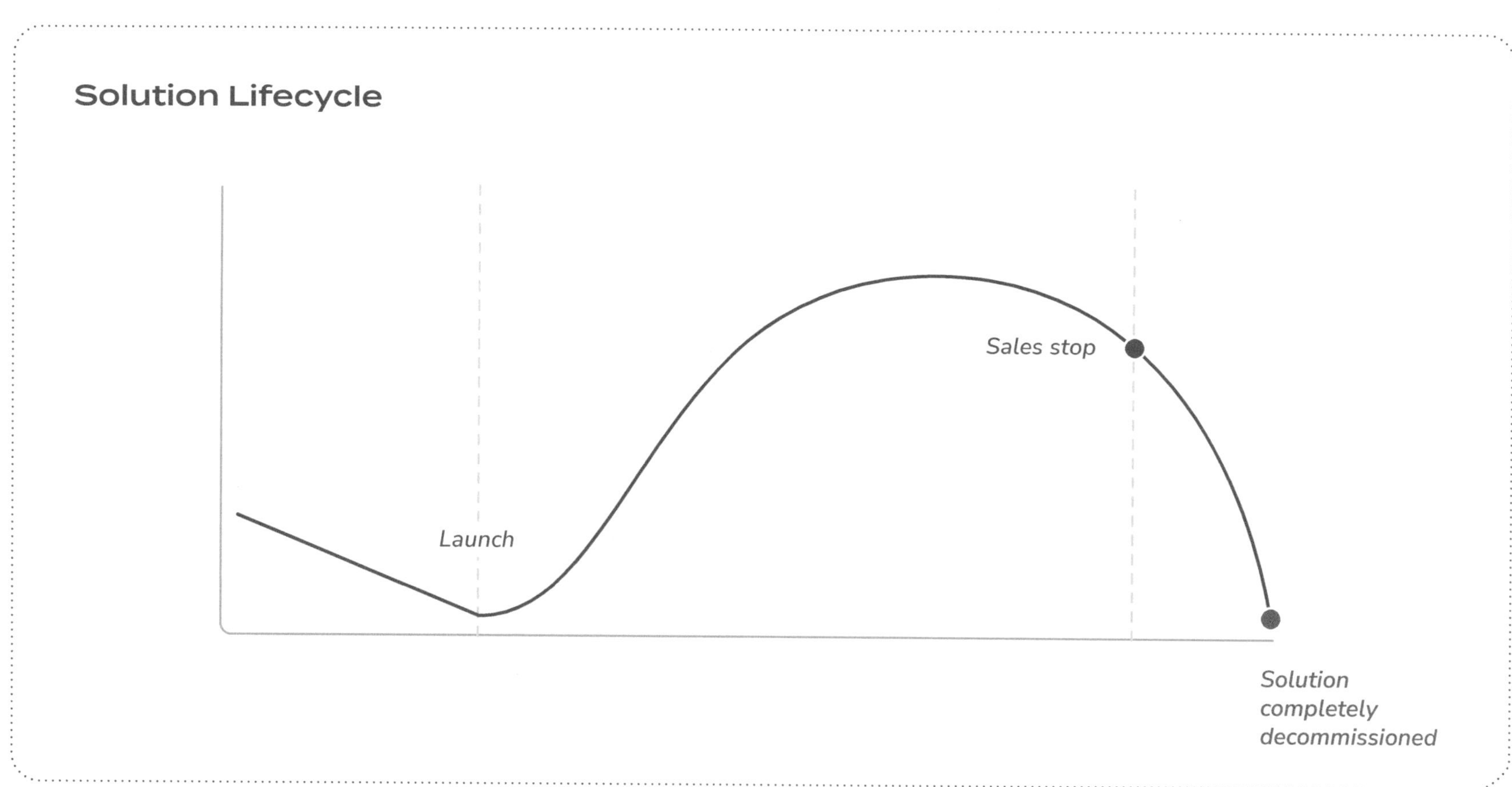

PERCENTAGE OF INVESTMENT ALLOCATION TO EACH CATEGORY OVER TIME.

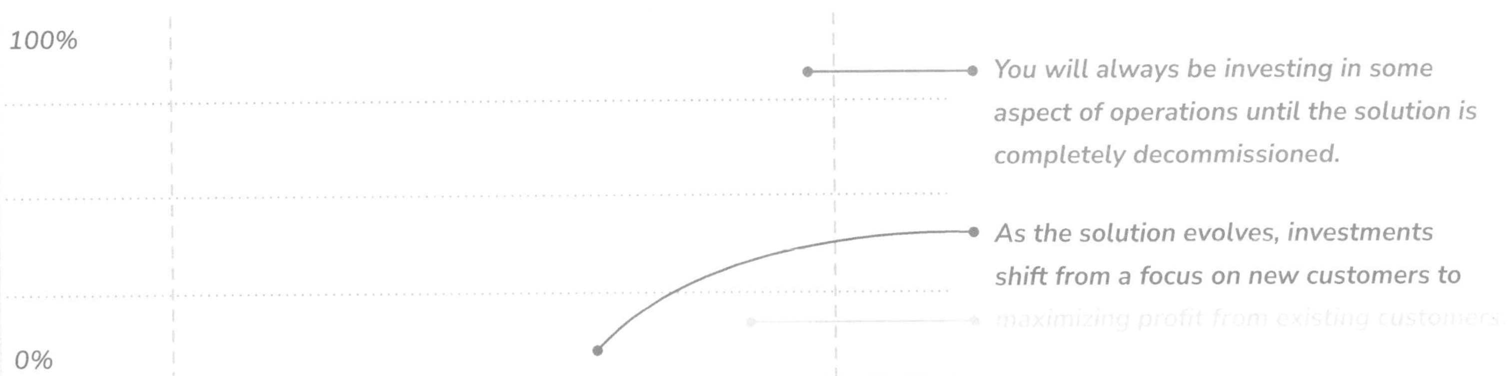

You will always be investing in some aspect of operations until the solution is completely decommissioned.

As the solution evolves, investments shift from a focus on new customers to

maximizing profit from existing customers.

Note that the total investment in each category changes based on the economics of the solution. The total amount invested on attracting new customers in the growth phase may increase even if the percentage of the total investment on new customers is decreasing.

REVENUE, PROFIT, AND INVESTMENTS OVER TIME

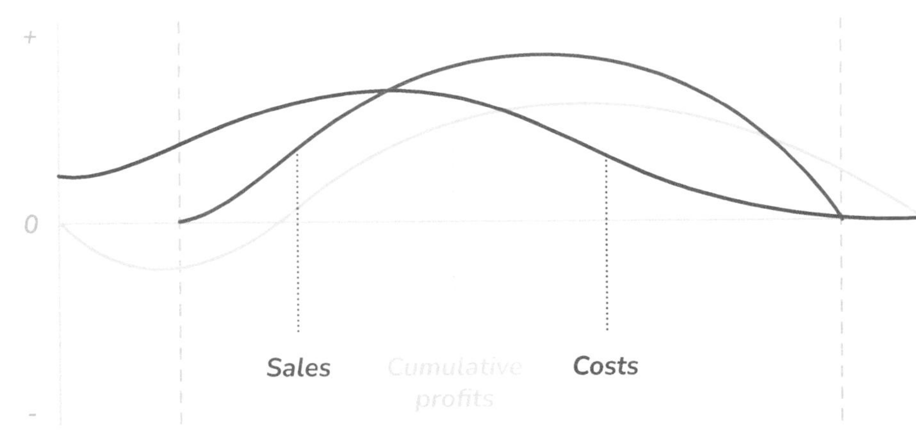

This curve captures the shape of costs, sales revenue, and profits over the Lifecycle of a healthy solution.

Visit www.profit-streams.com/profit-curves to explore other curves and how to improve them.

Adjusting prices

Adjusting pricing means adjusting one or more aspects of the Pricing Model in response to a trigger.

The most common changes are raising and lowering prices and adjusting policies.

Changes to Strategy influence all other elements.

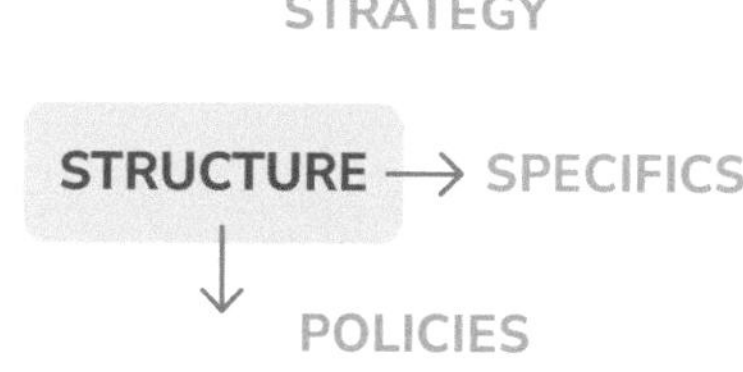

Changes to Structure will influence Specifics and Policies.

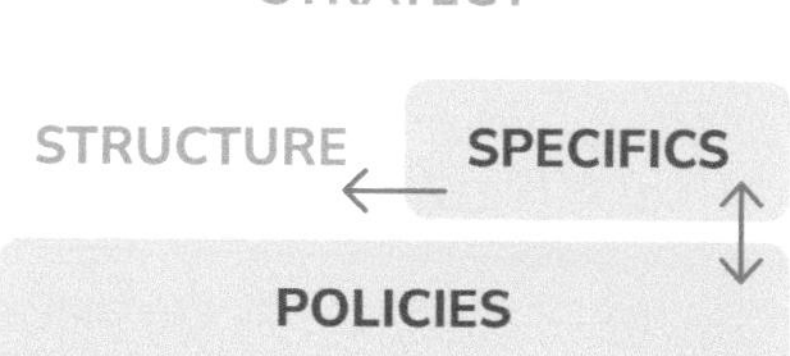

Changes to Specifics and Policies may be isolated or may influence other aspects of the model.

SIX STEPS TO ADJUST PRICING

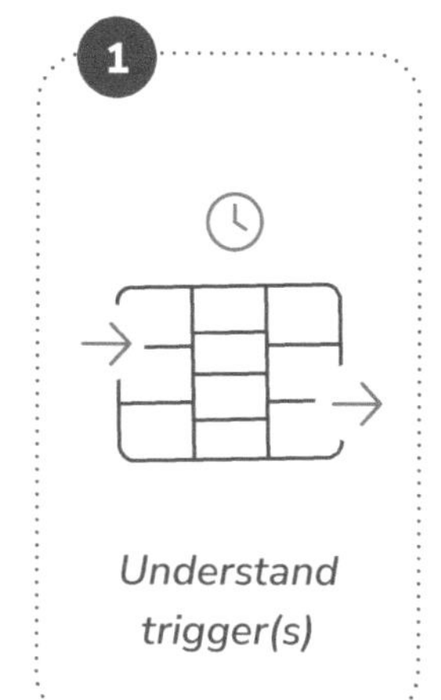

Understand trigger(s)

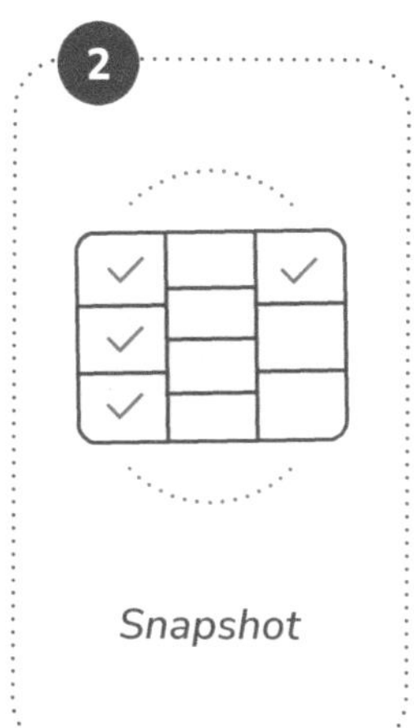

Snapshot

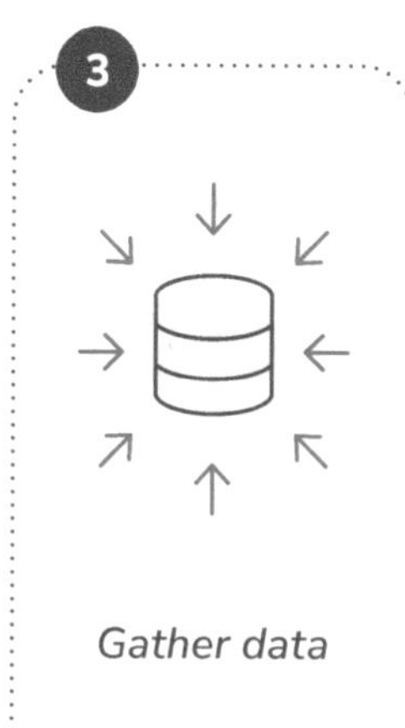

Gather data

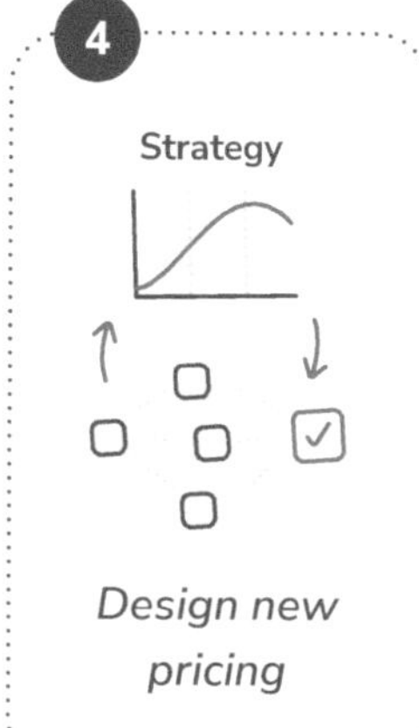

Design new pricing

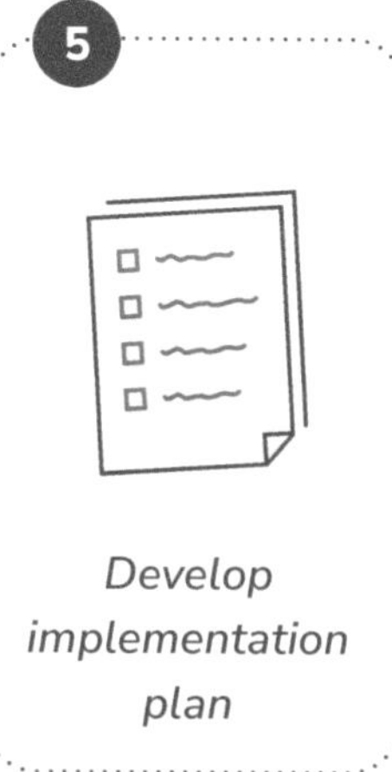

Develop implementation plan

Implement price change

UNDERSTAND TRIGGERS

Each of the triggers for adjusting prices creates an expectation of the pricing adjustment. Clearly identifying these triggers creates alignment on the likely responses and helps prepare the organization for the work that lies ahead.

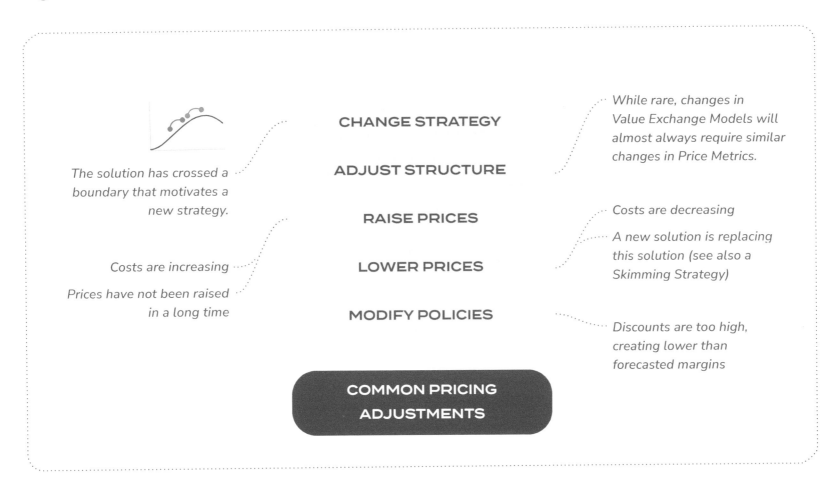

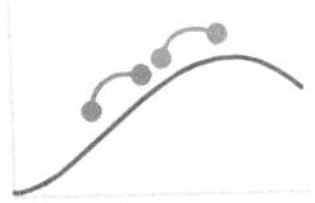

The solution has crossed a boundary that motivates a new strategy.

Costs are increasing

Prices have not been raised in a long time

CHANGE STRATEGY

ADJUST STRUCTURE

RAISE PRICES

LOWER PRICES

MODIFY POLICIES

While rare, changes in Value Exchange Models will almost always require similar changes in Price Metrics.

Costs are decreasing

A new solution is replacing this solution (see also a Skimming Strategy)

Discounts are too high, creating lower than forecasted margins

COMMON PRICING ADJUSTMENTS

SNAPSHOT

Create a snapshot of all relevant pricing, ROI, and related artifacts. This helps ensure you're assessing all necessary artifacts in the price change.

Include:

- **Pricing literature used in sales and marketing**
- **Web pages that include pricing**
- **Price calculators**
- **Customer ROI tools**
- **Solution ROI models**
- **Customer License Agreements that include pricing or price structure**

Don't forget to snapshot your Customer Benefit Analysis!

Add version identifiers to all pricing artifacts that align with solution versions to make tracking changes easier.

The result of this snapshot is a clearly stated and commonly agreed upon pricing model →

STRATEGY

STRUCTURE
Metrics, Fences

SPECIFICS
Levels

POLICIES
Discounts, Policies by buyer archetype

3 GATHER DATA

Gather data that will inform the price adjustment.

- **Surveys and interviews with customers** *(See page 182 for recommended research techniques)*
- **Feedback from customers, partners, sales, and support**

- **Macro-economic data, such as inflation**
- **Pricing strategy**
- **The relationship of solutions in a solution portfolio**
- **Competitor pricing**
- **Solution ROI Model updates**
- **Assessment of the effectiveness of your Profit Engine(s)**

These will help you understand how much you can raise or lower prices based on cost triggers.

Avoid gathering too much data. Gather just enough data to inform better, but not necessarily perfect, pricing.

4 DESIGN NEW PRICING

Focusing on the pricing block, use the explore-assess-select pattern to explore specific pricing changes, assessing the impact on other blocks and the economics of your Solution ROI.

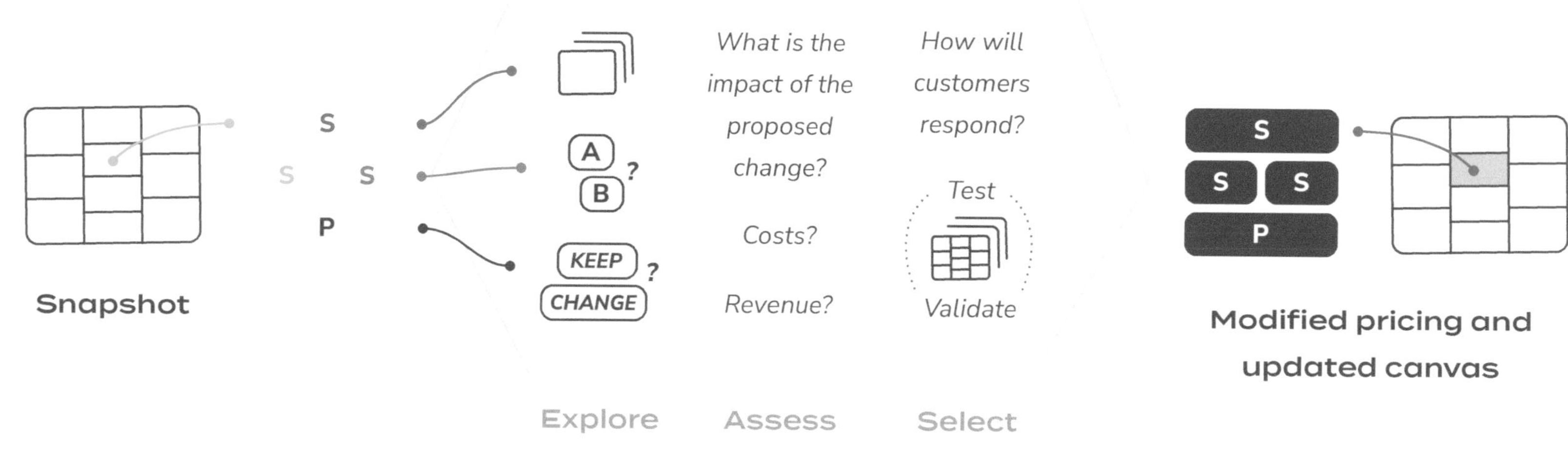

Like every design process, you will generate and explore alternatives and assess potential choices.

When modeling a price increase, add an estimate of how many customers you will lose because of the increase. You can minimize churn through effective implementation.

When modeling a price decrease, such as when a current solution is replaced by a new solution, include an estimate of customers who will not upgrade.

Remember to include the Total Cost of Ownership in your pricing adjustments as increases or decreases to the total solution cost will impact your pricing.

TESTING AND VALIDATING PRICING CHANGES

It is prudent to test and validate pricing changes before finalizing your choices. A small investment in **research with existing customers** can **prevent substantial problems** during **implementation.**

5 DEVELOP IMPLEMENTATION PLAN

Your implementation plan defines how you will execute your pricing changes. The best implementation plans are based on using your snapshot as a checklist to ensure you're not missing key steps.

Internal checklist

- ☐ *Communication plan*
- ☐ *Schedule*
- ☐ *Sales training*
- ☐ *Sales collateral*
- ☐ *Website updates*
- ☐ *Customer License updates*
- ☐ *Financial model*
- ☐ *Customer support*

External checklist

- ☐ *Communication plan*
- ☐ *Operations plan*
- ☐ *Policy changes*

Which customers are impacted?

How?

What do customers need to do? What options are available?

Why communicate price changes to customers?

→ ***Budgets.*** *Your customers need to adjust their budgets to account for the price increase.*

→ ***Sales.*** *A price increase is an opportunity to sell additional solutions as part of a larger deal.*

Your **Communication Plan** should include the following elements:

- [ ] **Current plans/pricing**
- [ ] **Rationale for change**
- [ ] **New plan/pricing**
- [ ] **Overview of benefits and value**
  + Higher quality + New features + Enhanced features
- [ ] **Timeline**
- [ ] **Actions your customer must take** (optional)
  + Do they need to sign an updated terms of service or license agreement?
- [ ] **Options your customer may consider** (optional)
  + Instead of renewing with an older solution, you might let customers apply a renewal to a new solution. + Discounts for pre-payments
- [ ] **Contact information for questions and follow-up**

Visit www.profit-streams.com for sample templates.

TONE:

- **Be direct**
- **Don't apologize**
- **Personalize when possible**

SEQUENCE:

- **Pre-Announcement**
- **Price change**

After the price change is implemented, consider additional emails to help your customers get the greatest possible Value from your solutions.

IMPLEMENT PRICE CHANGE

The complexity of implementing a price change varies based on the nature of the change and the relationship you have with your customers.

A low cost, B2C solution might announce a price change via an email.

A sophisticated B2B solution may need weeks or months to implement a price change, especially if this change requires updated Customer Licenses.

As the complexity of the implementation increases, build in time to adjust the plan based on customer feedback.

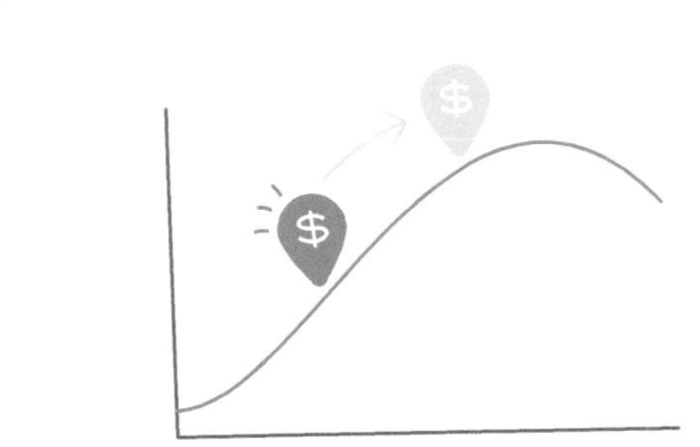

Conduct a retrospective at the end of each price adjustment to better understand how you can improve future price adjustments.

12 tips to **perfect your pricing**

1. **Use special offers to lock-in customers.**
When adjusting pricing, consider any number of strategies to promote longer term, lock-in relationships.

Example: SaaS providers who bill monthly can offer a discount to customers who convert to an annual plan, generating more up-front revenue and reducing future churn.

Example: B2B providers can include professional services as part of a price increase to help ensure customers are maximizing the solution's value.

2. **Pull revenue forward through pre-payments.**
Consider allowing customers to pre-pay for the solution at current prices for a limited time — you get more revenue, your customers get a lower price.

3. **Offer trade-in or trade-up discounts.**
Uniquely suited for solutions based on hardware value exchange models, trade-in and trade-up programs create incentives for customers to upgrade to the new solution by receiving some form of a credit for the current solution.

4. **Leverage API lockin to increase prices.**
APIs are incredibly sticky: once a customer is using your API, they won't want to change it. This can create more opportunities to raise prices more aggressively.

5. **Design additional fees around upgrades.**
Solution upgrades and replacements can create additional fees for value-added services. Unlike including services as part of a price increase, this strategy is about designing services around a specific event. Both approaches are valid and the specific approach you choose will be based on choices you've made in the past.

6. **Clean up internet website pricing.**
There are a number of websites that capture and share pricing information. As you adjust pricing, make sure you clean up any websites that might have older pricing data.

7. **Offer stable pricing.**
Stable pricing is a strategy designed to remove variability in pricing. You can use stable pricing when increasing prices to help customers better absorb the price increase.

8 **Use price changes to remove 'most favored nation' contract clauses.**

A 'most favored nation' ("MFN") clause (also referred to as a 'most favored customer' clause) is a contract clause that guarantees that the supplier does not (and will not) charge a customer fees that are higher than the fees charged to any other customer for the same solution. In simpler terms, an MFN clause guarantees the customer will always pay fees equal to the lowest amount paid by any other customer. MFNs are most often imposed by B2B customers who are trying to protect themselves or use their size to negotiate favorable terms from smaller companies. While you should never agree to an MFN, they do exist, and price changes provide a good opportunity to remove them from your contracts.

9 **Don't always provide a rationale.**

While it is generally good to provide a rationale for a price adjustment, it isn't strictly required. Accordingly, consider the benefits and drawbacks of including - and avoiding - a rationale for a price adjustment.

10 **Use a price adjustment for cross-selling, upselling, and bundling.**

A price adjustment provides a natural opportunity to offer additional solutions.

11 **Delay the price increase for current customers.**

Raising the price of the solution for new customers while delaying the price increase for existing customers creates goodwill and provides current customers more time to prepare for the increase.

12 **Remember your segmentation.**

Consider price adjustments for each segment to create more options. You may decide to raise prices for all segments or only for selected segments.

Bonus: Avoid tiered or "legacy" pricing.

Freezing pricing for a part of a customer's investment in a solution at a certain price or period in the solution history, also called grandfathering, creates drag when it's time to renew. move, or account for these licenses. Tiering can also occur when applying successively higher discount levels for greater quantity. Why is this a bad idea? Managing, accounting for, and paying for such tiers adds weight to several processes for both customer and provider, without much benefit.

Adjusting packaging

The evolution of the solution across the Solution Lifecycle creates opportunities for business leaders to modify packaging to better meet market needs.

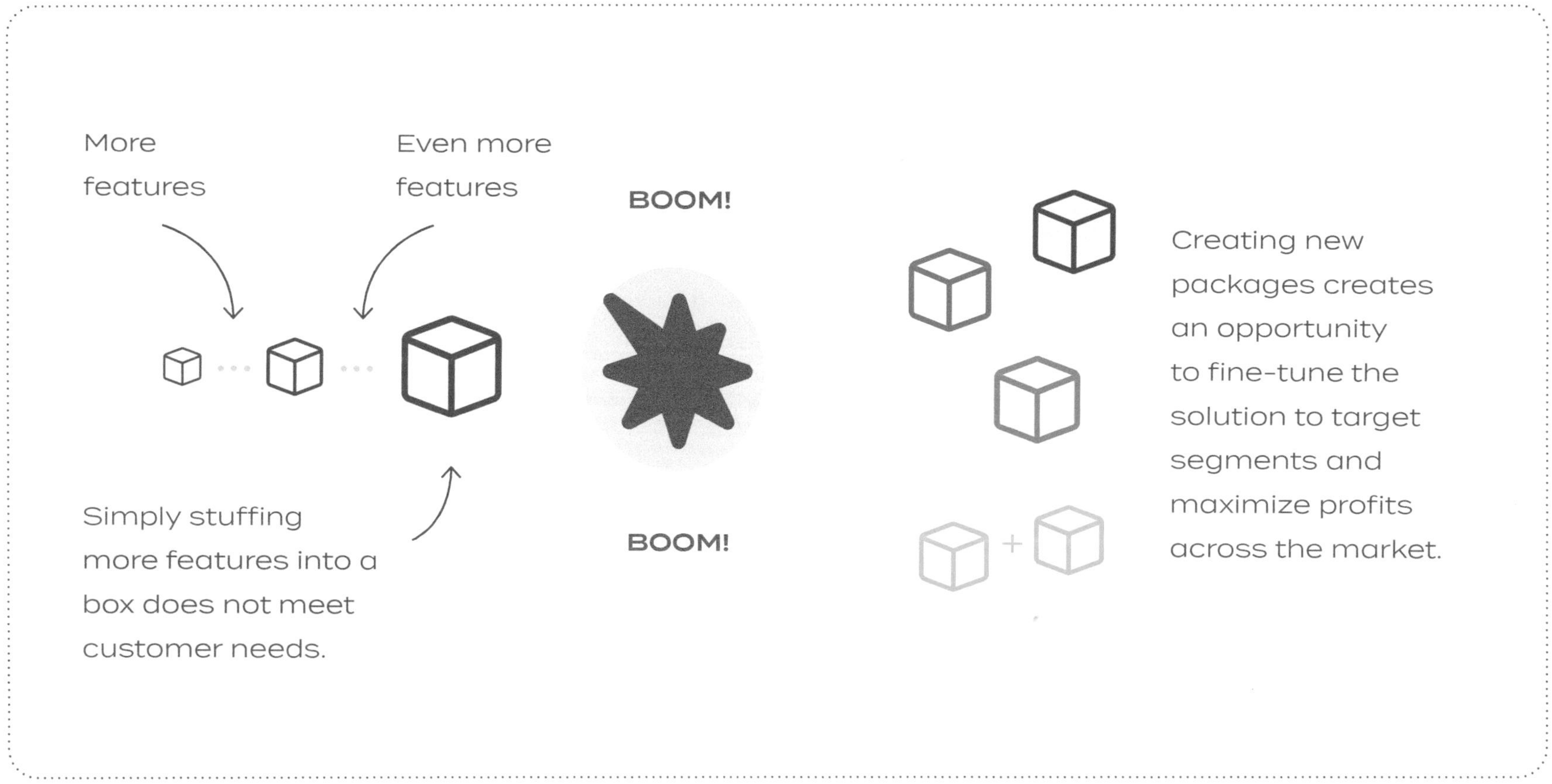

More features
Even more features
BOOM!
Creating new packages creates an opportunity to fine-tune the solution to target segments and maximize profits across the market.
Simply stuffing more features into a box does not meet customer needs.
BOOM!

The process for adjusting packages is similar to the process for adjusting prices.

The process for **adjusting packaging** is similar to the process for adjusting prices.

That's by design, while new pricing may not involve new packaging, new packaging almost always involves new pricing.

We advocate adjusting packaging and pricing at the same time, using the process outlined in adjusting process along with the process to adjusting packaging.

SIX STEPS TO ADJUST PACKAGING

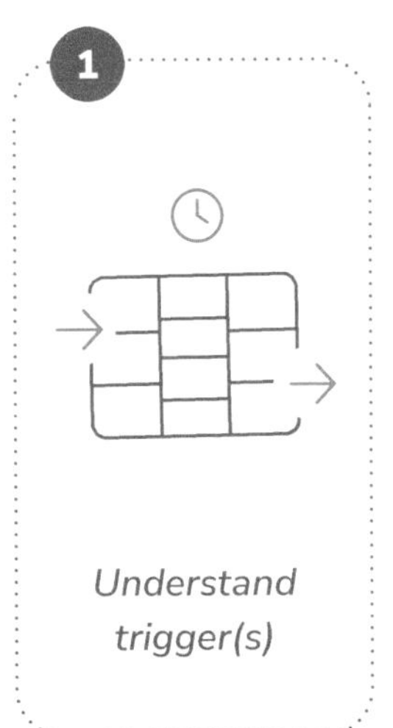

Understand trigger(s)

Snapshot

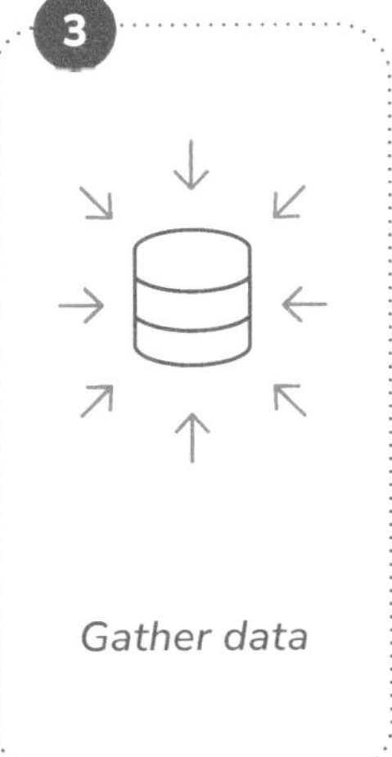

Gather data

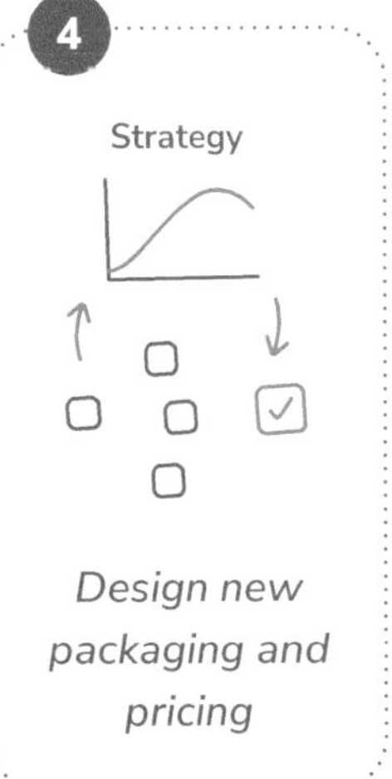

Design new packaging and pricing

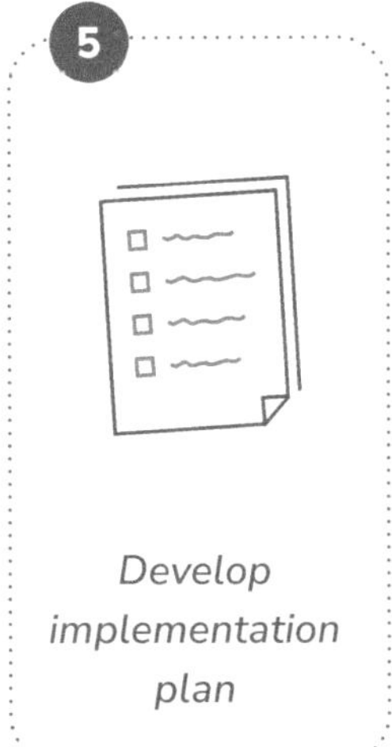

Develop implementation plan

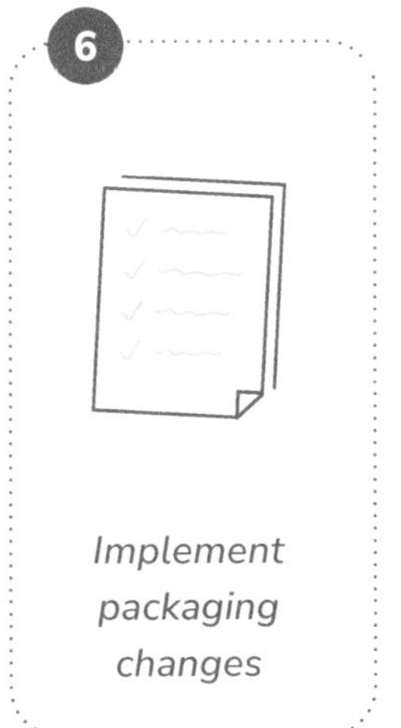

Implement packaging changes

SIX STEPS TO ADJUSTING PACKAGING

UNDERSTAND TRIGGERS

Triggers that indicate packaging needs to be adjusted tend to come from operational and sales data.

Your Solution Benefit Map doesn't align to customer usage patterns.

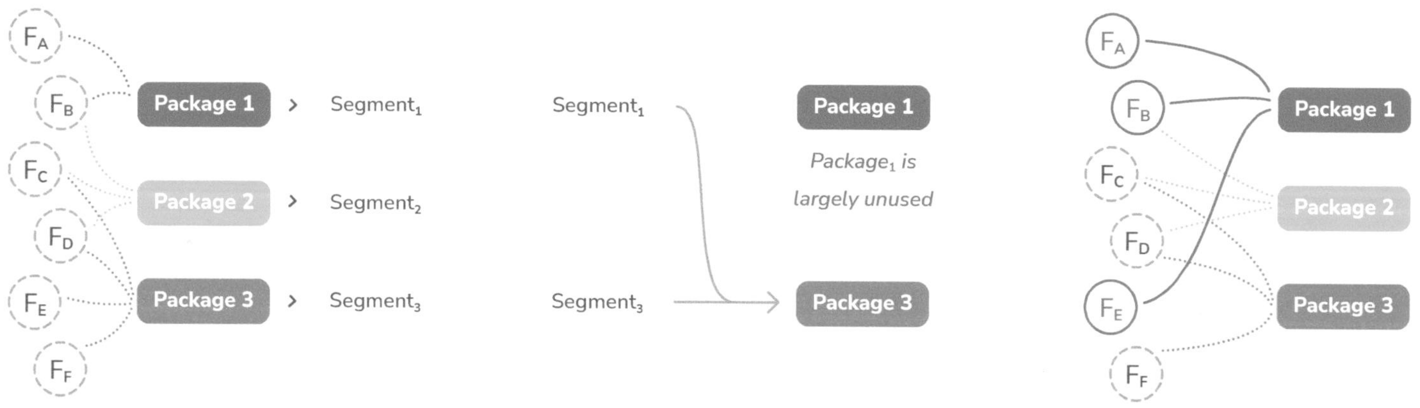

F_A F_B F_C F_D F_E F_F

Package 1 > Segment_1

Package 2 > Segment_2

Package 3 > Segment_3

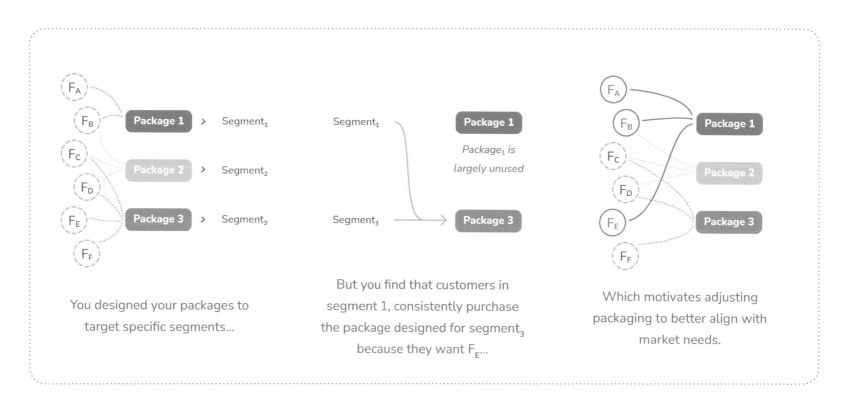

You designed your packages to target specific segments...

Segment_1 Package 1

Package_1 is largely unused

Segment_3 → Package 3

But you find that customers in segment 1, consistently purchase the package designed for segment_3 because they want F_E...

F_A F_B F_C F_D F_E F_F

Package 1

Package 2

Package 3

Which motivates adjusting packaging to better align with market needs.

Note that adjusting features within a package can include adjusting performance parameters, such as the transaction rate or data storage associated with a given package.

A more extreme version of customer usage patterns not aligning with package design occurs when customers of freemium packages fail to upgrade or when customers presented with a product pyramid never purchase the higher-tier offerings.

In both cases the response is the same:

- → **Substantially reduce the functionality of the freemium offering, or the lowest tiers.**
- → **Consider providing one-time incentives or discounts to motivate customers into premium, fee-based offerings.**

ⓘ Ideally, never offer freemium!

The differences between a **GOOD-BETTER-BEST** Pricing Strategy, different packaging of a solution, and different market segments are both subtle and profound.

GOOD-BETTER-BEST
Is a product pyramid pricing engine. It is often expressed through different brands that target the same core set of functional needs.

A given solution can be sold in different configurations, or packages, to better meet the individual needs of customers within a common segment.

Different market segments have different functional requirements and need different solutions. Even when technical components are shared, the solution is different.

Each brand offers a 4-door SUV, targeting the same functional need through a product pyramid.

Cadillac

Buick

Chevy

Once a brand is chosen the customer can select among several packages

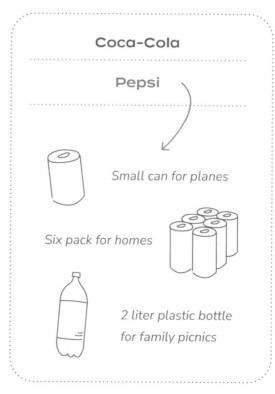

Coca-Cola

Pepsi

Small can for planes

Six pack for homes

2 liter plastic bottle for family picnics

Your Solution Context changes

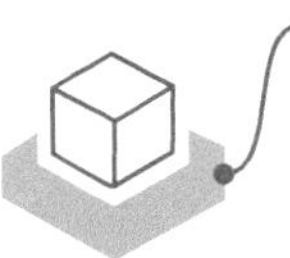

The **Solution Context** is provided by your customer or another company. Your solution, and how it is packaged, will evolve based on changes made by its provider.

Providers of mobile application platforms, such as Apple, Samsung, and Google, regularly add and remove capabilities.

Providers of web infrastructure, web application hosting, and Platform-as-a-Service companies, such as AWS, Google Cloud, Microsoft Azure, or Salesforce regularly add and remove capabilities.

*These changes can be highly beneficial when they enable you to create new packages or improve existing packages. Providers of the **Solution Context** may even help you develop new packages to promote their platforms. You might even be able to remove features, simplifying your solution.*

*These changes can be extremely frustrating, especially when the provider of the **Solution Context** offers a capability that neutralizes one of your competitive differentiators.*

SNAPSHOT

Create a snapshot of all relevant pricing, ROI, and related artifacts. This helps ensure you're assessing all necessary artifacts in the packaging change.

Include:

- **Pricing literature used in sales and marketing**
- **Web pages that include pricing**
- **Price calculators**
- **Customer ROI tools**
- **Solution ROI models**
- **Customer License Agreements that include pricing or price structure**

Don't forget to snapshot your Customer Benefit Analysis!

Add version identifiers to all pricing artifacts that align with solution versions to make tracking changes easier.

The result of this snapshot is a clearly stated and commonly agreed upon pricing model associated with each package →

STRATEGY

STRUCTURE
Metrics, Fences

SPECIFICS
Levels

POLICIES
Discounts, Policies by buyer archetype

GATHER DATA

Gather data that will inform the new packaging.

- **Surveys and interviews with customers** *(See page 182 for recommended research techniques)*
- **Feedback from customers, partners, sales, and support**
- **Macro-economic data, such as inflation**
- **Pricing strategy**
- **The relationship of solutions in a solution portfolio**
- **Competitor pricing**
- **Solution ROI Model updates**
- **Assessment of the effectiveness of your Profit Engine(s)**

These will help you understand how changes to packaging will impact your ROI.

Avoid gathering too much data. Gather just enough data to inform better, but not necessarily perfect, packaging.

SIX STEPS TO ADJUSTING PACKAGING

DESIGN NEW PACKAGING

Focusing on the customer and solution blocks, use the explore-assess-select pattern to explore specific packaging changes, assessing the impact on other blocks and the new economic models of your updated packaging.

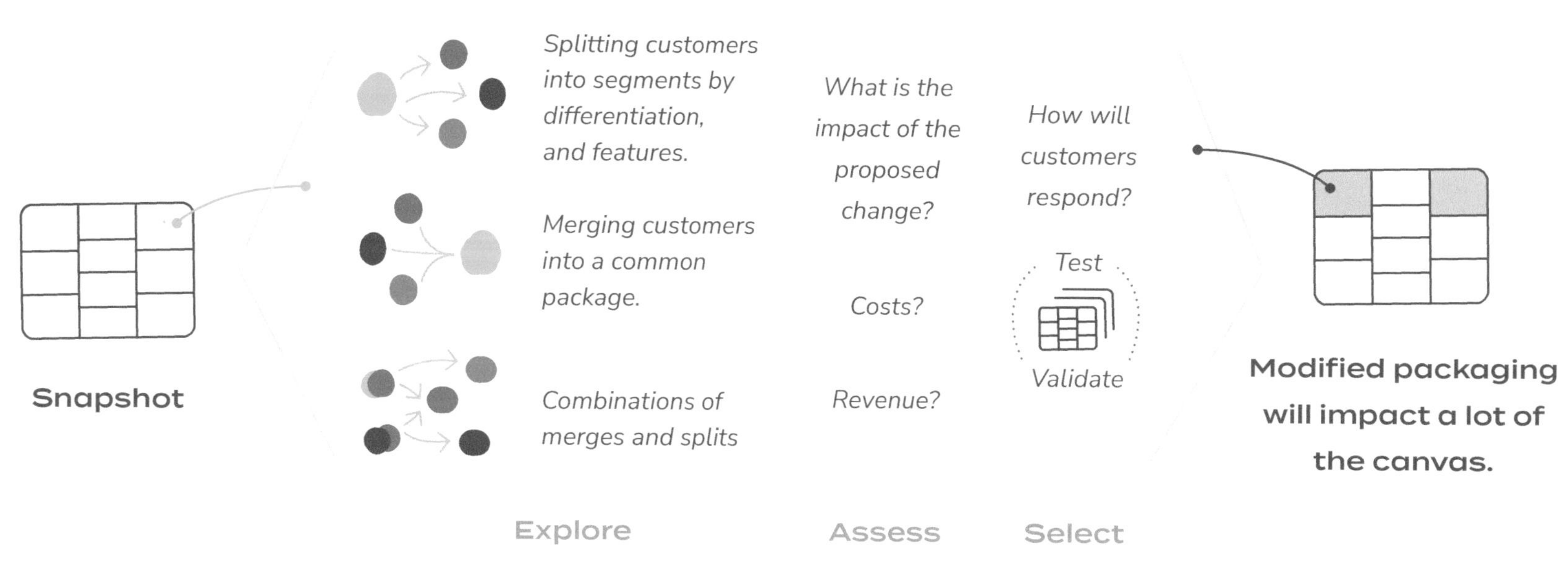
Snapshot
Splitting customers into segments by differentiation, and features.
Merging customers into a common package.
Combinations of merges and splits
What is the impact of the proposed change?
Costs?
Revenue?
How will customers respond?
Test
Validate
Modified packaging will impact a lot of the canvas.
Explore
Assess
Select

Like every design process, you will generate and explore alternatives and assess potential choices.

When modeling a packaging change, include an estimate of how many existing customers will stay on the current package.

5 DEVELOP IMPLEMENTATION PLAN

Your implementation plan defines how you will execute your packaging changes. The best implementation plans are based on using your snapshot as a checklist to ensure you're not missing key steps.

Internal checklist

- ☐ *Communication plan*
- ☐ *Schedule*
- ☐ *Sales training*
- ☐ *Sales collateral*
- ☐ *Website updates*
- ☐ *Customer License updates*
- ☐ *Financial model*
- ☐ *Customer support*

External checklist

- ☐ *Communication plan*
- ☐ *Operations plan*
- ☐ *Policy changes*

Which customers are impacted?

How?

What do customers need to do? What options are available?

Changing packaging will require changes to your operational systems.

SaaS providers will need to design and test changes to account capabilities. Customers may need to be migrated to new packages, with policies defined to handle data changes.

On-premise solutions, ranging from an app on a smartphone to enterprise software to sophisticated hardware must be adjusted to reflect new packaging. This often requires a phased implementation, as customers on current packages are migrated to new packages over time.

Your **Communication Plan** should include the following elements:

- [ ] **Current packages/pricing**
- [ ] **Rationale for change**
- [ ] **New packages/pricing**
- [ ] **Overview of benefits and value**
  + Higher quality + New features + Enhanced features
- [ ] **Timeline**
- [ ] **Actions your customer must take** (optional)
  + Do they need to sign an updated terms of service or license agreement?
- [ ] **Options your customer may consider** (optional)
  + Instead of renewing with an older package, you might let customers apply a renewal to a new package. + Discounts for pre-payments
- [ ] **Contact information for questions and follow-up**

Visit www.profit-streams.com for sample templates.

TONE:

- Be direct
- Don't apologize
- Personalize when possible

SEQUENCE:

- Pre-Announcement
- Package changes

After the package changes are implemented, consider additional emails to help your customers get the greatest possible Value from the new packages.

6 IMPLEMENTATION

Changing packaging can be more disruptive than changing pricing, as new packaging almost always encompasses changes to features, functionality, and operations.

Customers may need special and/or additional information to leverage the new packages.

Internal sales and support teams will need to be educated on the new packages and be given clear instructions on how to respond to customer inquiries, especially from customers who perceive a loss in functionality.

Fine-tuning Profit Engines

No matter how you define it, your sales funnel is how you acquire your customer, and that transaction represents your first sale.

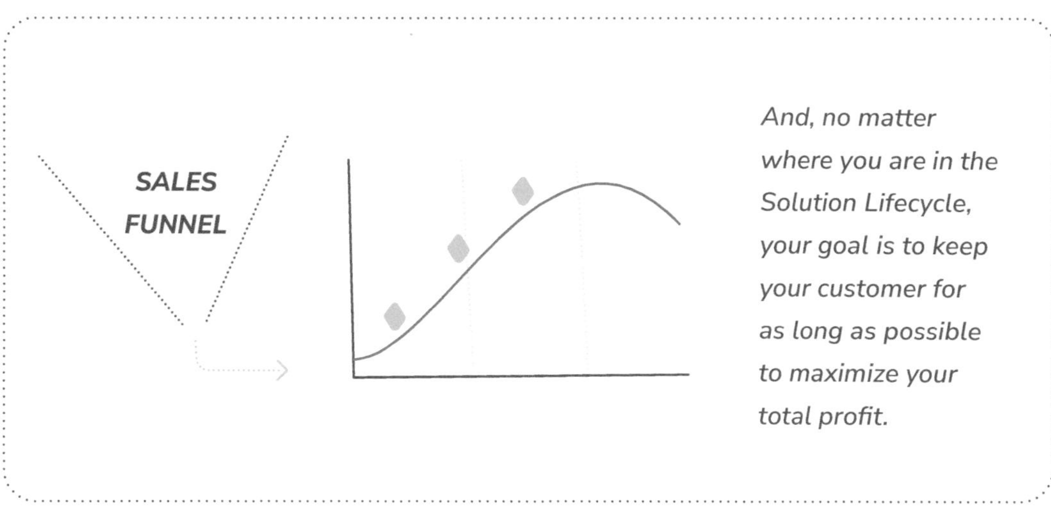

And, no matter where you are in the Solution Lifecycle, your goal is to keep your customer for as long as possible to maximize your total profit.

As outlined on page 229, a profit engine is an underlying set of business model choices designed to create additional or repeated value exchanges or increase the profit of a single value exchange.

Here are some ways you can fine-tune your profite engine(s) to maximize profit.

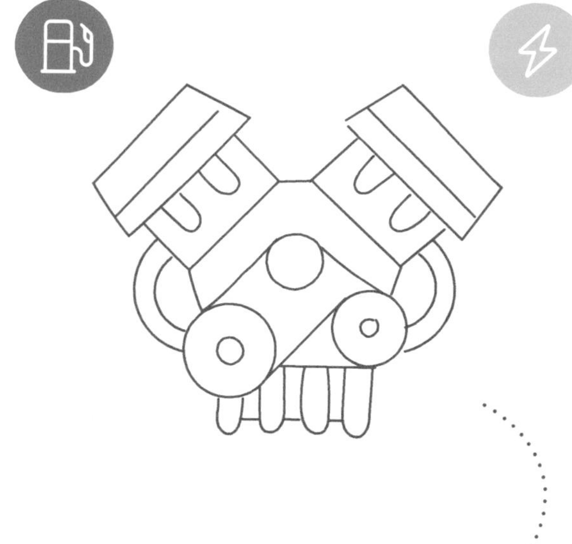

Tuning an engine refers to adjusting various parameters to improve performance.

In **gasoline engines,** this may include air-to-fuel ratios to reduce emissions and fuel consumption.

In electric motors, this may include adjusting the amount of current or voltage to increase or decrease the motor's power output and torque.

Tuning upgrades and new releases

The three main parameters you can adjust about upgrades and/or new releases are the frequency of releases, the magnitude of the change, and the costs associated with the change. Collectively, these influence your customer's perception of value and your ability to leverage the installed base.

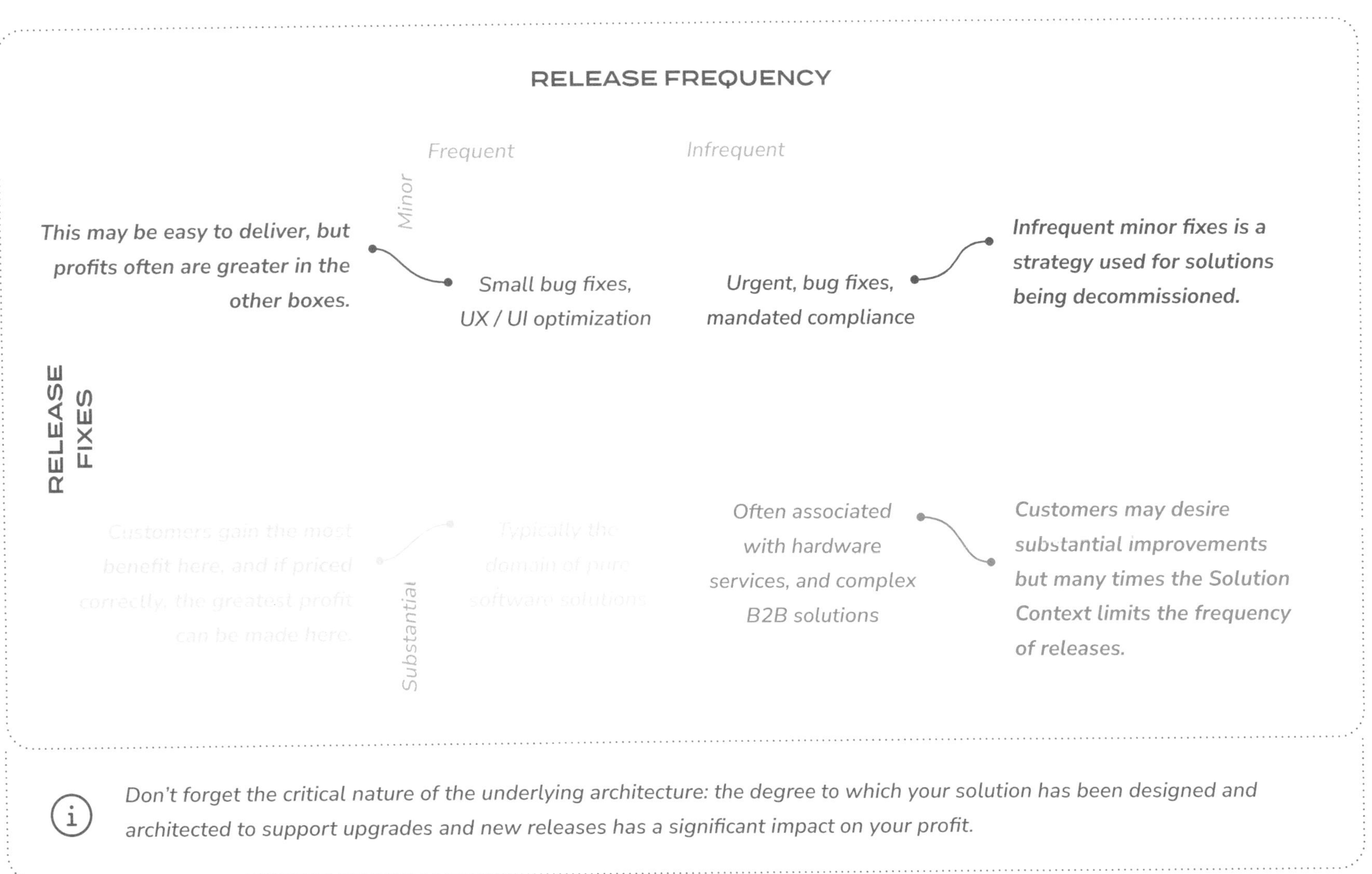

RELEASE FREQUENCY
Frequent
Infrequent
RELEASE FIXES
Minor
Substantial
This may be easy to deliver, but profits often are greater in the other boxes.
Small bug fixes, UX / UI optimization
Urgent, bug fixes, mandated compliance
Infrequent minor fixes is a strategy used for solutions being decommissioned.
Customers gain the most benefit here, and if priced correctly, the greatest profit can be made here.
Typically the domain of pure software solutions.
Often associated with hardware services, and complex B2B solutions
Customers may desire substantial improvements but many times the Solution Context limits the frequency of releases.

Don't forget the critical nature of the underlying architecture: the degree to which your solution has been designed and architected to support upgrades and new releases has a significant impact on your profit.

Tuning the product pyramid

Tuning a pyramid is based on adjusting the packaging of features at each tier. Follow the process for adjusting packages, with the goal of maximizing profit across the tiers.

Tuning the platform ecosystem

The primary parameter to tune in a platform ecosystem is the boundary between the solution and the solution context, and the underlying performance parameters of the platform end points.

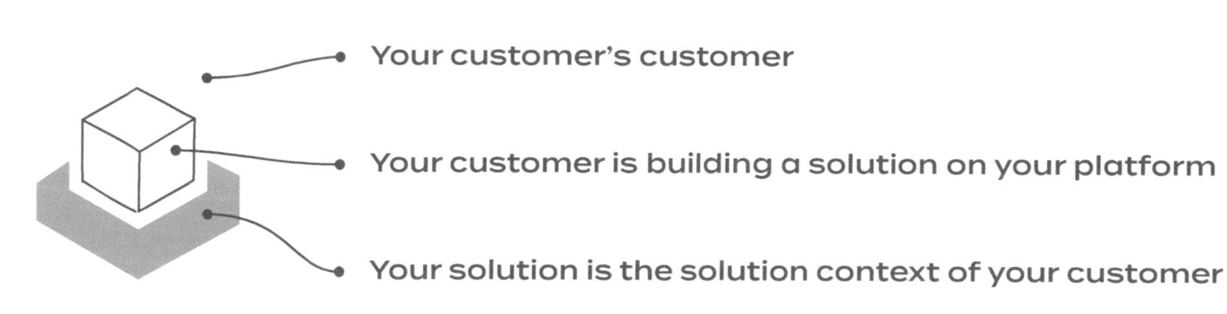
Your customer's customer
Your customer is building a solution on your platform
Your solution is the solution context of your customer

These boundaries and the performance of the solution context, such as an API, can be modeled and managed through versioning, packaging, and bundling.

Tuning the 'Think Solution'

The primary parameters to adjust in a 'think solution' profit engine are the relationships between the elements that compose the solution.

> A common strategy is to use services to address deficiencies in the software, eliminating these services over time as the software improves.

SECTION 04

Not the end

e end

Closing Thoughts

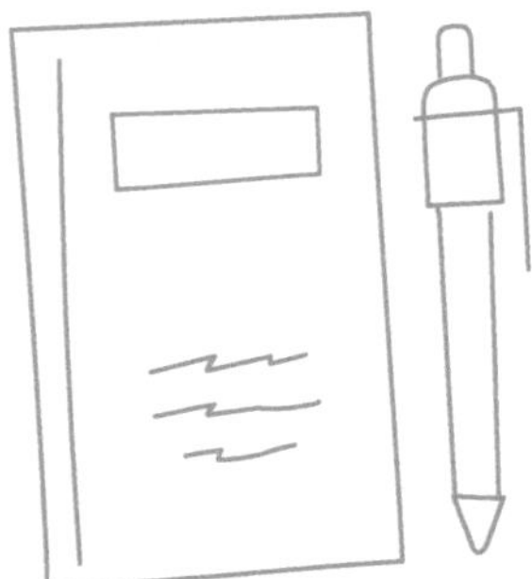

In the early part of 2021, Jason started working on a book to help companies create sustainably profitable software-enabled solutions through more effective pricing.

The key phrase in that statement is **pricing.**

There are hundreds—thousands!—of books that cover positioning, problem solution fit, product market fit, market research, agile development, business modeling, and so forth. And while these books are important contributions, as a consultant and educator, Jason knew this book was needed because without sustainability, none of the other books matter.

In 2022, Jason invited Luke to join him... Actually, Luke bugged Jason to let him into the party, because Luke agreed that this book needed to be written.

Guided by a few simple principles, we committed to creating the most beautiful book ever written on the subject of software pricing.

A book that would be an enduring contribution to the industry we serve and love. A book that helps the industry evolve from value streams to Profit Streams.

A book that, as one reviewer shared, doesn't just advance the thinking, but instead advances how business leaders are able to think.

A book that creates the foundation for evolution beyond the confines of this book at www.profit-streams.com and the Profitable Software Community.

We're not artists. We knew that we needed an extraordinary designer to realize our vision. We found that person in Federico González (Fede), who also joined the team in 2022. We are forever grateful for his brilliant work in designing and illustrating this book and bringing our vision to the world.

Together, we are proud of the book that you're holding in your hands (or reading online).
Jason, Luke, and Fede.

Here are the principles that guided our work. They'll guide you, too, as you use this book to create more sustainable software-enabled solutions.

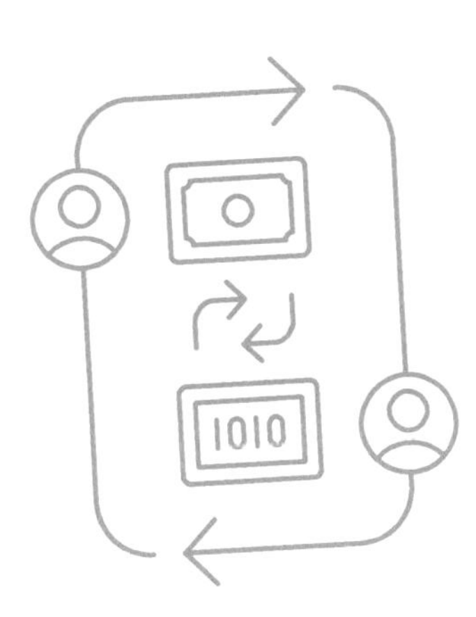

Profit fuels sustainability.

Pricing is a system, not a number.

Pricing evolves.

Total value for customers must be greater than total cost of ownership.

Business models must generate a Profit Stream—a revenue stream that is greater than total costs.

Profitability is a team sport!

We hope you have as much fun storming your castles as we have had in storming this book.

JASON TANNER / LUKE HOHMANN / FEDERICO GONZÁLEZ

Book's collaborators

Jason Tanner

Jason Tanner is CEO of Applied Frameworks, establishing the company's strategy and leading its growth. A Scrum Alliance Certified Scrum Trainer, he has led Agile transformations at several Fortune 500 companies, including MassMutual, Capital One, and CoStar Group. An in-demand speaker, coach, and facilitator, his engagements focus on strategy, product, and portfolio management. Jason served nine years as an officer in the United States Marine Corps, commanding an infantry rifle company of over 100 Marines and directing operations for over 1,500 Marines. He studied engineering at Cornell University and earned his MBA from Duke University.

Luke Hohmann

Serial entrepreneur Luke Hohmann is Chief Innovation Officer of Applied Frameworks. Luke also founded Conteneo, a collaboration software company acquired by Scaled Agile. Author of five books and a principal contributor to the SAFe® Framework, Luke is a popular keynote speaker and has engaged audiences around the world. He co-founded Every Voice Engaged Foundation, a 501(c)(3) nonprofit that collaboratively solves problems through civic engagement. Hohmann graduated with a BSE and an MSE from the University of Michigan.

Federico González

Brand and product designer Federico González has more than fifteen years of experience in graphic and product design. He spent a decade as a creative lead at a software consulting firm working with top global brands and holds world-class expertise in branding, art direction, UX, UI, design systems, prototyping, illustration, and video.

About

Founded in 2003, Applied Frameworks is a boutique strategy consulting firm helping companies of all sizes create more sustainably profitable software-enabled solutions. Our internationally recognized team of Strategy, Product Management, Scrum, SAFe, and Agile consultants have helped invent, design, deliver, and sustain B2C, B2P, and B2B solutions.

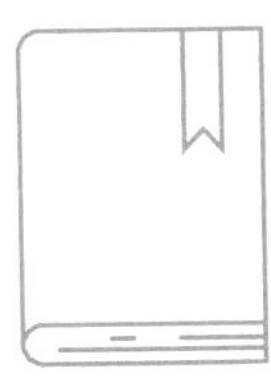

THIS BOOK

The foundation of Profit Streams

ASSESSMENTS

Evaluate and track your progress

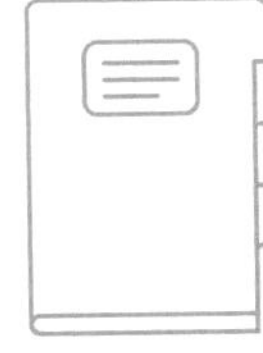

TRAINING

Learn from experts

CONSULTING

Accelerate mastery

CERTIFICATIONS

Validate and communicate your achievements

COMMUNITY

Join a global community of practitioners and experts

Learn more at

www.appliedframeworks.com

Bibliography & References

(1) *"Why Software is Eating the World"* by Marc Andreesen https://a16z.com/2011/08/20/why-software-is-eating-the-world/

(2) Definition of Technical Architecture is adapted from the book: *"Beyond Software Architecture"* by Luke Hohmann

(3) Theodore Levitt, *"Marketing Success Through Differentiation—of Anything"*, Harvard Business Review, January, 1980 https://hbr.org/1980/01/marketing-success-through-differentiation-of-anything

(4) *Prune the Product Tree* is described in the book *"Innovation Games"* by Luke Hohmann

(5) The classic book on the S-shaped curve of adoption is *"Diffusion of Innovation"* by Everett M. Rogers. Get the latest edition!

(6) *"Crossing the Chasm"* by Geoffrey Moore. Another classic... and do get the latest edition.

(7) *The Pace of Technology Adoption is Speeding Up, Rita McGrath.* https://hbr.org/2013/11/the-pace-of-technology-adoption-is-speeding-up

* *Profit from the Core* by Chris Zook and James G. Allen. *Publisher: Harvard Business Review Press; Updated ed. edition (Jan. 26, 2010)*

* *Software Product Management and Pricing: Key Success Factors for Software Organizations* by Hans-Bernd Kittlaus, Peter N. Clough. Publisher: Springer; 2009th edition (Jan. 15, 2009)

* *Winning the Profit Game: Smarter Pricing, Smarter Branding* by Robert G. Docters, Michael R. Reopel, Jeanne-Mey Sun, Stephen M. Tanny. Publisher: McGraw Hill; 1st edition (Jan. 2, 2004)

* *The Strategy and Tactics of Pricing: A guide to growing more profitably 6th Edition* by Thomas T. Nagle, Georg Müller. Publisher: Routledge; 6th edition (Nov. 16, 2017)

* *Beyond Software Architecture: Creating and Sustaining Winning Solutions* by Luke Hohmann. Publisher: Addison-Wesley Professional; 1st edition (Jan. 30, 2003)

* *Fundamentals Of Software Licensing* by H. Ward Classen * Copyright (c) 1996 PTC Research Foundation of Franklin Pierce Law Center. IDEA: The Journal of Law and Technology 1996. 37 IDEA 1

* The Anatomy of SaaS Pricing Strategy - Price Intelligently - https://www.priceintelligently.com/

* *Software Pricing Trends* by Galen Gruman, Alan S. Morrison, Terril A. Retter - McKinsey - https://www.pwc.com/

* *The Good-Better-Best Approach to Pricing* by Rafi Mohammed. Harvard Business Review (Sep-Oct 2018)

* *Usage-based pricing: How to lay the foundations for success* by Griffin Parry. Venture Beat (Mar. 16, 2022)

* *Aligning Product and GTM Teams with Better Segmentation* by Zeya Yang and Baker Shogry

* *Don't Just Roll the Dice - A Usefully Short Guide to Software Pricing Paperback* by Neil Davidson. (Oct. 1, 2009) Publisher: Redgate books

* *Monetizing Innovation: How Smart Companies Design the Product Around the Price* by Madhavan Ramanujam, Georg Tacke. (May 2, 2016) Publisher: Wiley

* *Marketing Success Through Differentiation* - of Anything by Theodore Levitt. HBR (Jan-Feb, 1980)

* *Marketing Intangible Products and Product Intangibles* by Theodore Levitt. HBR (May-Jun, 1981)

* *Value Proposition Design: How to Create Products and Services Customers Want* (1st Edition) by Alexander Osterwalder, Yves Pigneur, Gregory Bernarda, Alan Smith, Designed by Trish Papadakos

* *Testing Business Ideas: A Field Guide for Rapid Experimentation* by David J. Bland, Alexander Osterwalder

* *Business Model Generation: A Handbook for Visionaries, Game Changers, and Challengers* by Alexander Osterwalder, Yves Pigneur

* *Power Pricing: How Managing Price Transforms the Bottom Line* by Robert J. Dolan (Author), Hermann Simon

* *Winning at New Products: Accelerating the Process from Idea to Launch, Third Edition* by Robert G. Cooper

* *Product Management (McGraw-Hill/Irwin Series in Marketing)* by Donald Lehmann, Russell Winer

* *Marketing Imagination Expanded Edition* by Theodore M. Levitt

* *SAFe 5.0 Distilled: Achieving Business Agility with the Scaled Agile Framework* by Richard Knaster

* *Financial Accounting (9th edition) An Introduction to Concepts, Methods and Uses* by Clyde P Stickney, Roman L Weil

* *Principles of Corporate Finance (6th edition)* by Richard A. Brealey, Stewart C. Myers

* *Marketing Management: Millennium Edition (10th Edition)* by Philip Kotler

* *The Profit Zone: How Strategic Business Design Will Lead You to Tomorrow's Profits* by Adrian J. Slywotzky, David J. Morrison, Bob Andelman

* *The Product-Led Organization: Drive Growth By Putting Product at the Center of Your Customer Experience* by Todd Olson

* *Stories Of Scaling With Usage - Based Pricing* by Kyle Poyar. 2022 - OpenView Partners - https://openviewpartners.com/

Index

People

Companies and Solutions

Topics

Index

Index

CPSIA information can be obtained
at www.ICGtesting.com
Printed in the USA
BVHW061655050423
661817BV00003B/28